Praise for *In One Ear*:

'This is a wonderful book of pop music history. A man obsessed with the beauty of creative artists and wanting to create his own legacy and to enable other musicians to have a voice by releasing their magic. We need more people like him in a world full of mass-produced mediocrity'

Elton John

'A beautiful, insightful and honest look into the life of legend and musical polymath Simon Raymonde'

Cillian Murphy

'Simon and his father Ivor have soundtracked many chapters of my life. Their musical journey makes for a fascinating read that's a very British take on the story of rock 'n' roll'

Don Letts

'Simon Raymonde likes to credit serendipity for the storied life that music has given him – seemingly unaware that his genial *joie de vivre* might have influenced the outcome of his successes. Therein lies perhaps the greatest of this book's myriad charms'

Pete Paphides

'I was engrossed in *In One Ear* from the start and just gorged on it from then on, hungry to learn what happened next. The depth and honesty when describing everything from Simon's youth, to being a vital part of one of the most influential bands ever, to setting up and running probably the most important independent label of this era is addictive. Oh yeah, and the lad can write, books as well as heartachingly beautiful songs'

Pat Nevin

'Simon's book is nothing short of a gift for us lifelong Cocteau Twins fans. Beautifully executed and absolutely riveting. I felt transported. Indeed, an honour and a thrill to witness in such perfect detail the band's unfolding, as well as Simon's personal journey from record-store clerk to legendary musician'

Jason Lee, actor and skateboarder

'Simon Raymonde has helped write some of the most celestial and influential music ever created and that is just one part of his remarkable story. He recounts it here with great command, insight and wit. So moving, so honest and disarmingly charming. I was riveted and I remain devoted'

Shirley Manson of Garbage

'Simon Raymonde spent fifteen years making beautiful music with the Cocteau Twins, he has subsequently spent almost thirty years bringing us beautiful music via Bella Union. He brings us that beauty again in the pages of *In One Ear*. As highly recommended as *Treasure, It'll End in Tears* or *Heaven or Las Vegas*'

Merck Mercuriadis

In One Ear

SIMON
RAYMONDE

In One Ear
'Cocteau Twins, Ivor and Me'

NINE
EIGHT
BOOKS

NINE
EIGHT
BOOKS

NEB 031

First published in the UK in 2024 by Nine Eight Books
An imprint of Black & White Publishing Group
A Bonnier Books UK company
4th Floor, Victoria House, Bloomsbury Square, London, WC1B 4DA
Owned by Bonnier Books, Sveavägen 56, Stockholm, Sweden

X @nineeightbooks

@nineeightbooks

Hardback ISBN: 978-1-7887-0938-5
Special edition hardback ISBN: 978-1-7851-2223-1
eBook ISBN: 978-1-7887-0937-8
Audio ISBN: 978-1-7887-0936-1

A CIP catalogue record for this book is available from the British Library.

Publishing director: Pete Selby
Editor: James Lilford

Cover design by Chris Bigg
Typeset by IDSUK (Data Connection) Ltd

Printed and bound in Great Britain by Clays Ltd, Elcograf S.p.A

1 3 5 7 9 10 8 6 4 2

Nine Eight Books is an imprint of Bonnier Books UK
www.bonnierbooks.co.uk

MIX
Paper | Supporting
responsible forestry
FSC
www.fsc.org   FSC® C018072

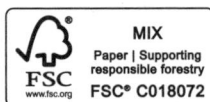

To the memory of Ivor and Nita, to Elizabeth and Robin for bringing me into the fold, to my wife Abbey, my sons Stan and Will, my brother Nick and to all those who hold me dear

'*A book read by a thousand different people is a thousand different books.*'

Andrei Tarkovsky

CONTENTS

INTRODUCTION

During 2001, I met a gent and fellow Spurs fan Phil Howells who had started a label called City Rockers. I should say that in starting my book with 'I met a gent', I may be swiftly creating the impression that I am a sociable sort. It's not that I *can't* be, it's more that I prefer dogs. That will become clearer as we progress through the book.

Phil was, like me, a genuine enthusiast about new music, and as our joint football hero Glenn Hoddle was also managing Spurs, we found we had a lot to talk about. If I have, by the middle of only this second paragraph, now created the notion that in fact I only like dogs, music and football in that order, this will also prove to be quite false. The purpose of starting the book with my meeting with Phil is to signpost the chain of events that it kick-started. So I guess there's Life Before Phil, and Life After Phil, but Phil is where we must begin.

You could say that in 2001 I was a few steps into my 'second' career. Or I could say it. Makes more sense if I say it.

In 2001, I was running – if sporting terminology was appropriate here, 'limping along' would probably be more accurate – an independent record label that my former bandmate Robin Guthrie and I had started together back in 1997, just prior to the sudden but kinda-to-be-expected demise of our beloved band Cocteau Twins when singer Elizabeth Fraser called me to say she couldn't continue. Something about difficulties being in a band with her ex-boyfriend and father of their daughter, and a whole host of related and unrelated issues.

It still seems strange to me that in 2022 I celebrated twenty-five years of running the record label, Bella Union, especially given how bad *our* experiences were in the last couple of years at 4AD and again during *all* of our time signed to Fontana, part of the major label conglomerate Universal. This running a label thing was never a career path I considered, even during the first few years of doing it. It just sort of happened.

Robin exited Bella Union stage left soon after, moving away to France, and I continued to stumble from one near-disaster to another, like Oscar Isaac in the Coen Brothers' *Inside Llewyn Davis*. The sole reason for the existence of Bella Union was initially only to release Cocteau Twins music, so to have spent the last quarter of a century putting out *no* Cocteau Twins records at all, does make me laugh. Apart from when it makes me cry.

So back to Phil.

Phil loved a new band he'd heard called Solomon and wanted to play me some music with a view to me producing them. 'That's not going to be their name though, don't worry!' he offered, before I had a chance to say that I wasn't at all worried.

INTRODUCTION

Within a minute of hearing each of the two demos, I was in love, and within a week Phil had booked us into a recording studio in Brighton called Metway, a fine place run by local heroes the Levellers. I won't get overly sentimental but I am still close friends with all the members of Solomon, twenty-three years on from that session, so I think we can say it went OK.

The night we finished the final song (we recorded and mixed six tracks for an EP/mini album), we drove back home to London with one rather pressing matter still unresolved. Phil had booked the mastering studio for the next morning and the band had promised him that along, with the mixes, they would also be delivering a brand-new band name, replacing the aforementioned 'Solomon'.

Before dropping everyone home, we stopped by the old Bella Union label office in Twickenham to unload some drums and amps, all the while time slipping away with dawn fast approaching, the deadline looming, and singer Liela frantically looking around the office for some divine inspiration for her new band name. She stumbled across a pile of books in the corner that belonged to Cocteau Twins' singer Elizabeth that she had left behind after quitting the band several years before, and began thumbing through one of them.

My abiding memory is of her shouting out three words that jumped out of the page – THE DUKE SPIRIT. It was perfect.

The recording session in Brighton had been a lot of fun, Liela, Dan, Toby, Olly and Luke were wonderful people to work with, and together with my close friend and Bella Union 'house engineer' Giles Hall, we felt very much at home in their company.

On the third day of recording, something odd happened to me. You know when you've been swimming and you get water in your ear and for a day or so after you're trying to 'pop' your ears, or tilting your head to one side and banging your ear in some vain hope that the water will just fall out? Well, I hadn't been swimming. But I was producing an album and certainly had *no* time for an ear infection. I was sitting at the mixing desk with Giles when it first started to block up. It was annoying because I couldn't really hear very much at all out of that ear, but it was probably just the start of a cold, or maybe I just needed to get my ears syringed. I figured as I was away from home for the next week or so, I would sort it when I got back if it was still bothering me. It didn't really hinder my ability to produce the record, but you'll be a better judge of that than me.

The doctor booked me in to clean the wax out of my ears as she said she couldn't see if there was an infection or not. They flush warm water through your ears and it all just unblocks. It feels very weird, but ultimately supremely satisfying. Normally. But this time, the blocked feeling remained and still I couldn't hear much on that side. The next step was to go and have an audiogram hearing test. At the conclusion of the test, the gentleman with the machine said I would need to go and have an MRI scan. 'That sounds a bit serious,' I suggested. 'Just a precaution,' he responded.

The scan was booked the same day, which also seemed a bit odd. I thought these things took ages to arrange? Anyway, I thought no more of it. The MRI scan isn't a barrel of laughs itself but I was more bothered about just finding out what was causing the blockage.

Within an hour of the scan, I was in an office at the hospital looking up at my brain on one of those light boxes hung on the wall that you see on the telly on *Casualty*. Quite a wonderful sight in many ways, the organ that is responsible for everything we do, see, touch, think, imagine, create, all up there in bright lights on the wall. Being housed so adroitly in our heads, wrapped so tightly in skin, and surrounded by hair (barely in my case), it is a rare sight to see it in an X-ray, without all the expressive moving parts that tell us so much, the glint of an eye, pursed lips, the raising of an eyebrow, the forehead frown, the twitch of a nose.

There was something there I didn't recognise though: a large oval shape on the right side, like a big egg, one that would make one hell of an omelette all by itself.

'This is an acoustic neuroma,' said the bearded man rising from his chair and pointing at the egg with a yellow pencil.

I didn't know what that was but I blurted out nervously, 'As a musician, I like the sound of that but what exactly is it?'

After he said the words 'It is the reason for your loss of hearing – it's a brain tumour', I can't really remember an awful lot else. A giant Stephen King-sized fog descended in front of my eyes, and I didn't regain clear focus again until I was being shown out of the office into another room.

It so happened that the leading brain surgeon for acoustic neuromas in the country, Professor Bell, was *in* the hospital visiting/ consulting for the next two days, and they had managed to get him to come and see me shortly after I'd received the news. He was clearly eminent because he said he could operate on me later that day and remove the tumour. My mum had been waiting to get her hip done for about thirteen months, so 'same day service' seemed to suggest something unusual was going on here.

Bear in mind, this conversation with the eminent Professor Bell is maybe fifteen minutes after I had first been given the news that I had a brain tumour. I can only equate it to pressing play and forward on a cassette machine at the same time and I couldn't clearly process any of the audio that was coming out. And not just because I was deaf in one ear.

I do remember asking him what the operation would entail.

'Well, we drill a hole, so big (he made an 'O' shape with his thumb and index finger the size of a ping pong ball) behind your ear, and then we carefully remove the tumour.'

I asked if by removing the tumour I would regain my hearing in my right ear.

'No. Your hearing is never coming back I am afraid. There are risks of course as it's a glutinous mass and when removing it we have to take great care as it's connected to the part of the brain that controls all of your nerves on that side of your face and body, and it's not a simple operation. But as I am here, you couldn't be in a better position as I am willing and able to do it later today.'

I didn't want to argue, but I was pretty sure I *could* have been in a better position. Like half asleep on a hammock between two palm trees on a deserted beach in Hawaii for one.

I asked what the success rate for the operation was.

'About 94 per cent,' he said.

'Wow, that's terrible!' I said. 'So six out of 100 people don't make it?'

'Those odds are excellent, Mr Raymonde.'

I want you to think about those odds for a second, and I am still wondering if you would have felt the same as me.

I didn't allow Professor Bell to operate on my brain that day, nor did I ever let him operate on my brain, though I realise that on another day, I may have felt differently, less bullish and perhaps I would have just relinquished myself to his eminence's circular drill, skull saw and incredibly sharp knives.

But doesn't this decision illustrate so well the peculiar essence of our lives? That moment when we choose this path over that one, based on what exactly? Not very much indeed. A hunch, a gut feeling. I've always tried to trust mine. I've felt for a while that instinct certainly seems to define so much of my life.

I can only hope that my eventual exit from the world isn't as dramatic as my entry into it. In April of 1962, I was born more than a month early and was immediately whisked away from Mum, diagnosed as having infant methemoglobinemia, a rare condition where the skin turns blue due to a lack of haemoglobin, a blood protein which carries oxygen around the body. When the blood is unable to carry oxygen around the body, the baby turns blue (cyanotic, looks lovely written down, but doesn't sound as good when the doctor is explaining why your baby is being rushed into another room seconds after being pulled out of yer womb). Mum wasn't able to see, feed or hold me until I was about two weeks old, and this I know was very traumatic for her. Probably for me too. So growing up my family always referred to me as 'the blue baby'. Thankfully this was pre-Smurfs.

Even as a crawling baby, it seems that I was already making strangely independent decisions that while clearly unwise, appeared to make me stronger not weaker. My mother, Nita Mavis Raymonde (née Archer), with three other young children to look over, took her eye off me for a minute in 1963, in Croydon where we lived in a two-up, two-down in Coombe Lane, and as Mum tells it, I managed to crawl out of the front door and a few yards up to the edge of the road where I stumbled, lurched backwards and cracked my head open on a manhole. I recovered, of course, though as I write this I am now wondering if maybe the brain tumour was as a result of this 'soft baby's head on metal' incident. Or was it perhaps a combination of this and the next one a few years later when I fell off Dad's lap on to the sharp corner of a marble table in Marbella and cracked it open again in the same place, during a game of 'Banbury Cross' – a questionable blend of a robust 'bouncing up and down on the knee' diversion along with a sing-song, the lyrics to which haven't dated so well:

Ride a cock horse to Banbury Cross
To see a fine lady upon a white horse
With rings on her fingers and bells on her toes
She shall have music wherever she goes

Dad's own career in music, which bears such an influence on this book, I'll return to in due course, but anyone hearing him sing 'Banbury Cross' that morning in Marbella would not have imagined that he actually had a beautiful singing voice. Mum often said proudly that he sounded like Sam Moore of Sam and Dave. Dad would whisper 'More like Chas 'n' Dave!'

With my bloody head wrapped in my swimming towel, I was rushed off to the nearby hospital.

Hospitals in Marbella in the 1960s didn't seem to be much more than a large tiled bathroom that smelled of Dettol with a drawer full of sticking plasters. It is just now dawning on me fifty-odd years later that we probably just went to the large tiled bathroom round the back of the swimming pool.

But all this gleeful reminiscing about childhood head trauma is distracting me from what I have really believed is the reason I now have this funny egg in my head.

I must just say this, I did love a pager. Thirty-five years later and my digital radio in the kitchen is using still the same painfully slow wandering text technology, but they were a lot of fun for those really crucial 'I'm leaving now, I'll be home soon' messages.

Then when those first small Nokia mobile phones arrived, I eagerly signed up and, ignoring the scaremongering headlines of hazards to health, would defiantly spend far too long cradling this almost too hot to hold mini microwave up to my right ear, talking exactly the same nonsense I could have waited a few hours to share in person. Ho-hum.

Four and a half years of those early mobile phone prototypes steadily and secretly boiling the egg inside my head, until this moment of awful diagnosis. Four and a half minutes for the perfect boiled egg, so they say.

Whatever caused it, the reality was now kicking in, and from the moment I arrived back home from the hospital, I sat on the computer solidly for two weeks, feverishly reading everything I could find on the internet, to understand what this tumour was and how many people had it, how many different treatments there were and most importantly for me (a dad with two young children) what my life expectancy was going to now be!

For sure, according to the pages and pages of medical testimony I read, Professor Bell was indeed very eminent, but his haste in trying to get me on the operating table within hours of my MRI scan had spooked me. All I could picture now when I thought of Professor Bell was Laurence Olivier in *Marathon Man* playing Dr Christian Szell. Terrifying. *Is it safe, Simon?*

I found some recent research pioneered by another professor, Michael Brada at the Royal Marsden Hospital in Chelsea, of a treatment that claimed 100 per cent success (apart from the hearing coming back bit – I knew that was gone forever) and decided I needed to go and find him.

Sometimes you just have to go and seek people out.

I remember standing outside BBC Broadcasting House in 1981 in the pouring rain, with a cassette of my first band the Drowning Craze in my clammy palm, waiting for the DJ John Peel to arrive to present his radio show. A little handwritten note to him was also in the envelope. I was a little anxious I would miss him.

Was I a few minutes too late? Had he already arrived?

He was, after all, like a god to all of us. I don't use the word god lightly, but I had spent all my teenage years with a little radio under my pillow religiously listening to his show on BBC Radio 1 every night before I fell asleep.

I suddenly saw his silhouette coming down Portland Place towards still-teenage me as I sheltered under the dome of All Souls Church on Langham Place and I must have startled him as he peeked out from beneath his umbrella. But despite my ambush, he was charming and seemed genuinely happy that I had made the effort to see him, especially given the downpour. I mumbled something incoherent and handed him the envelope. It was clearly an exchange that he was familiar with and he thanked me and continued on his way into the beautiful art deco building in front of us.

I didn't think anything would ever come of it but was thrilled just to have mumbled with him for a few seconds. I don't think my big gold dream back then was to even get a record deal. It was to be played on the John Peel show, and well, even if he never played us, I still owed him so much. Near enough every band I went to see and every record or tape I bought during the '70s and '80s, I heard on his show first.

Two weeks later, just as I walked in the door from work, the phone rang in the Earl's Court flat I shared with my best friend Stan, and it was John Walters, Peel's producer from Radio 1, who said that John 'loved the music' and wanted to offer us a session at Maida Vale.

My brain slowed to a pause. He 'LOVED THE MUSIC'. He didn't say he 'liked' it, he LOVED it.

I felt like a kid with a massive teacher crush.

She said she 'loved my essay'. She must therefore love ME!!

Seeking people out can work, I thought, as I drove up to the Royal Marsden Hospital in Chelsea to meet Michael Brada.

It was a blustery but sunny morning as I pulled into the hospital car park. As I walked into the building, I had an overwhelming feeling of calmness and positivity, neither of which were my natural default settings.

In my late-night internet scrolling, I had read that the Royal Marsden was so named in honour of its founder Dr William Marsden who, after losing his beloved wife Elizabeth to cancer in 1851, vowed to dedicate the rest of his life to studying the disease and looking for new treatments.

And maybe knowing this small titbit of info on the history behind this place, and that it had been studying cancers and tumours for 150 years within these very walls, gave me a comforting feeling as I climbed the stairs up to the Oncology Unit. I hoped Michael Brada would be like Professor Xavier and he would save me.

Professor Michael Brada had a kindly and intelligent face, a gentle welcoming smile below bright shining eyes clearly fronting the sharpest of minds. I liked him instantly, and his serene demeanour reminded me of Robin Williams when he played Oliver Sacks in *Awakenings*. Part-scientist, part-psychologist, and after he read my notes and looked at my scans, he began talking. While some of it went in one ear and well . . . not out the other one I guess, I trusted every word. The bits I remembered (doctors look away now) were that I have a vestibular schwannoma (also known as an 'acoustic neuroma'), a benign tumour that whilst generally very slow-growing is attached on one side to the stem of the brain and on the other to the nerves connecting my ear. When he said the words 'vestibular schwannoma', I'll be honest, all I could think of was Mike Myers as Wayne Campbell saying it in *that* voice, with Garth tittering, saying it sounded like a vicar getting a hard-on.

The surgical procedure as previously proposed by Professor Bell was tricky, a bit like trying to get one of those price stickers off the front of old vinyl records. More often than not, even the most delicate slow removal resulted in you taking some of the beautiful sleeve with you. Even if you are precise, as Professor Bell no doubt was, if the glutinous tumour is too tacky when you start to gently pull it away, it can damage OTHER nerves as well, meaning that as well as losing my hearing, I could also lose control over the right eye muscles, the right side of my mouth, right arm, leg etc. You'll hopefully now understand my reticence in submitting to the knife that day.

Michael Brada's treatments at Royal Marsden, however, were non-invasive. His speciality is called fractionated stereotactic radiosurgery or Gamma Knife Surgery. He thankfully described it simply, as my reaction to long medical words was to either look blank or think of scenes from comedy films, usually *Young Frankenstein*.

'You would come into the hospital every morning for a month, we would put something like a crash helmet on your head and we blast tiny zaps of radiation at the tumour and break it up. Half an hour a day. Then after a month, you're done.'

Scrambled egg, I thought.

Perhaps the bit I have to be most thankful for is what he said next.

'Does it bother you?' he asked.

'Which bit?' I queried.

He paused. 'Well, some people just cannot deal with there being a tumour in their head, and often just want rid of it immediately. For some it just feels like the monster from the movie *Alien* inside there and they need it removed. How do you feel about it? Does it bother you?'

'No, not particularly. Certainly not if removing it is going to potentially cause me further problems.'

'OK, good. Then let me suggest this. Go away. Live your life. You seem like a busy chap, go be you. If you change your mind one day and suddenly feel anxious or if the tumour suddenly grows and impacts your balance or something along those lines, call me up and we'll book you right in. That could be tomorrow or in twenty years . . . or never.'

It was that paused 'or never' that has stuck with me all this time. His confidence, reassurance, almost nonchalance over the whole saga of what had happened to me over these last few weeks gave me such strength moving forward from that meeting, a stark contrast to how I had felt since my first diagnosis.

Within a year of meeting Michael Brada, my wife Karen and I separated.

I know what you're thinking but the curious thing about this, which I didn't discover until many years later, is that she wanted us to break up a year earlier but what with my sudden loss of hearing, and then the diagnosis of the brain tumour, she just felt terrible about it all and didn't want to put me through any more drama. Bless her. We first met in 1980 when we were both eighteen years old and eleven years later had two wonderful children, but the last few years we had grown apart and fallen out of love with each other. I take responsibility for that. Cocteau Twins had taken over my life to a large degree and it was never a job that I felt able to leave 'at the office'. I always seemed to be at the office too which didn't help.

Turning forty was supposed to be a time for reflection, and yet the approach hadn't been troubling me at all. However, within a year, I was divorced, deaf in one ear and housing a brain tumour. I couldn't tell my children, they were too young to understand and I didn't want to worry them, and I felt any credibility I had earned in music, as a musician, an A&R man or a producer, would be in serious jeopardy if anyone found out. So I kept it a secret from everyone apart from those close to me.

'If you want to keep a secret, you must also hide it from yourself.'
George Orwell

CHAPTER ONE

School

My dad, Ivor, was from a family of Polish Jews who along with tens of thousands of similar families had escaped to London in the 1880s fleeing the pogroms and persecution in Russia and the Pale of Settlement. My grandfather, Hirsch Pomerance, was born in Warsaw in 1886 when it was under Russian rule and was brought to England shortly after his birth and the family settled initially in East London. They moved to Marylebone in 1914 when Hirsch married his sweetheart, Sarah. Hirsch was a tailor's machinist and managed to get work in the rag trade. Dad always talked about the love that his family had for each other, and I certainly saw that growing up whenever we had family get-togethers with his brothers and sisters. Ivor was one of five children and they all lived together in a terraced house in the Marylebone area, not far from Broadcasting House, home to the BBC which would one day be like a second home for him. He had two brothers and two sisters. There were the twins Gertrude and Len, ten years his senior, then Lillian two years older, then Ivor and finally Harold.

Dad wasn't a child prodigy exactly, but like his sister Lillian was a massive show-off (his words not mine) and he was already entertaining the large family at a very young age, singing and playing anything he could get his hands on. His grandmother had bequeathed his mum, Sarah, an ancient Zimmermann auto-harp and Dad would play tunes on that. Lillian was obsessed with dancing, and still brimming with sibling pride he would tell me with that beautiful wide smile on his face that she actually preferred dancing to walking and usually waltzed her way home from school every day, then would later shimmy her way upstairs to bed, imagining she was Ginger Rogers. With her vibrant red hair, maybe that wasn't so far off.

Dad was given piano lessons for his sixth birthday and, by the time he was nine, had won a scholarship to the Trinity School of Music which he attended for free every weekend until he was sixteen. Hirsch, his father, was not earning very much at all, yet with five children to look after, even then Ivor knew that a scholarship like this was a godsend. Like me, he preferred music to his school work and was soon excelling at the piano. But the war was coming and all that would soon be coming to an abrupt halt.

For all those families living in London, a plan was devised to get the younger children out of the city with the capital about to become the target of so many German bombing raids, and Ivor was sent away to the country with his younger brother Harold in September 1939. They went to stay with a family at number 8,

Hoadlands Cottages, in Handcross near Haywards Heath, Sussex, only a few miles from where I live now. I took a drive out there last September and just sat in the car for I'm not sure how long as rain began to fall steadily, the drops hitting the roof in rhythm. I opened the window and took a deep breath of that earthy petrichor scent as it permeated the air. I imagined the fear Dad and Harold would have had as they arrived at this house those seventy-odd years ago.

The children of course hated being away from their family, living with strangers in the country, but when Dad was allowed to return to London briefly for his bar mitzvah in October on his thirteenth birthday, he managed to persuade his mum and dad to let him stay home a bit longer as the bombing had not begun, though when it did his school in nearby Clipstone Street was totally destroyed.

Finally, when he came back to London, a letter was waiting, offering him, as a result of his exceptional music grades, a free place at University College School in Hampstead, a place he described as 'a posh fee-paying school that I never in my wildest dreams would have imagined I would attend'.

He hated it from day one. Being a scholarship boy would have been difficult enough, but he was also one of only two Jewish boys in the entire school and soon discovered to his confusion and dismay that anti-Semitism was also rife in his own tiny circle. Given that his family had come to England precisely to find a safe haven from such hatred, he found that baffling, but he decided, after putting up with it for a couple of months, that he had to get out. His plan was to simply refuse to do *any* work.

At all. Pens down! For a scholarship pupil, this was educational suicide, and with his reports subsequently going from bad to worse, he was indeed asked to leave. Naturally he feared the wrath of his parents, but they were a large loving family and never said a cross word to him about it. They simply found him a different school in Chelsea, where thankfully he was able to thrive.

'I ran away from three different boarding schools before joining a circus school and eventually I became an actor. The only thing I learned at boarding school was never to send my child to one.'

Vincent Cassel

At *my* first school, we were allowed to take an instrument home for a night or two to see how we got on with it. I was given an oboe. Even in the mouth of a healthy six-year-old, an oboe will make the sound of a dying duck. But my asthma was terrible in childhood – probably some residual issue following me being a month premature, fed from a bottle and in an incubator for two weeks – so possibly I should have thought about that before taking it home. In front of my expectant proud parents, one of whom was a professional musician, it sounded like the duck had already expired and this was merely the slow death rattle. I could see the look of disappointment, nay horror, on their faces as I once more wheezed feebly into the reed. The following day, having decided overnight that music was not for me, I returned home from school with a violin. After tea, it was time for another round of humiliation. Now, *no* child ever in the history of the world got a round of applause playing violin for the first time, and terrible though it sounded to me, their faces were at least not quite as tortured as they were the previous night as I scratched away, dying inside. They encouraged me to 'give it a go for a bit', and not one for disappointing them again, I feigned enthusiasm. I returned to school in the morning and smiled weakly when Miss Allen, the teacher, asked me how I'd got on. 'Shall we put you down for some violin lessons?'

Dad had become a professional musician, playing, arranging and songwriting for some of the biggest names in pop music, and his musical prowess was well known within the school. I am sure that this was why before too long I found myself as first violin, leader of the orchestra *and* singing in the school choir. I'd come to *hate* playing the violin and did the bare minimum of practice, but somehow got to Grade 5. School reports were always of the '*clearly has some talent and aptitude but Simon is always talking and distracting others, can do better*' type, and I am sure by now, Mum and Dad, with the other three children now 'adults', just wanted some peace and quiet, so it was decided to ship me, the youngest, off to boarding school.

After Dad's own bad experiences with schools, the anti-Semitism, the war and his working-class roots, it was perhaps surprising that he and Mum considered sending me off to a boarding school at all in the early '70s, but when I asked him about it later in life, he said they just thought it was the right thing to do. His success in music in the '60s had afforded him, Mum and the children a nice house and maybe he thought it *was* going to be OK. That *I* was going to be OK.

I am completely sure it was *not* the right thing to do. The first year was brutal and I considered running away about ten times. It felt like we were not far from the scenes in both Lindsay Anderson's *If. . .* and *Tom Brown's School Days* which were set almost a century apart. Nietzsche once said, 'What doesn't kill you makes you stronger,' and in my first year a new boy, who had come over from Canada, jumped off a bridge near the school and did kill himself. Then, only a week later, one of the older boys in my house, who had been nice to me after I gave him the last two of my cigarettes, died of a heroin overdose. I swiftly settled into the brutality because you had no choice really.

About twenty-five of us first-term boarders slept in a large dormitory on the second floor, with each bed separated by a wooden partition.

First-termers – 'yearlings' was the parlance back then – had to be in bed by 9 p.m. and 'lights out' was shortly after. One of the 'monitors' (this school's vernacular for 'prefect') would shout out to stop talking, then switch the lights off, and then we'd hear the huge dorm door squeak loudly on its way to its final gentle clunk as it shut. We usually waited a few minutes before daring to make a sound, because the housemaster would often be heard coming through, on his way to his rooms on the other side of the house, to say 'goodnight'. To be more accurate, you could smell him coming through as he had a pipe permanently embedded in the corner of his mouth. Even now on the rare occasions I smell someone with a pipe, I am transported back to this time.

By the way, this isn't one of those nice 'nostalgia' smells of childhood like lead petrol, the fresh pages of a *Beano* annual at

Christmas or a girl walking past wearing Charlie perfume that I *want* to remember. This is the smell of fear and remembering something you have tried with all your might to forget.

There were twelve houses in the school; the one I was in was built in 1872 and felt like nothing had changed in the hundred or so years since. Our housemaster was Colin Davies, who everyone called 'Stump', apparently due to his diminutive dimensions. If they were to make a movie with his character in it, he would have been played by Kenneth Williams with no method effort required on his behalf. He had an old basset hound called Claire that stank to high heaven and looked like Clement Freud. He was also our Latin teacher in the first year. Colin that is, not the basset hound. The house did also have a matron who, to continue the *Carry On* theme, *was* just like Hattie Jacques, strict and no-nonsense.

'There is no such thing as dead languages, only dormant minds.'
Carlos Ruiz Zafón

Audere est facere: to dare is to do.

I didn't learn that at school, I learned it at Tottenham Hotspur Football Club. This succinctly sums up my education.

One night in my first term, the lights had been switched off shortly after 9 p.m. and after a few minutes' silence, the rumble of twenty or so restless children whispering grew increasingly louder. Even though there were wooden dividers between the beds, there was no 'roof' so you could just stand on the bed and chat to your neighbour or, as was more common, come out of your area altogether and go into someone else's and sit on their bed and chat or just scream at each other and have fights and throw things. Many children stayed in bed and slept, tried to at least, but hey, what a surprise, I was never one of those. I had several close friends who also liked smoking, music, football, being daft and bending the rules as far as they could be bent. Simon Crisford was one of those and, even aged twelve, was obsessed with horse racing. Before too long, he had infected quite a few of us with the bug.

I was sitting on his bed, studying form for tomorrow's racecard in his copy of the *Sporting Life* (I was quite sure even back then that no other twelve-year-old schoolkid had a dog-eared copy of the *Sporting Life* always in reach) while he was lying on the floor drawing out some of his favourite jockey's colours in a book, when the large overhead lights suddenly came on and flooded the room. We froze in silence. Occasionally the 'monitors' would just pop their heads in when the noise level was maybe increasing a little too much, and then leave again without incident and we could continue mucking about. But within a few seconds, we knew that *this* 'monitor' had turned off the lights, pretended to leave and then just remained hidden in the dorm this whole time, stealthily waiting in the dark to strike. This felt more like when the German officers in Colditz burst in while the POWs were digging a secret tunnel. As we quickly tried to empty the metaphorical sand through the holes in our pyjamas, the commandant kicked the flimsy door of Simon's cubicle open and marched in.

The 'monitor', a power-crazy son of a Greek shipping tycoon, grabbed the racing paper and ordered me back to my bed.

Damn! I had even circled a few dead-cert horses in red pen and now he had them! He was built like a small tank and carrying a hockey stick as he followed me. Ominous.

As I slipped quickly and sheepishly under the sheet, he lifted his arm above his head and cracked the hockey stick down and across my shins.

Fuck *me* that hurt.

I'll say I didn't scream because I don't remember, but I bet I fucking did. I know I didn't play football for a few weeks which hurt a lot more than the horrible dark purple and yellow bruises that the sadistic little prick left me with. As I lay back alone in my little metal bed in the heavy silence that now hung over the rest of the dorm, I thought long and hard about digging for escape.

That first year progressed with many more incidents, not quite as dramatic and immediately painful as the hockey stick across the shins, but it all seemed like an elongated initiation, seemingly never-ending at times. I guess looking back on it now, we didn't really learn very fast, because we continued to get caught, but the punishment always seemed so wildly inappropriate and always unchallenged. The psychological effect of what went on at school has lived deep within me for a long time. I learned both how to cope emotionally but also how to suppress a lot of emotion. I am sure the reason I still can't sleep well at night stems back to these early traumas.

One day, one of our young friends reported some money missing from his cubicle. A search was instigated with no success, but Stump let it be known in no uncertain terms at lunch that the culprit would be caught. It was like a little school whodunnit.

25

The next afternoon, *another* theft was reported and almost immediately a heavy bell was rung slowly and portentously. This solemn summons meant everyone in the house (about 120 pupils) had to congregate at once in Founders Court which was situated outside our house. The huge bronze statue of Thomas Sutton had sat there since 1911, three hundred years after he founded the school, and his big fat bronze head and disapproving glare beamed down upon us as we all lined up on the gravel on one side of the courtyard. The housemaster started with us 'yearlings'.

'Hold your palms out in front of you, and as I walk past you, turn them over and then back again.'

One of the boys started crying. I could see his shoulders shaking and bouncing up and down.

It turned out that Stump had put some special invisible ink on a wallet in one of the cubicles after the first theft, and ensured it was left out in the open, in a kind of primitive 'sting' operation.

The blue 'ink' would only reveal itself after several minutes and was impossible to wash off. Credit where credit is due. It was ingenious.

Caught blue-handed.

The boy was suspended from school. Lucky bastard. I didn't steal *anything* and had a limp for a month.

I often wonder if, by the time we get to school, we are already predisposed to behave or misbehave. It seems that the more brutal the regime, the more we would rebel, but I guess we just got smarter in how. In a school of around 800 pupils, it's impossible to keep track of everyone all the time, and as the years wore on, either we became more masterful in avoiding being caught, or the 'monitors' were less bothered about punishing boys who were growing fast and catching them up physically. The language of cruelty and violence wasn't only spoken by the sons of the upper classes, and in those early years of trying to work out who you were, it just spread like a virus.[1]

So I made it through the first couple of years. Just. Football certainly helped, as it always has, and I found my own very small group, other boys who to me had no airs and graces, no affectations, who were just ordinary kids who hated the stuffed-shirt entitled sadists too – the ones you knew, even at the age of twelve, would turn into the likes of Jacob Rees-Mogg. In fact, at the age of twelve, they were already like Jacob Rees-Mogg.

Being tall, and decent enough at football and music, gave me a distinct advantage at a boarding school. Such things were valued highly, if not always by the staff but certainly by your peers where it was survival of the fittest. These fortunate assets also conveniently masked my lack of ability in any other subjects.

---

[1] I never went back to a school reunion as I couldn't wait to get out of there, but I kept getting the invitations and kept ignoring them year after year, until finally thirty years later they stopped. I did get asked to a house reunion several times in my fifties, and when my best pals Stan, Simon and a group of good friends said they'd go if I'd go etc., etc., I thought, *well, it can't be that bad*. I hadn't seen any of these great people in decades and it was just a dinner in some fancy restaurant. As I walked in, I immediately saw the perpetrator of my beating for the first time in forty years, sitting there at the table laughing and joking. I reverted to the thirteen-year-old me, sat at the table and barely spoke a word all night and couldn't even bring myself to eat. I left as soon as I could without saying a word. The brain is fascinating isn't it? It retains EVERYTHING.

After my O levels, it was discussed with Mum and Dad that maybe this wasn't quite the place for me. No shit. I had taken and retaken maths O level eight times (and by the time I had left school, eleven times) in an attempt to get good-enough grades to stay, but the musical prowess and the burgeoning football skills *just* about kept me there.

However, when the violin lessons began to clash with football practice, without warning I quit. My teacher was an absolute monster so it really wasn't a difficult decision. If she could have got away with hitting me with it she would have. Scraping away doing my scales over and over with this gorgon screeching at me, while I looked out of the window over the playing fields to all my mates running about having fun, I knew I'd done the right thing. Stump and my parents weren't so sure.

Of course, like all football-loving kids, we wanted to emulate our heroes. For school I played up front as centre-forward, imagining myself as Spurs striker Martin Chivers and behind me in midfield was Dave Allison, who played in the style of Spurs legend Glenn Hoddle. Dave wore Adidas and I wore Puma. Pelé and Johan Cruyff wore Puma and while I did once have a pair of Stylo Matchmakers as worn by George Best, they weren't very comfortable. I loved the look and feel of the Puma King and while it wasn't quite the golden slipper story, they did make me feel special when I slid my foot inside. Maybe for a few minutes per game, knowing that these same bits of leather were being championed by two of the most skilful players on earth, my game was mildly elevated – until I got clattered by that thundering tackle from behind by the kid with calves thicker than my thighs.

So Dave and I wore different boots and we were in different houses *and* classes, plus he was a year ahead of me. In a school so large, your closest friends would generally be your immediate peers through proximity so we didn't really know each other *that* well at the time, but we both loved Spurs. In Ivor's family, you either supported Spurs or Arsenal, and Dad took me several times to White Hart Lane in the late '60s, and as quality time with him was so rare and precious, my enthusiasm was quite boundless. Half a century on, it remains so.

In our last year at school, Dave and I had the chance finally to bond properly when we shared a room on a weekend trip away to play against Repton for the school and, corny as it sounds, our connection on the pitch was real. He was the Hoddle to my Mark Falco. Actually no, Mark Falco wasn't that good. How about Dave was the Hoddle to my Steve Archibald? No, that doesn't really work either. Dave was the Hoddle to my Chris Waddle? That's better because when I ran I did definitely waddle. When we were in the school first XI together, we couldn't have known what would happen in our futures, but Dave and I continued to play football together for many, many years after we left school – well into our thirties – most auspiciously in Nigel from Rough Trade's team Red Star in one of the Sunday Leagues.[2]

---

[2] Happy to report that even though I was only fifteen when I first met him, Nigel House and I have been firm friends since then too. He is absolutely one of the best people in our strange business, and his commitment to his shop and to promoting the music he believed in remains as strong as it did fifty years ago.

Dave's a writer and a poet now, and when we go for long walks every month or so with our dogs, we talk about everything. Apart from my wife Abbey and my brother Nick, Dave is the only person I feel I can share stuff with. I have trust issues, find it hard to let people in too close, and similarly I know that I distance myself from others, so it feels good that Dave has been a true constant in my life for almost fifty years. We have both been going to Spurs since the 1980s, still both have season tickets, and still sit next to each other, with his son Leo, and my youngest Will, and our friend Judy. Dave was also my best man when Abbey and I got married in 2013 in Carmel, Monterey and I couldn't think of a lovelier friend to have had all these long years. He does have a lifelong obsession with Andy Latimer from Camel that I would love to understand but cannot. I didn't leave school with anything educationally notable, three very-below-average A level passes, but having Dave in my life is infinitely more valuable to me than a redundant qualification.

CHAPTER TWO

The Dawning of an Age

While I was back in London during the half-term school holiday in October 1976, my musical enlightenment truly began, when Stan Frankland and I started listening to John Peel on Radio 1 and going to the early punk gigs. Stan was the same age as me, but he was *that* smart, he went straight into the year above the rest of us. But on the days we were at school in 1976–77, we still went to Record Corner in the town near school together every week to pick up our seven-inch singles of the songs we'd heard on John Peel the night before. I had a little pocket radio that I kept under my pillow so I could listen to his show at night.

Stan was a beautiful, handsome boy, talented at everything; cricket, football, all the classes. All the boys fancied him, all the girls fancied him, and he was aloof and androgynous and no one knew if he was into boys or girls or both. He was quite the enigma. He already had all the Bowie and Roxy Music albums, and we would listen to them constantly, but now he also had *Horses* by Patti Smith and a New York Dolls album. Being fourteen and with music coursing through my veins, soaking up the punk scene like a sponge seemed the most natural thing in the world, and it was the first time I felt part of something that resonated with me, not just physically but emotionally and socially. We took the train to London from school as often as we could get away with it. Stan bought 'New Rose' by the Damned back to school and I bought 'Spiral Scratch' by Buzzcocks and both were worn out within a few days. It was the start of our obsession. When the Roxy opened in late 1976, we went as often as we could. We saw Eater (their drummer Dee Generate was fourteen, the same age as we were), Generation X, Slaughter and the Dogs, the Lurkers and, early in '77, the Vibrators and the Drones. On the weekend of my fifteenth birthday, Stan and I went there to see X-Ray Spex on the Saturday and then, on my actual birthday the next day, we heard from Nigel at Rough Trade that the Pistols were playing a free secret gig at the Screen on the Green in Islington, this time with Sid Vicious on bass. Sadly, we couldn't get in, but to be honest, it just felt exciting enough being outside.

If we weren't at the Roxy, we were to be found at the Marquee or the Nashville, the Hope & Anchor or Vortex. Then we'd some-times go to the bigger rooms like the Music Machine in Camden where we just about survived Eddie and the Hot Rods with Sham 69, a terrible pairing of clashing genres with that kind of awful tension that was par for the course at football matches in the 1970s. Occasionally we would go to the Rainbow in Finsbury

Park. Stan and Nick bought us all tickets for my sixteenth birthday in '78 to see Patti Smith here. Before the gig I saw John Lydon outside standing talking to some people. I went up and asked him for an autograph.

'Fuck off,' he snarled.

We went to the Lyceum (home of *The Lion King* since 1999) where we saw Peter Perrett's Only Ones (*another* Spurs man – respect, Pete!) and UK Subs, to the Electric Ballroom where we saw Pauline Murray's Penetration and, a year later, Joy Division. Add all of this together and our teenage years were being defined for us every night. From 1976 to 1981, we were getting the best education possible, but none of it was at school. School taught me who I *didn't* want to be.

That whole year of '77 was a blur of London, school and learning the bass. My brother Nick gave me a jazz bass that he had swapped for his green Baldwin Double Six twelve-string guitar.

'The bass is just like a big violin really,' Nick told Mum who was still sore at my recent reckless abandonment of the fiddle. I think she wanted me to be the next Itzhak Perlman as she kept sending me his latest cassettes. I remember opening one care package at school hoping it was going to be some biscuits and cake and finding one tape of 'Itzhak Perlman Plays Fritz Kreisler' and the other was Perlman and John Williams playing together. Perlman, like Dad, was of Jewish Polish parents and only recently in writing this book have I finally got round to listening to those records. I placed the cassette tapes in my drawer underneath my pants. As kind though the thought was, I was only really interested in the Clash and Wire at that moment.

At first I wasn't sure what to make of the 'big violin', but when *Never Mind the Bollocks* came out later that month, I tried playing along with the album in my bedroom and it seemed easy enough. In one short afternoon I had the whole album nailed and I figured I would be ready to stand in for Sid if something terrible happened to him. The other album I tried to learn was *My Aim is True* by Elvis Costello, but his bassist Johnny Ciambotti was clearly in a wholly different league. I figured I had a long way to go before I could get up to that level.

When I reluctantly returned to school after summer to start my A levels, they had changed their centuries-old policy and now allowed girls to board too.

Lindsay Anderson's *If . . .* has always been a favourite film because it so beautifully articulated those feelings of loneliness, confusion, rebellion and obsession all festering away, creating so many anti-establishment urgings. I'm sure the only reason the school avoided more major incidents was their brainwave of allowing girls into the school for the last two years. Of course, at that impressionable and sexually confusing age, after being in separate schools since I was six years old, the close proximity of hundreds of girls suddenly appearing out of nowhere quickly put paid to any ideas of a revolution.

As a fifteen-year-old still discovering what the fuck was going on down below, this influx was both incredible and a disaster. Certainly for my studies anyway. It was in this sixteenth year that I lost my hitherto closely guarded virginity. But not as you might now be imagining, at our newly mixed school, but rather at Stan's brother Nick's birthday party at his flat in London.

I won't bother you with the mucky details, but suffice to say, as the party was entering the witching hour, I was sitting slumped in an armchair, sleepy and drunk while a friend of Nick's, whom we will call Verity, was sitting atop me, for quite some time stroking my hair telling me how lovely it was while whatever was going on down there, went on.

I don't recall any particular pleasure in 'the moment' and I'm pretty sure she didn't either, but after she sweetly kissed me goodbye – *I feel it was more of a 'there, there' kiss than a 'thank you'* – I slipped into a hunched, haunted sleep in the armchair with my long black overcoat over my body. A kinda sheet of shame.

CHAPTER THREE

1979

Whenever I get asked my favourite year in music, I always without hesitation say '1979'.

Now bear in mind this was the year Michael Jackson released *Off the Wall*, Supertramp *Breakfast in America*, Fleetwood Mac *Tusk* and AC/DC *Highway to Hell*, along with other huge sellers by the Eagles and Pink Floyd, but these names and albums meant nothing to me.

These are just a few of the records from 1979 that meant *everything* to me, and I am bound to them for life.

The Slits: *Cut*

After Stan and I went to see the Clash at Tiffany's in Purley in late 1978, our lives were never really the same. The Slits were the support on that 'Sort It Out' tour and we thought they blew the Clash off the stage that night and I *loved* the Clash!

Their set back in April at the Rock Against Racism event in Victoria Park was electric, unforgettable. I had just turned sixteen and met a petite punkette called Liz that day on the RAR march from Trafalgar Square, and was immediately smitten as we walked together for hours. I came up to London the following weekend to see her, but in the evening when we went back to this squat where she was staying and we lay down on her mattress, she reached into her bag, brought out all her drug paraphernalia and began the dark and depressing ritual of injecting heroin into her arm. I stayed with her until Monday morning but knew that as much as I liked her, this wasn't something I could handle. *Should I Stay Or Should I Go.*

That slightly all over the place dub-punk energy of the Slits was the blueprint for so much of my musical taste that I have carried with me since and is still firmly with me today.

The album was produced by Dennis Bovell, with Budgie replacing original drummer Palmolive on drums, and features the classic line-up of Ari Up, Viv Albertine and Tessa Pollitt, and came out on Island Records. Still sounds as fresh now as it did then. Imitators won't get close.

Wire: *154*

My room-mate in my second year at school, Simon Crisford, loved a lot of the punk singles that Stan and I would bring back, but horse racing was still his main obsession and whenever I could, I would accompany him down to the bookies in town as I was tall and could pass for older when he needed me to put a bet on. One of the punk bands Simon *did* love was Wire, especially their debut

Pink Flag. I loved this and the second album *Chairs Missing*, both fantastic records, but their third *154* was when I really connected with Wire in a deeper way. I imagined for a long time what the meaning of the enigmatic title might have been. Was it some magical number with spiritual significance? No. It was called *154* after the number of gigs the band had done up to that point. That's really the only disappointing thing about the whole album. It has sad poignant love songs such as 'I Should Have Known Better' which opens the LP, along with classic pop songs like 'Map Ref No. 41°N 93°W' which I played over and over when I first bought the LP. The production by the band and Mike Thorne is remarkable and streets ahead of other records from this period. Ken Thomas was engineer and his CV was peerless. (He was to work with my own band Cocteau Twins on our 'Aikea-Guinea' EP five years later in 1984 at Jacobs Studio in Farnham.) Thorne did a lot of work for the band's label Harvest, but in the next few years also produced 'Tainted Love' by Soft Cell, 'Uncertain Smile' by The The and many other very special releases.

I've asked myself, 'Why 1979?' many times. Was seventeen just the age when I was starting to work things out, when I was super-receptive to all these new sounds and styles? Punk had been such a brightly burning comet passing through. It got us all riled up, in a good way, focused our attention on all the shit that was going on. But then it all went wrong, and ended up as the exact opposite of what had been so important and life-changing in the first place. This did leave a bitter taste in the mouth. Thankfully, the music that followed was exactly what I needed to cure the hangover, the post-punk comedown.

Public Image Ltd: *Metal Box*

And *Metal Box* by PiL – try to forget what PiL later became and focus on *Metal Box* itself – for a few of us anyway, signalled the death of punk and the birth of whatever the next thing was going to be. Arriving in a metal container that looked like it might house a film spool, and with the album split across three twelve-inch singles, this *felt* subversive and said so much about the stodgy old rock albums by the stodgy old supergroups that dominated the charts, and showed that you could create beautiful objects in an artful way all the while making music that had courage, was original *and* striking. This line-up of John Lydon, when he was still both stylish and had something interesting to say, Jah Wobble (another lovely man who shares a love of Spurs with me) with his wandering dub basslines that ARE the backbone of this eclectic collection of sounds and rhythms, and Keith Levene (RIP), whose wonderfully strange and inventive guitar lines influenced a whole generation of my friends, was the *only* line-up of PiL that truly thrilled me and reinforced why I wanted to be in a band of my own.

The Pop Group: *Y*

A similar refusal to obey any rules may explain the attraction to me in Bristol's the Pop Group and their 1979 album *Y*. The production, also by Dennis Bovell who had so masterfully guided the Slits' *Cut* deep into my heart, was rough around the edges but it is always *at* the edges where interesting things happen in music. Drummer Bruce Smith (who had replaced Budgie in the Slits when the latter got the call from Siouxsie and the Banshees following the departure of *their* drummer Kenny Morris) and bassist Simon Underwood created this sensual underbelly of funk, dub and jazz, but not like anything I had ever heard before. The guitars of John Waddington and Gareth Sager were jagged and unhinged. Over the top of this maelstrom of guitars, the words and tone of vocalist Mark Stewart (RIP) were urgent and provocative, distorted and echoing. I lapped it all up. As well as this, in the same year they released 'She Is Beyond Good And Evil' which, nearly forty-five years later, is still my favourite track to play on the rare occasions I get to play my vinyl records at clubs. That unholy screech of guitars at the beginning makes the hair on my skin stand to attention every time. *Y* the album is as vital a record as I own.

Joy Division: *Unknown Pleasures*

The sound of isolation, desolation and loneliness. And the darkness that it reflected was real and long-lasting. It was the Winter of Discontent. Literally. The country was in a mess, with continual strikes and industrial disputes and when Labour's James Callaghan lost the general election to the Conservative leader Margaret Thatcher, we were about to enter a dark age of government that we have never really come fully out of. The new prime minister became Europe's first elected female head of government and that really is the only positive thing I could say about her.

Unknown Pleasures captured this time so perfectly, whether by fate or design. I got to see them play on four occasions and as I think back to each one, when it replays in my mind, it is in black, white and grey and I am standing transfixed by the twitching, compelling awkwardness of Ian Curtis. Time, conversely, standing completely still.

Talking Heads: *Fear of Music*

Their third album, as brilliant as it is and following two of the greatest albums of all time – *77*, then *More Songs about Buildings and Food* in 1978 – is not even their best which was coming a year later. With Brian Eno back at the controls, it was loose and more minimal than previous records, and felt like a reinvention. Not too many bands make *four* of the best albums of all time in *four* consecutive years. Talking Heads did. (Rory in my office insists Black Sabbath did too but I'll have to get back to you on that.) I don't know how but they are one of the only bands I never got to see from this era. Talking Heads and Television were two of my favourite bands and I never saw *either* of them in their pomp. I did go to see Television in 1992 on their first 'comeback' tour having been away for about ten years. It was a massive disappointment.

Linton Kwesi Johnson: *Forces of Victory*

On one of my many trips to the Rough Trade shop in Notting Hill with Stan, I met a couple of black punks, one of whom was called Dennis. We got talking up at the counter because it turned out that we were buying the same single 'Germ-Free Adolescents' by X-Ray Spex. We kept seeing each other out and about around West London and became friends over the next few years, and he would always come to the early Drowning

Craze shows until he moved away to Birmingham around 1982. He was lovely and funny, and we often bumped into each other at the Nashville or the Roxy and I was with him down the front of the Reggae Regulars set at the Rainbow with Patti Smith the night before my sixteenth birthday.

I saw him one afternoon probably late 1978, shuffling slowly down Westbourne Park Road. I asked if he was OK and he told me that he'd been stopped by the police just walking to the corner shop to get cigarettes around midday a couple of weeks before, that they'd jumped out of a van and told him to empty his pockets. While he was doing it, one of the police took a truncheon and cracked him across the back of the legs forcing him to fall on to the pavement. While down and in excruciating pain, he asked why they'd done that, as he had done as they'd asked, and the same policeman hit him again on the front of his legs this time. They hauled him into the police van and he spent the night in a cell at the station with no medical attention. He was never charged with any offence and he physically recovered over time, but seeing him depressed and without his usual zip was sad and upsetting. The inherent racism and injustice dished out by the very people who were supposed to be protecting ordinary citizens going about their business taught me an invaluable early lesson in how 'the authorities' operate. These incidents were not isolated; the experience of 'black Britain' in the late 1970s was shameful. There was a law passed called the 'sus law' (suspected person) which allowed the police to stop, search and arrest anyone they deemed 'suspicious'. None of my white friends were ever stopped.

To explain why I've always loved Linton Kwesi Johnson is probably partially rooted in my friendship with Dennis. I have a tattoo on my arm of the cover of his *Bass Culture* album that came out a year later. But most tellingly and why it resonates with me so deeply, on his debut LP *Forces of Victory*, on the A side of the vinyl, is a song called 'Sonny's Lettah (Anti-Sus poem)' which is a heartbreaking tale of Sonny and his younger brother, Jim, written from Sonny to his mother while in prison. Like Dennis, police pulled up in a van, jumped out and grabbed Jim while he was minding his own business. As the inevitable beating ensued, Sonny couldn't stand by and watch, so he punched one of the police officers who fell to the ground, crashed his head on the kerb, and died. The letter to his mum concludes with the tragic news that Jim was charged with sus while he himself was charged with murder. Sonny tells her not to be too downhearted but to have courage. In one song, so much is told with such grace and dignity in the face of so much brutality.

Linton remains one of the most important lyricists/poets in Britain today and his debut LP is far more than just a reflection of the time. I cannot recommend it highly enough.

David Bowie: *Lodger*

Lodger isn't my *favourite* Bowie LP – that would probably be *Low* or *Heroes* – but it is the one that soundtracked so much of my year. Every single opening bar brings back so many memories.

By 1979 we were getting used to brief mini-encounters with some of our musical icons of the day, but all were trumped on 15 February when Stan, his brother Nick and I went to see the

Human League and Scars at the Nashville Rooms. We loved this venue not just because we could walk there from the flat, but we had discovered a little ruse. We had seen that there was a wooden box at the back of the pub and inside its little door, a ladder that took you up to a small platform. I think it was used for lighting – they always had three chairs up there – and because we were there so often, we had soon worked out that it was often empty during the gig. In recent weeks we had seen a double bill of Echo and the Bunnymen with the Teardrop Explodes in August and then the Cure a week later. On both occasions, we managed to creep up to our private box and watch the bands from the most brilliant raised viewing position.

On the night of the Human League gig, we strolled casually to the little door at the back as we often did, careful not to draw any attention to ourselves. As we began to climb the ladder, someone reached over the top and shouted down, 'Sorry, lads, already occupied up here.' Mildly dejected that our secret was seemingly out and public knowledge, we went back out to the room, grabbed a couple of chairs and pulled them up against the back wall of the wooden box. Stan and I stood on the chairs and Nick stood next to us as Scars walked onstage. Scars were great but as the night wore on a rumour started to whip around the crowd that David Bowie had been seen in the club.

The second we heard it, we knew of course where he was hiding. As the anticipation grew for the Human League, I reached into my jacket where I always kept a tatty little green Letts pocket diary. I ripped out a page, not very neatly as it happens, and placed it on the shelf above our heads, along with a little red 'bookies' pencil. A hand took it off the shelf and then a minute or so later, tapped me on the shoulder and handed it back.

'Bowie '79'.

He had signed it.

Fuck me.

After the Human League finished their perfect set, and the room began emptying out, we stayed close to that back wall and as the little wooden door opened, out walked David Bowie with two minders, looking like a superstar despite having been hunched up in a tiny dark box for an hour in the back of a pub. Ultra stylish as ever wearing a trilby and a tweed jacket, he walked up to the three of us, standing there gormless and star-struck, and enquired which of us had wanted the autograph. I waved or did something daft with my face to indicate it was me and he came over and shook my hand while smiling genuinely and kindly, then did the same with Stan and Nick. I will never forget that day. Nor will I ever forgive the person back at school who stole the page from under my pillow that term.

We were now way beyond the invisible secret ink trick in our schooling, so I sucked it up.

'Bowie '79'.

What a year that was.

CHAPTER FOUR

Stan

By 1980, I was living with Stan in Earl's Court at his elder brother Nick's flat. As music obsessives, days were spent hanging around Beggars Banquet record shop in South Kensington, Rough Trade near Portobello Road and playing pool in the Three Kings. And at night, every night, I was going to a gig with Stan and Nick. For a good year or so we were inseparable. I got a job working at the Beggars Banquet record shop – the boss there, Steve Kent, said that I spent so much time in the shop that I may as well help him out and get paid for it.

My own band at the time – the Drowning Craze – was solely instrumental, though I think that was mostly because we just hadn't found any singers that we really liked yet. Steve Kent's brother Peter worked upstairs from the record shop running a label called Situation 2 who had recently signed the Associates, a band Stan and I had seen a few times and loved. I plucked up the courage to invite Peter to come and watch us rehearse the following week. Miraculously, he said he'd love to work with us, and mentioned a girl from New York who was moving to London whom we should try out on vocals. She'd played with Bush Tetras whom we were already fans of after hearing them on the John Peel show and Peter seemed very excited about it.

When nothing is happening for the band, life seems to move so slowly, and the inertia was hurting us. To suddenly have Peter's help, things just began to happen at speed. He was a man of action, and I loved that. After just one rehearsal, Angela Jaeger joined the band and one week later we went into the studio to record our first single for Situation 2, 'Storage Case/ Damp Bones', at Alvin Studios in London, with my brother Nick helping us out as producer. Two weeks later we played our first show with Angela at Farnham Art College. She was absolutely perfect. That was also the night I met a girl called Karen who was doing an art foundation course there.

Our debut seven-inch single came out on Situation 2 on 24 June 1981. *NME*'s Paul Morley and *Sounds*' Dave McCullough wrote effusively about it. If I could have picked the two journalists I'd have wanted to support our band from the start, it would have been those two. Such brilliant writers, and we somehow made Single of the Week in both papers. I cut the reviews out and stuck them in a blue folder which I still have forty years later, so the significance is not lost on me. Both reviews had name-checked a few bands as reference points for our music: Moby Grape and Pearls Before Swine I had never heard of, but Public Image, 23 Skidoo and Delta 5 were bands we all loved, so for one hot second, the Drowning Craze had a moment in the sun. But storm clouds were a-gathering a few miles in the distance. Our guitarist Paul and I were close and generally felt similarly about things. Paul was an exceptional talent and he had that angular funk side like Malcolm Ross of Josef K, but could also be our Keith Levene at times, creating little counter melodies and weird sounds.

Just when we were planning to go back into the studios to record a follow-up to 'Storage Case', Angela called to say she wanted to go back to New York to finish art school, and before we had a chance to bask in any residual glory at all from those favourable reviews, that chapter ended as quickly as it had seemingly begun. Undeterred, Peter set about finding us a replacement. Frankie Nardiello from Chicago, who had been in a band with Ministry's Al Jørgensen, was someone Peter felt would be different enough from Angela as to avoid direct comparison. He was both a wonderfully charismatic frontman and an adorable person, so within a few weeks we had our second American singer. When John Peel's producer called me to offer us a Maida Vale session, we hadn't had much time to rehearse with Frankie, but this was a Peel session and we could not mess this up. It *had* to work. This was everything.

Our performance was passable.

But momentum *was* starting to pick up again, and two more seven-inch singles followed in quick succession with Situation 2, 'Trance' (also in 1981) and 'Heat'/ 'Replays' (1982) before we got offered a couple of our biggest shows. The first was with my heroes the Birthday Party at the Africa Centre in Covent Garden, and the second with legendary drag queen Divine at Heaven under the arches in Charing Cross in London. As crazy as that combo of gigs sounds, both artists were misfits, and also both signed to Beggars labels, so we just looked at them as 'family'.

The Birthday Party were a phenomenal live band – heavy but artful and the perfect visual and sonic replacement for the black hole that punk had left us. Tracy Pew, the band's singular bassist, looked like a character from *Midnight Cowboy*, one who would eat anyone who got in his way. I could barely believe I was getting to share a stage with him, yet as we crossed on the stairs at the Africa Centre, I somehow found the courage to ask if I could use his bass rig.

'Absolutely not,' he quietly intoned, no doubt imagining chewing on my feeble carcass as he ambled past.

These were our gods. Singer Nick Cave, Mick Harvey, Rowland S Howard, Tracy Pew and Phil Calvert, all as important to me as the Stones and the Beatles were to my older brother and sisters. And even though the Birthday Party were probably only five years our senior, it felt like we were simply blessed just to be in the same room as them.

The reality was we just weren't good enough to be in the same room as them.

Whether it was this, or the disappointment of the Peel show, I was having trouble fighting off the self-doubt ahead of the Heaven show supporting Divine.

His film *Polyester* had come out earlier in the year, and Peter took Stan and me to see a John Waters triple bill of Divine at the Paris Pullman Cinema near Earl's Court where we lived. At weekends the cinema screened sci-fi or horror all-nighters, even all of Bowie's early films would screen every now and then, and we came here most weeks when we needed a break from gigs. They would show movies by Bergman, Renoir, Herzog and Fassbinder (his *Veronika Voss* was the last film to show there before it tragically closed down in 1983), but when *Polyester* came on, we were handed a special 'scratch and sniff' card ('Odorama'), with the numbers one to ten printed on the reverse of the card with the direction 'Do not scratch until you receive instructions from the film'. It was everything you'd expect from a John Waters film, with additional gross smells prompted by the numbers flashing up on the screen. Not quite enough to make you retch but as close as you'd want to be out in public.

Situation 2 were releasing his first singles 'Born to be Cheap'/'The Name Game' so supporting Divine made some sense, and Heaven was heaving that night. I felt like heaving too.

After the show, the writer Paul Morley, who had waxed so rhapsodically in the *NME* when our first single was released, came up to me and said, 'That didn't really work at all, did it?'

I didn't want to admit it, but he was totally right. Guitarist Paul and I knew it hadn't really been working for a while and Morley had just succinctly voiced what I had been unable to do. And as Heaven turned out to be our final show as a band, I could swear there was still a lingering whiff of the shit from the Odorama card in the air that night as I walked back home to our flat.

Thankfully, the record shop was keeping me busy, and a constant stream of artists who worked with the Beggars Banquet label family would come through on their way to visit.

Artists and staff had to walk through the shop to get upstairs to the office where 4AD Records, the Beggars label and Peter's Situation 2 were all based, and one morning in early 1982, Lydia Lunch came to visit 4AD's boss Ivo Watts-Russell. Lydia appeared on the Birthday Party's EP 'Drunk on the Pope's Blood' and her appearing in our tiny shop felt like a big deal. It was like visiting royalty. She was striking and quite beautiful with her pale complexion and luscious ruby-red lips. I was a shy gormless teen with bright orange spiky hair. But she kept commenting on my hair, and how much she liked it, each time my face going a deeper shade of rouge. My *mum* loved my hair, but no one else had ever said anything nice about it – because they weren't my mum. Lydia announced – far too loudly for my liking given that the shop was busy – that she was about to leave but wanted to give me a kiss. She asked Steve my boss if that was OK. While I was thinking that she should probably have asked me first, she leaned across the counter and kissed me full on the lips. It wasn't my first kiss but it certainly felt like it. A weird sensation. I felt mortified and amazed at the same time.

My brief encounter with Lydia Lunch's red lips was soon trumped a week later when Billy Mackenzie, singer of the Associates, arrived for a label visit. Billy was not just blessed with the most celestial voice I'd ever heard, but he was also a lovely, sweet man. He arrived with two adorable small grey whippets and asked me if I'd be OK to walk them around the block a few times while he went upstairs and had his meeting. They were striking-looking dogs and it was a pleasure wandering around South Kensington with them and I've loved Billy Mackenzie – and whippets – since that day. I know what a horrible time he had while he was signed to Warners, and I thought about him a lot during our own difficult time with Universal in the '90s after we had left 4AD.

I was still in a state of shock about my own band's break-up when I heard the awful news that he had died in early 1997. Later that year, Nude Records contacted me to ask if I would work on some recordings Billy had begun before he died. I didn't hesitate and those sessions for *Beyond the Sun* were among my favourite as a producer. I worked on the tracks at September Sound, the studio we had moved into in 1989 ahead of recording *Heaven or Las Vegas*. I definitely felt a presence in the studio while we were mixing those sad, sparse tunes. One night, alone, when I had one of those doubts that I'm sure all producers have about a sound or a direction, and was wishing I could just turn and ask Billy if he thought the mix sounded okay, it suddenly felt like soft hands were being placed gently on my shoulders. It wasn't the last time a spectral figure entered those studios during a session of mine, but it was the first.

Chaperoning Billy's whippets while he had his label meeting is a memory I have always cherished, but it was another chance encounter at the shop in the spring of 1982 that changed the course of my life, starting a chain of events that is still reverberating today.

The record shop opened daily at 10 a.m. and usually by 11 a.m. most of the label folks from 4AD and Beggars were in the office above. Steve and I would usually get in by nine to catch any early deliveries, have a coffee and catch up on what bands we had seen the night before. One such morning, we were opening some boxes when there was a gentle knock on the door. I looked up to see three people peering through the glass, all of a similar age to me. I walked over to unlock the door.

'Hi, we aren't open until ten. Are you able to come back in an hour or so?'

In a barely audible whisper, the bigger one asked, 'Is Ivo in?'

Ivo-Watts Russell ran the label 4AD but was *never* in before ten.

'No, sorry, the label people won't be in for quite a bit yet. Can I help? I just work down here in the shop though.'

'Could you give him this tape? It's our first record,' replied the softest spoken voice in the world.

'Of course. I'll make sure he gets it on his way through, but if you'd rather give it to him yourself, I am sure he'll be here before too long?'

'No, that's OK. If you can give it to him, we have to get the bus back to Scotland soon.'

This first record that I was entrusted with to pass on to the 4AD supremo was in fact a cassette by Scottish trio Cocteau Twins, and I had just spoken to guitarist Robin Guthrie, who was accompanied by singer Elizabeth Fraser and bassist Bill Heggie. I think about this moment often.

What if . . . I had not been working that day? What if I had been in the bathroom and Steve had answered the door instead of me? Would I be writing this book? Well . . .

Whether it was *because* of this initial encounter with them, with me as the unwitting messenger delivering this magical music gift from the future to the handsome, enigmatic boss man upstairs, or for some other less *Twilight Zone*-esque reason, over the next year or so we became firm friends.

In 1983, Bill left Cocteau Twins and Robin and Elizabeth moved away from their hometown of Grangemouth to head down to London. I saw more of them now they were nearby, and discovered that they were fans of the Drowning Craze records. That made me happy. While they seemed terribly shy in public situations, each time I met them, I could feel a connection. They were private and certainly not party animals, which I also liked. We were all the same age, on the dole and liked the same music. We all had the similarly self-administered spiky haircuts that were pretty standard for the time, wore clothes mostly from charity shops, and I remember Robin had some excellent pointy boots and was fond of red and black plaid shirts and black jeans. I hadn't moved on stylistically too far from the John Lydon early-PiL era look, but none of us were that bothered by fashion; our interests were pretty singular. In these early days, I always looked forward to the next time we would get to hang out.

Elizabeth was quiet at first, and while I sensed some sadness behind her big cerulean blue eyes, she always seemed gentle and kind, and when she laughed, it was with every part of her being, and it always made me happy to see that. I went to see them on their headline tour that year in a few cities around the UK, usually with Ivo, and after one show, we were chatting and Robin mentioned how he loved being in studios but wanted to record in one without engineers fussing around him. I invited them both to come and use this little sixteen-track studio I was helping out at over in Camden Town at the weekends. I certainly wasn't an engineer, really more of an assistant at this point. So when they arrived, I showed them around and said, 'Let me know if you want any tea or anything.'

'What did you have in mind?' Robin enquired in his soft Scottish brogue.

'Well, I think there's some Earl Grey?' I replied.

'No. We thought you wanted to write some songs with us?' he replied matter-of-factly, almost sounding put out that I wasn't already aware of that.

'Wow, er . . . no, I just thought you guys might want to use the studio yourselves and as the owners were away, I thought you'd get better use out of it than me!'

'Well, have you got any basslines kicking around? Why don't we just plug in and make some noise?' Robin asked gently.

I didn't reply. I just went to the cupboard and pulled out a bass and plugged it in, still somewhat in shock, but pretending like it was the most normal thing in the world. Liz announced that she was going out to get us all chips and left Robin and me alone.

I did have half a bassline kicking around, yet within half an hour, we had recorded pretty much the whole of an instrumental piece, bass, drums and guitars. Like a *real* song with a structure. It kinda just . . . recorded itself. I have no idea how. This had never happened to me before. When Liz walked back in, her eyes bright and wide, her face lit up.

'That is one of the most beautiful things I've ever heard. Fucking gorgeous!'

Hearing that gave me goosebumps. I didn't appreciate the significance of this at the time, but I've sure thought about it a lot since. Making music with people I barely know has always terrified me – indeed I am still not that comfortable with it these days – but because *my* involvement in this session was so unexpected and unplanned, I didn't have time to worry about it.

I certainly had more questions than answers as to how that just happened. Three relative strangers meet up in a room with nothing and shortly after, leave the room having written a song.[1]

'I'll play it first and tell you what it's called later.'

Miles Davis

I don't remember much more of that day. It was a glorious blur that seems like someone else's dream. On Monday morning, I returned to my nine to five at the record shop.

In the meantime, Karen – the girl I had met at our debut Drowning Craze show – and I had started seeing a lot more of each other and after she finished her course, we talked about moving in together somewhere. Life at the flat in London with Stan and his brother was great, but I was starting to tire a little of the nightly bong sessions, and waking up with a thick head each morning, so before too long Karen and I found a tiny bedsit nearby in Earl's Court, just a few yards from the Tube station. I was still working at the record shop around the corner at this point and Karen had started doing some graphic design work in a company over in Chiswick.

---

[1] That exact recording at the wee Camden recording studio became the first track we wrote together and appeared on a compilation called *The Pink Opaque*. The song was called 'Millimillenary'.

Our landlady was a larger-than-life Irish woman called Sheila with a shock of curly, dyed-blonde hair and was, as she proudly reminded us many times, the reigning 'London's Miss Dolly Parton'. Not a singer, but a lookalike champion. Thankfully, I don't now need to describe her physical appearance, but her boyfriend Gerald was even more fascinating to us. He dressed like he was playing Malvolio in *Twelfth Night* and always with a feather in his cap. This was his everyday attire. The New Romantics scene of the late '70s / early '80s had by and large come and gone, and he would have fitted in perfectly with the Blitz crowd, but unless I was much mistaken he was certainly not a casualty of that era. Maybe it was an affectation, his way of trying to compete with the attention 'Dolly' would have attracted, but I'll admit his flamboyant style did certainly turn heads.

Our accommodation wouldn't pass any stringent test for privacy, security or safety these days, and clearly either they had a friend who was handy (two left hands I'd suggest) with a saw and some nails, or Gerald was more multi-talented than I'd given him credit for. At the back of the ground floor, they'd built – maybe *erected* is more accurate – two different areas, one of which was to be ours. In our youthful naivety, we must have thought it was fine. Sheila pointed to the 'room' next to ours, and explained there was to be 'another nice young couple like you' moving in there soon.

We had something that resembled a front door, and we did have our own key, to at least enhance the facade that it was 'private' but that door was flimsier than wet cardboard. We put a couple of small mattresses side by side on the floor in one tiny space on the left next to a narrow passageway which had a portable cooker in it. On the right-hand side we had just enough space for a small two-seater sofa and a little Sony Trinitron TV next to the sink where we could watch *Brookside*, *Boys from the Blackstuff* and *Tiswas*. It was probably about 75 square feet at best and, not to put too fine a point on it, was a total shithole. But it was *our* shithole and we were happy enough, young love and all that.

Karen's lovely mum, Jane, and her boyfriend Tony were coming to stay so we needed a minute to tidy up. It's funny, these first steps you take after leaving home, to show your parents that you are grown up now, and you aren't going to be murdered in your sleep, and that they really don't need to worry about you. Karen was very close to her mum, and while it seems *insane* now that we thought for a second that showing her our bedsit in bedlam would be reassuring, this is what we did. Indeed, to their great credit, they even stayed the night! We lent them one of our mattresses and when we lifted it off the floor to rearrange our sleeping quarters, we noticed that there were mushrooms growing on the carpet underneath it. Jane and Tony were very kind liars, but I was sure they were quietly horrified at the squalor of the room. Seeing it through their eyes for a second, I think I was too.

We didn't stay there much longer and soon moved to Shepherd's Bush. I didn't see Stan quite as often after the move as my own music was starting to keep me busy. Then the Cocteaus happened and I soon lost touch with most of my other friends from school. And then as time wore on, I lost touch with reality altogether.

But when we had our first child, we called him Stan.

CHAPTER FIVE

In the Beginning

During 1982 and 1983, after the Beggars shop closed down, I found a job at Our Price Records, the chain of high street record shops in the UK and Ireland that at the time was second only to Woolworths in terms of market share. By accident rather than design, I found myself managing, at various times, three of the main London stores: the Charing Cross Road, King's Road and Tottenham Court Road branches. It wasn't like working in the Beggars shop. No visits from the likes of Lydia Lunch and Billy Mackenzie, though I did serve Jeremy Beadle once, the presenter of the TV programme *Game for a Laugh*, a 'light entertainment' show whose basic premise was to make fun of unsuspecting members of the public. I gave him the wrong change to see if he *was* actually game for a laugh, but he came back saying we had short-changed him £5. No sense of humour at all.

When Genesis drummer Phil Collins released his second solo album *Hello, I Must Be Going!* in November 1982, I was doing a stint in the Charing Cross Road branch, one of the flagship stores right next to the iconic Foyles bookshop. Collins' new album was, to these ears, a dreadful collection of faux-Motown inspirations, essentially the folly of a pale, pasty-faced man from a hairy-arsed rock band trying to reinvent himself by injecting cod R&B rhythms and grooves with his wholly unrhythmical lyrical sense and particularly ungroovy style. Of course it was a runaway success. Phil Collins, Paul Young, Rod Stewart, some regular blokes with blokey names, all had golden moments dabbling with that soulful sound in the '80s. You could be a regular bloke with a regular bloke's name *and* be famous back then. Or you could be Sting.

Hello, I Must Be Going! was top of the Our Price chart for weeks on end and indeed was to be a permanent feature in the Our Price chart for the next twelve months. OK, so I didn't like it, but they didn't give me the manager's job to determine what records were brought into the shop, or the chart. Although I'll be honest, I'm still not quite sure why they *did* give me the manager's job. But this was a triple platinum album, which meant about 900,000 copies on vinyl were sold in the UK alone, so boxes and boxes of this awful music would arrive every week and it was our job to unload it, price it up and sell it. It was so popular we barely had time to get them on the shelves before it was sold out again.

Everything at Our Price Records in this period was ordered in centrally by the suits in head office, while the staff and I mostly had a brilliant time in our own little bubble of oblivion, listening to music all day, pretending to be DJs and befriending everyone who came into the shop. Even if they didn't buy anything, we would make sure they'd come back.

But as the year wore on, the decree came down from on high that the staff should be playing mostly chart stuff and we should not be coming out on to the shop floor to chat with customers, but should stay behind the counter and 'sell'. We all felt it was becoming a bit like flipping burgers, so when area manager Norris came in for his monthly inspection, I had prepared a little speech on behalf of my brothers and sisters about how we wanted to have the flexibility to be out on the shop floor at certain times talking to people and helping them with their purchases to build that customer loyalty. We *knew* that sales technique worked.

Norris himself was an unattractive man, a likely casualty of the financial crisis who had left the City looking for any job where he could act out his inner Captain Mainwaring.

He began his inspection, summoning me towards him with a wagging finger, his pale cheeks reddening with rage, aghast that there was no Phil Collins on our chart wall and demanding to know why. I explained in my best Sergeant Wilson voice that we had ordered it last week and reordered it again on Monday but that it still hadn't arrived. Being a day without Phil was bad, but a week was unforgivable.

I skulked behind Norris while he scuttled around the shop like an angry crab who'd been flipped on his back and decided now was probably not the time to deliver my Gettysburg moment. He opened the door to the basement – a space that was currently being used to prepare the stock for the soon-to-open Tottenham Court Road branch – and descended the stairs. I stayed at the top. He seemed to be examining two large boxes at the bottom and turned his head with a look that said, *'You might want to come down here, boy.'* Yep, you guessed it, 300 pristine copies of *Hello, I Must Be Going!* I was forthwith demoted with immediate effect to assistant manager.

Thanks, Phil.

That night I went back home, chastising myself for not telling him where to stick his demotion.

Out of the blue, Robin Guthrie called me the following morning to say how much they had enjoyed working on the song together last month in Camden and asking if I'd like to come to Scotland in a couple of weeks to write and record a new Cocteau Twins EP.

Whilst I could not have possibly imagined in that moment what lay ahead, my gut told me that this was exactly where I wanted to be. *Needed* to be. I didn't even ask for time to think about it and said 'yes' immediately. Then I called Mr Norris.

'Hello, I must be going!'

*   *   *

That first session in Scotland went almost *too* fast. I wanted to press pause on it. So many new foreign feelings and experiences to take in, my head was exploding every day. Robin was extremely laid-back about it all and I think that helped to calm me down, and Elizabeth was blessed with this beautiful and strange mixture of a child's wonder and the wisdom of someone thrice her age. The dying embers of my old band the Drowning Craze now finally extinguished and this new adventure was already stirring the fire I knew was in me.

After we returned to London, rehearsals began almost immediately for a tour the following month. I was terrified of the water as a child until Dad threw me in at the deep end, and then I could swim. And so it was here. I may have been thrown into the band without a life jacket, but in all honesty I was lucky to have been thrown in at all. Even being allowed to possibly drown in their burgeoning success was a blessing and I would never take this new opportunity for granted.

My debut Cocteau Twins show was on 11 February 1984 at Ratinger Hof in Düsseldorf's old town, an artists' pub that the crew told us was the birthplace of German punk. Bands I had bought records by like 999, XTC, Wire and Pere Ubu had all played here so I was keen to get through this momentous night without any major mishaps. As I had only been in the band a month or two, most of the nine songs we performed during this tour were written before I joined. 'Pearly Dewdrops' Drops' and 'The Spangle Maker' were the only two I had co-written, so I felt a small bubble of pressure each night to make sure I played those older songs as well as I could.

With all the drums recorded onto tape, I couldn't afford any mistakes. If I messed up, I would likely throw Elizabeth off and then the whole thing would just fall apart, so any 'shoegazing' on these early tours was really just as a result of me concentrating extra hard on my fingers and where they needed to be. Looking out casually into the crowd as I had maybe done in my previous band was now very much a thing of the past.

Within that first month of performing with the band, we played eight shows in the Netherlands and Germany and then my ninth appearance was on the BBC TV show *The Old Grey Whistle Test* at Television Centre. I had been here once before, but it was when I was a child for a taping of *Jim'll Fix It*, so the less said about that the better.

I must have had some butterflies of course to be performing on the telly, but this was all happening at such a pace since I joined that I didn't really have the time to be nervous. We'd smoke a joint and we'd feel fine. That seemed to be the answer to everything back then. The TV show was presented by David Hepworth and Mark Ellen, great friends and respected music journalists who had at various times both been editors of *Smash Hits*, and as we arrived in the studio any nerves gave way to excitement seeing that we were going to be on the show with Aswad, a band from Ladbroke Grove that Stan and I had seen previously at the Notting Hill Carnival. We closed out that memorable month of February 1984 with our tenth, a sold-out headline show at Victoria Palace in London (now home to the musical *Hamilton* no less) playing to 1,500 people, by far the largest crowd I had ever stood before.

While my own gaze was still firmly locked on my guitar and my fingers during each song, hoping and praying they would land on the right frets each time, I was still able to notice the extraordinary effect that Elizabeth was having on audiences everywhere we played. The unusual qualities of her voice and her unique movements onstage were mesmerising and quite unlike other artists of the time that I had seen. The only other performer

I had seen live who affected people in such a profound way was Ian Curtis. I am not sure Ian or Elizabeth were even fully aware of what their bodies were doing once the song had begun. It was just *happening*. Endorphins released during singing are the body's mechanic for killing pain. Literally morphine. And I felt for many years that as shy and nervous a performer as she could be, the greatest freedom she had was when she was singing.

The love that the band received over the extraordinary period when we were together will be in large part due to Elizabeth's creations, on record and live. Not to diminish the music that we made in any way but this woman was in a league of her own.

Even though we had to pre-record the drums for the tape machine that accompanied us live, we never prepared an 'encore'. Not once. For more traditional band set-ups, where everything is 'live', you can finish your set, go off, and decide there and then if you do indeed even *deserve* an encore, and subsequently discuss amongst each other backstage what song or songs would be right for this particular crowd on this specific occasion. Because we were a slave to the drums on our tape machine, it felt wholly wrong to sit in our studio a month BEFORE the tour and think about what song we should play as an encore. It felt conceited. Arrogant even. How can we even say we would or should get an encore at any point? So we never prepared one.

This was great. But probably in hindsight, for the audience anyway, rather a disappointment. That's not to say we never performed an encore song. Oh we did, but it would always just be one of the songs we had already played. Stop the tape machine, rewind it a bit, play it for a second to check whereabouts the tape now was, rewind it again and so on until it landed on the right song, and then we could start it. Probably *not* a great spectacle either now I come to think of it.

On that first tour, our encore song would just be a 'second' version of 'Pearly Dewdrops' Drops' which had just been released and was our first 'minor hit' single, scraping into the top thirty at number twenty-nine.

Technology was always a blessing and a curse for us. When our drummer was a tape machine, we had no real choice, and married with our idealist approach, the encore was always going to be a moot point. In years to come, samplers gave us more choice, but it wasn't until the '90s when we actually involved a real drummer and we had significantly more songs to choose from that we could plan the set to include more songs at the end bit. But I still do admire the bands who acknowledge the mild absurdity of going off after playing a full set and then waiting for a load of hollering and screaming before coming back on.

As we continued to tour throughout 1984, and with the release of the album *Treasure* imminent that winter, we had begun to add a few more songs into the mix, so that by the time we played our final show of the year at Brighton Dome in late December, eight of the twelve songs in the set that night were ones we had all written together. I felt more at home now, playing the parts I had created. It was good, but we were just getting started.

Robin and Elizabeth had already moved to London away from their hometown of Grangemouth, near Falkirk. For a year or two, and during the making of *Treasure* in Scotland – our first full LP working together – they both resisted every time I asked if they'd take me to see where they grew up. When they finally relented a few years later, after a couple of hours wandering around Grangemouth visiting friends, I asked, 'When will we be going into *town*?'

'This IS the town. This is it.'

Cocteau Twins' sound and vision even in their early iterations to my mind weren't solely reflective of their environment, and while the darker, spikier edges of the first album *Garlands* hinted at their desire for escape, it was the second album *Head Over Heels* that certainly felt full of flavours of the blossoming romance between Robin and Elizabeth. But even I could see how a small town with limited opportunities and possibilities could not have held them for long. All the music they loved and wanted to be part of was not there. The labels they could see being a part of were not there. The move was inevitable.

A bunch of their pals wanted to take me to a football match over in Glasgow that afternoon and, being diehard Celtic fans, they got us tickets for the Old Firm derby between Celtic and Rangers at Celtic Park. I'd been to plenty of Spurs vs Arsenal North London derbies, so figured this would be a feisty affair along those lines. When you live in a smallish town where you either work in one of the local industries or you're on the dole, then it's not hard to see why football takes on such significance come the weekend. Grangemouth has a huge BP oil refinery and for most of the 1980s, 20 per cent of the town's entire population of around 16,000 people would have worked there, including our esteemed guitarist Robin, who at one point was an instrument technician there before the band took off.

Unemployment was rife everywhere. In Glasgow, around 20 per cent of the population was out of a job, compared to London where it was bad enough at 7 per cent, but with a ticket for this match priced at just £2.80 – for comparison a pack of twenty Rothmans King Size was £1.40 and a pint of Kestrel was 80p – back in the 1980s, football was still a game that was fully in touch with its working-class roots. An average annual wage for a footballer at the top was only £28,000. Because of that, it was affordable even for those without much.

However, when you throw in the religion and the politics – all far too complex for a soft southerner like me to analyse succinctly in this light-hearted memoir – the deep-rooted hostility between the rival fans was palpable during this period. As my new friends pointed out – and, sorry, but some generalisation is necessary here – in a nutshell the majority of the Rangers support in Scotland was from the Protestant community and the Celtic support mostly from the Catholic. For many years Rangers even had a club policy not to sign any Catholics, so this was as much about Northern Ireland as it was Scotland, as much about the Loyalists and the Republicans. There are several additional layers of complexity which add to the ferocity of this rivalry. Historically in the west of Scotland, Rangers fans were 'Ulster' Scots and Celtic fans were 'Irish' Scots and at the games you'd see Rangers waving the Union Jack, while the Celtic fans would be waving the Irish tricolour flag, so this wasn't 'just a football match'. I got *that* bit totally wrong.

After a forty-minute ride on the Celtic supporters' bus from Grangemouth to Glasgow, we entered the ground. 'The Jungle' was a standing enclosure in the north stand of Celtic Park and as soon as we walked in, I was immediately hit by the smell. Piss mostly but mixed with cigarettes. This was probably a decade before you could leisurely wander on to a concourse and grab a pie or a burger. In fact the only food I could see was a fella carrying a box of macaroon bars and spearmint chewing gum. Given the overpowering odour, I grabbed a couple of packs off him and popped a couple of sticks in my mouth. It helped a bit.

Whilst I don't remember much about the actual match, I do remember the atmosphere: it was *intense*. Celtic won 3–1, but one significant thing lives with me to this day. It wasn't weird or unusual for us to be crammed into spaces that seemed barely able to contain us, and at most punk gigs in London this was actually part of the fun, and certainly the 1982 Cup Final replay at Wembley when my team Spurs beat QPR 1–0 my feet didn't touch the ground for pretty much most of the game so this felt familiar. And as Celtic scored, we all moved in waves across the concrete below. Strangers would hug and kiss each other in extraordinary outpourings of emotion. I loved the unbridled passion of it all. What wasn't expected happened just before half-time as I felt a warm trickle of liquid rolling down my spine. I turned round to see a lad putting his penis back in his trousers, and with eyes still fixed firmly on the game, he patted me on the shoulders in a very friendly way. Sort of a non-vocal apology as if to say, '*Sorry, big man, what else could I do?*'

Turns out that the loos were just so far away and packed for so long that people just pissed where they were standing.

At the pub, I raised a glass to my Aunt Lillian, Dad's beloved dancing sister, also a fanatical Spurs fan, who had tragically died during the match at Wembley at that replay back in May 1982, just fifty-eight years old. I thought of her and her incredible Jewish cooking and shed a private tear as the Celtic fans around us began singing 'Always Look on the Bright Side of Life'.

The weekend was enlightening and I had loved the experience and the friendship I was shown in Grangemouth. But as we returned back home to London, I could see why Robin and Elizabeth had felt the desire to leave. Whilst our respective childhoods, I imagine, could not have been more different, we had a lot more in common than appeared on the surface. And I certainly knew all about escaping the past while respecting your roots.

* * *

In the 1980s, it was still relatively uncommon for artists to produce themselves, and certainly when I first joined Cocteau Twins in late '83, Robin clearly knew *exactly* what he wanted his band to sound like. But he was still getting the vibe back from 4AD that he should consider working with a producer, despite the fact that previous records, where Ivo Watts-Russell and the Associates' sonic wizard Alan Rankine had both taken on production roles, had not been wholly great experiences for Robin. Some bands do just work better on their own and that could be for a million reasons; maybe due to temperament or anxiety, or maybe the lead singer is too shy to sing in front of a stranger and building a rapport takes too long and is too costly. Or maybe because the band totally know what they're doing. I have seen whole sessions wasted over the years working as a producer myself. Some bands take to the studio like ducks to water and some don't.

As I wasn't there for any of those early Cocteaus sessions, I can't speak with authority on how well or badly they went, but I know that when discussions were going on with 4AD about the producer for the upcoming album in 1984, Robin was adamant that we didn't need one. I felt that the 'Pearly Dewdrops' Drops' EP proved he was clearly right. But, more out of courtesy, we agreed to meet a producer that Ivo was particularly keen for us to work with.

And so in April 1984, Brian Eno and Daniel Lanois arrived at Ivo's flat and, barely half an hour later, left after Brian summed it all up fairly succinctly:

'Well it sounds to me that you have a pretty good idea how you want your band to sound, and really don't need a producer as such.'

Uncomfortable as it was, I had to admire Robin's couldn't-give-a-fuck attitude. I was a fan of Eno, and especially the recent *Apollo: Atmospheres and Soundtracks*[1] he had just released with his

---

[1] One little side note on the Enos' and Lanois' *Apollo: Atmospheres and Soundtracks* album. I had a very shoddy midi hi-fi system that I bought in Dixons around 1984 that incorporated a tuner, a CD player, a turntable and a double cassette player, and while this beautiful album sounded horrendous through the tiny tinny speakers that came with it, I left it on the turntable for about a month and listened to it every day when I was in the flat, and it was so peaceful and elegant. I went round to a friend's flat for a drink one night and we were chatting away while some music was playing in the background. I recognised it but couldn't work out what it was.

'This is the new Eno and Lanois,' he said. *What???* Turned out I'd been playing it for a month at 45rpm. Tell you what, though; while I do now appreciate the album at 33rpm, it is waaay better sped up! Try it!

brother Roger and Daniel Lanois, but even I couldn't imagine being in a studio with Eno *and* Robin. Their strong opposing personalities would certainly have clashed.

* * *

When discussing which studios and producers are appropriate for a band, some important points need to be considered. How do the band function as people? How do they write and record together as musicians? What are their strengths and long-term aims? The single most significant reason why *we* ended up with our own studios and producing our own music all those years was because it was the only way that made any sense. For us it was simply the conclusion we quickly reached after consulting our own checklist. It wasn't to be obtuse, or difficult. It was to enable us to focus 100 per cent on what we did best, without any third-party involvement. It wasn't because we were too arrogant to consider anyone else's input (OK, well maybe a little); it was because we were comfortable with this way of working.

So, my first full album with Elizabeth and Robin was written and recorded at Palladium Studios in Straiton, Scotland. Without Brian Eno or Daniel Lanois. Going away to a residential studio in the middle of nowhere is always a rare privilege, but when it is a little bit out of the city and the ground is covered by a thick blanket of snow, you wake up every day with the excitement of a child on Christmas morning.

Outside those soundproofed studio walls, Scotland was also going through a dark time, and in nearby Bilston, families were fighting on the picket lines during the bitter miners' strike, but inside our secluded pit head at Palladium, we tried to extract as much as we could in the few short weeks ahead.

Arriving at the studio with nothing prepared was both exciting and terrifying. I knew we could do it but a whole album did seem quite a daunting challenge.

There's always a gentle deception at play when bands tell their record labels that they're 'ready' to make the album, as well as during the recording when questions are asked as to how it's going. It was no different with 4AD. We told them we *were* ready and Robin assured me that he had every confidence that we would do it, and moreover felt this was the best way for us to work. I figured that if Robin and Elizabeth thought we were ready, then I certainly wasn't going to argue. They had recorded here before, for their second album *Head Over Heels* in 1983, so had some experience of the studio if nothing else. That allayed my nerves a little.

As I lay in bed that first night unable to fall asleep, worrying whether I was actually good enough for this, I reached over and picked up one of the books on the bedside table. It was, appropriately, George Orwell's *1984*. I loved this book, written just a few hours west of where I lay, on the Isle of Jura. I thumbed through the pages and a bookmark fell out on to the bed, and before I placed it back I read these words quietly to myself: *'In general the greater the understanding, the greater the delusion; the more intelligent, the less sane.'*

As my adventure was beginning, I was quietly comforted by this and drifted slowly off to sleep.

The studio was run by Jon Turner, jovial, avuncular and always cracking bad jokes. A brilliant pianist, he played with the Walker Brothers in the 1970s and then toured with Demis Roussos for many years before setting up Palladium within this cosy residential family house, about twelve miles south of Edinburgh. I was greeted at the bottom of the stairs each morning by a beautiful Doberman called Corrie, and then would walk straight into the kitchen for a hearty cooked breakfast courtesy of Jon's wife, Anne. In the whole time we were cocooned in there, I don't remember leaving the building once.

I felt initially that it must have been difficult for Elizabeth and Robin to have me sitting there in the room, having recently made such a great record by themselves. And like any new relationship, it did take time for us to settle into a rhythm. I did feel a little out of sorts for a day or two. I wasn't just figuring out how to be in the band, but how to be in a band with a couple. I felt they were probably working it all out too. We all did the best we could. There wasn't much talking about 'the music', but there was a lot of laughing, often hysterical. I liked them both a lot. I wasn't quite sure if I was fitting in, but there really wasn't time to sit back and examine this new dynamic too acutely. It was always on to the next song, trying to get something down on tape.

Robin would start each day by creating a drumbeat, a groove that we could play along to and hopefully a tune would materialise. Some of the drum parts he made on *Treasure* were truly brilliant, almost hip-hop beats. Tracks like 'Lorelei' and 'Persephone' came together quickly and the lilting, soulful swing of 'Pandora' was another progressive bold step. As the start point for everything we created on top, it was important for us to feel inspired by the beat, the vibe. The drums were created on an EMU Drumulator which I think Robin had used on *Head Over Heels*, but this time he had modified the Drumulator with the 'Rock Chips Set', which used samples of John Bonham's drums. After the initial two-bar drum guide for us to write the music to, Robin would then later go back and program the *whole* drum track with all the fills. Usually we would then add some real cymbals. Sampled cymbals back then just sounded *nasty*. I mostly just stuck to the bass on this album. Maybe Robin wishes I had stuck to it for *all* the albums; I don't know for sure. But he never looked particularly happy when on a rare occasion I did pick up a guitar. I could see why he might bristle if he felt like I was getting too big for my britches too soon.

Verbal communication was sparse, which sometimes I thought was down to me just being there, getting in the way, or them maybe feeling paranoid that I was surplus to requirements, but I soon realised it was more that in our own way, we just seemed better at articulating complex feelings by writing a song together than sitting around talking about it, and that our moods were actually dictated by the quality of our work. If I was playing something and Robin wasn't reacting positively, it didn't deflate me, it made me try harder. He may not have even been listening for all I know, but I tried not to get undone by making assumptions as to what had caused him to seem moody. And he probably wasn't even being moody; he might have just been concentrating!

And if I ever found myself doubting why I was there at all, I figured if Robin hadn't wanted me to contribute, then he wouldn't have called me to ask me to join the band. But for a wee while I wasn't sure if he thought he'd made a mistake. It's never easy inviting a stranger into your house.

None of us were confrontational, with each other at any rate, and therefore seemed to find solutions to any potentially awkward moments by plugging our instruments in and playing music together. The studio control room was like our happy place, full of instruments and gadgets. Robin and I spent most of every day in the control room trying to find the magic and Elizabeth was in other parts of the house during the day trying to concentrate on her lyric writing, and while she would pop down to the studio room in the evenings to hear what we'd been up to, it was probably as much for some company as anything. Her reactions to the music we were coming up with were crucial though. If she didn't like a piece we had started, then she would surely find it impossible to be inspired to find melodies and words. So the whole thing was pretty precarious, but somehow we did start and finish ten tracks instrumentally, and then in that final week, Elizabeth would transform these pieces into fully formed songs.

At Palladium studios, it felt like we were always up against the clock. We barely left the house the entire time we were there but we were getting to know each other and that takes time. If you force it, you can hear it for sure. We smoked and drank a fair bit but not to excess, just to aid the creative process and loosen up when we needed to. We were there to work but we laughed a lot through the haze, sometimes so much we cried. But I am sure that knowing we only had one week left would have, I imagine, put enormous pressure on Elizabeth to get cracking on adding her voice to all these pieces that we were creating. Most of the vocals on *Treasure* were done in the evenings. Robin and either studio owner Jon or engineer Keith would be on hand to help set things up for her in the vocal booth. I sat quietly at the back of the control room. I was just happy to be there, and she seemed fine with that. Elizabeth would spend a little time getting the blend of her vocals and then the music in her headphones right – sometimes a difficult and delicate thing to balance – but once she was happy, she would listen through once or twice then swiftly start to nail her vocals within two or three takes. Her lyrics were like poetry, playful and clearly personal. I could sense she was a little sensitive, even secretive, about them but I never pushed her on it because it was truly none of my fucking business, and I never found it to be as polarising a topic for conversation as everyone else. What she created over that last week or so in the studio was quite breathtaking and seeing it all unfold first-hand was something else. What she was capable of was of a wholly different scale to anything I had imagined.

When you're making music this way under such time constraints, it's bound to be a bit hit and miss, but you still have to commit 100 per cent to each idea. *Improvising* wasn't how we would describe it then, as it's a word that we usually associate with jazz and the attainment of complete control of your instrument to enable you to let go of your knowledge and ignore the boundaries of technique and education, like looking for a higher power. Our approach was born out of punk rock, not jazz, and our improvisation came from looking at it upside down. We made our limitation our strength. We didn't have a studied technique, we weren't schooled, and our knowledge was self-taught mixed with a heavy dose of bravado. I always feel a little strange saying we wrote our songs by improvising because it just sounds too learned, and a bit self-congratulatory when all we did was make shit up as we went along. But conversely when I say 'we just made shit up as we went along', that sounds so dumb and unbelievable.

We didn't always get it right and were our own fiercest critics. On *Treasure*, maybe we didn't get it right *all* the way through, but we would get the chance to try again soon.

* * *

After we got back to London, I met up with Scotland and Chelsea winger Pat Nevin not long after he joined the West London club. He too had been listening to John Peel for years and had seen Cocteau Twins back when they were a duo, so was already a fan, as was his wife-to-be, the very lovely Annabel. He contacted me out of the blue the day of our show at the Royal Festival Hall in 1984 by leaving a message at the box office beforehand to ask if we could meet up afterwards for a drink. As it turned out, we got on famously and arranged to hang out the following week in London.

Being a professional footballer, Pat was free most days after training finished at 12.30 p.m., and when I wasn't on tour or in the studio, I found myself in the same situation with time on my hands. We spent a lot of time together in those first few years and, after all that running about in the mornings, he liked to eat.

So we would meet at the Chelsea Kitchen on King's Road at least once or twice a week, and Pat would order – without fail – the following:

Starter: Small spaghetti Bolognese.

Main course: Large spaghetti Bolognese.

Pudding: Apple crumble and custard.

He may have deviated once or twice but only because the chef didn't have enough Bolognese left. He had always finished his food before I had started mine.

And not an *ounce* of fat on the fella. Very annoying.

He was a fabulous chap to spend time with, and was/still is a big music fan. He was described by the *NME* as the 'first post-punk footballer', and while that may have been true and a good attention-grabbing headline, the fact was that he was also very ahead of his time within the game. For a start he had been to university and had a degree, which was rare within the dressing rooms of most football clubs. He called out racism when he witnessed it – often within his own club – and had strong principles that his late father Patrick instilled in him.

He was also such a big fan of our band that he once asked the Chelsea manager if he could come off at half-time just so he could get to France in time to see us play. Incredibly, the boss agreed.

Pat also brought Barry Horne (Wales and Southampton) and Brian McClair (Scotland and Man Utd) to see Cocteau Twins play a few times – both excellent gents. I'd assumed, like all of you, that all footballers just liked Phil Collins, Dire Straits and Simply Red. Or jazz funk. To be honest, most of them did, but these were a few of the exceptions. Pat said he tried to play his music on the team bus but he never got past the first twenty seconds of the first song. He was an early adopter of the Sony Walkman for good reason.

One day he asked if I'd like to go to training. Sounded fun, and I assumed he meant to watch, but when we arrived at Stamford Bridge, he took me into the changing rooms and threw me a training top and bottoms, asked me my shoe size and grabbed a pair of fellow winger Paul Canoville's spare football boots and handed them to me. Five minutes later, I was out on the pitch with Pat and a full contingent of fit and athletic Chelsea squad players, wearing a Chelsea training kit that did feel a little . . . snug. And pulling that shirt on felt like I was cheating on my girlfriend. My asthma at the time wasn't great – probably something to do with the thirty Marlboros I smoked daily – and after the trainer sent us on a long jog around the pitch to warm up, I had to go to hide behind one of the goalposts and get my Ventolin puffer out and give it a right old blast or two down the lung hole.

Once I had recovered my composure, a new training manoeuvre was starting up, the same stuff we all do with our pals in the park. Pass the ball out to the wing and then run into the box and try to score. When my ball came across it was quite a way behind me and with my back to goal, I instinctively and very foolishly tried an overhead kick. To mine mostly but to everyone's amazement, it flew into the net. An absolute fluke. I returned to my feet nonchalantly as if I had just made the simplest tap-in and ran back round for the next turn. Pat still tells that story today, and while I am sure he is exaggerating, he did describe it on Steve Lamacq's show on BBC 6 Music recently as 'the best goal he's ever seen'. I told you, he's a very lovely bloke. The unlikely image of a post-punk footballer and a post-punk musician training together at Stamford Bridge in 1984 is so incongruous, so ludicrous, that I often question it myself. I didn't even tell Robin and Elizabeth about it. Football was so NOT cool then.

Pat was chairman of the PFA (the players' union) for many years, and would always get me a ticket to sit near him on their big awards dinner at the Grosvenor Hotel in Park Lane, London. I couldn't sit *next* to him because he was always on the 'top' table with the bigwigs, but he always tried to get me on a table with some Spurs players.

I loved it. Rather *that* than the Brit Awards for me. We would laugh that he would often rather be at a gig, and I would rather be at the football. One year I sat next to Leeds and Scotland legend Gordon Strachan. He was funny, interesting and *interested*. Asked me all about my job and seemed genuinely engaged. In stark contrast I once sat between Spurs' Teddy Sheringham (who I loved as a player) and Brian Marwood (who I didn't) and boy, what a way to shatter someone's illusions. I learned a lot about how expensive their cars and houses were and not a lot else.

But Pat's moral compass was always spot-on. His concern for player welfare and his standing within player circles meant that he was an excellent PFA chairman with a vision. I'm biased but I would say one of the best they'd ever had. When he moved away to Everton in the 1988 season, I sadly did see less and less of him for obvious reasons, but they were special times.

And soon after he left, our daily haunt, the Chelsea Kitchen, closed down and Chelsea were relegated to the Second Division. I mourned the former and rejoiced the latter.

CHAPTER SIX

BBC

Making a promotional pop video in the 1980s was, for many musicians, a fun and enjoyable thing to do. Come up with a concept, dress up wild, get a load of your friends along and have a fabulous time running about in a field or fannying around on the back of a boat with an entourage of fit and beautiful athletic bodies. Show the world what a wonderfully exciting life they can have, a glimpse into the glitz and glamour of being in a band. The pop video was a three-minute blast of hedonism, escapism and fantasy. Most bands that thrived in the early MTV era generally had at least one show-off. Think of ABC's Martin Fry, Boy George, Human League's Phil Oakey, Siouxsie, and even Robert Smith once he found director Tim Pope.

The Cure, I guess like Cocteau Twins, were initially saddled with the image of being depressing bedsit goths. But the subsequent collaboration between Robert and Pope that began with the video for 'Let's Go to Bed' changed that view almost immediately. The brilliant videos they made together from 1982 onwards helped to propel the band into the mainstream as MTV's cultural influence became significant all over the world. Their films were stylish, inventive and, most of all, laced with an irreverent humour that their music releases alone had only hinted at.

Cocteau Twins never found our Tim Pope, not that I recall we looked very far, and the videos we made remained, at best, atmospheric and colourful, a foggy backdrop to our abstract music. At worst they showed us to be camera-shy, awkward, depressing bedsit goths.

In 1984 I was a music snob, still idealistic and the punk inside felt that desperately seeking attention was a bit tasteless and not something I could – or would – pretend to enjoy. I'm guessing Robin and Elizabeth felt the same because we just continued to make the same blurry video for most of the fourteen years I was in the band.

If we *have* to make one, let's at least not look like a bunch of cunts.

Unfortunately, with the very first video we *did* make, for 'Pearly Dewdrops' Drops', that's exactly what we looked like.

We were naive. When making records and writing songs, we were in our comfort zone and in control, but producing videos back in the 1980s was often expensive and not something we had the time or interest to invest in. You also had to rely on someone else that you had maybe met once to take your vague ideas and make them a reality. We kept doing that over and over again. Making the same abstract colour field with someone else at the helm, until eventually some years later the penny dropped and I bought my own Super 8 and 16mm cameras and started

Dad sent this photo of himself to his mum and dad in the late '50s.

Dad's wonderful family at his brother Harold's wedding in the early '60s, London.

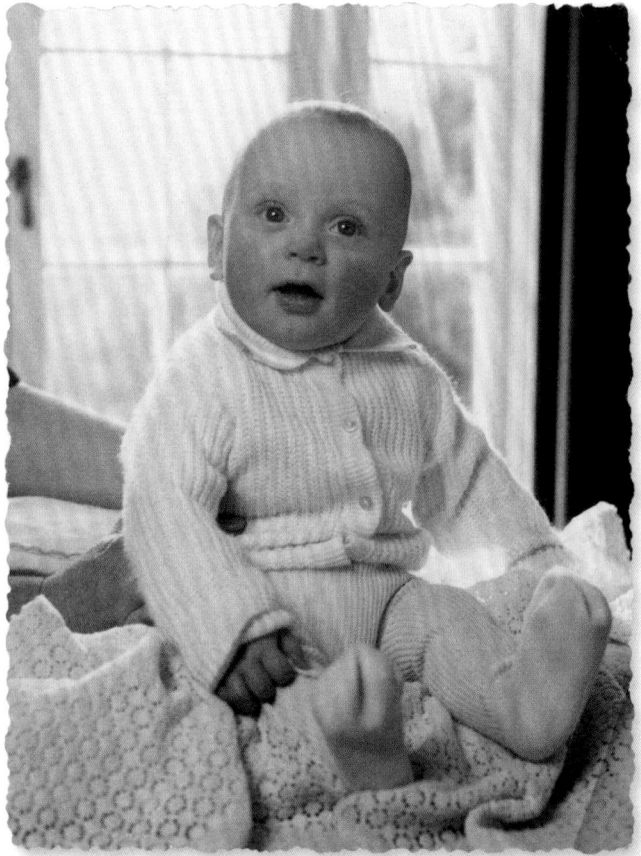

Right: I think I still look like this. From 1962, the year I was born.

Below: What a fine-looking couple they made!

Above: Dad looking like he just walked off the set of a Jean-Luc Godard film and remembering he had to take his sons out for the day. Nick all stylish and French and me just wondering when the ice cream was coming.

Left: On a barge in London in 1965. No memory of this. Why is there a hand coming out of my knee?

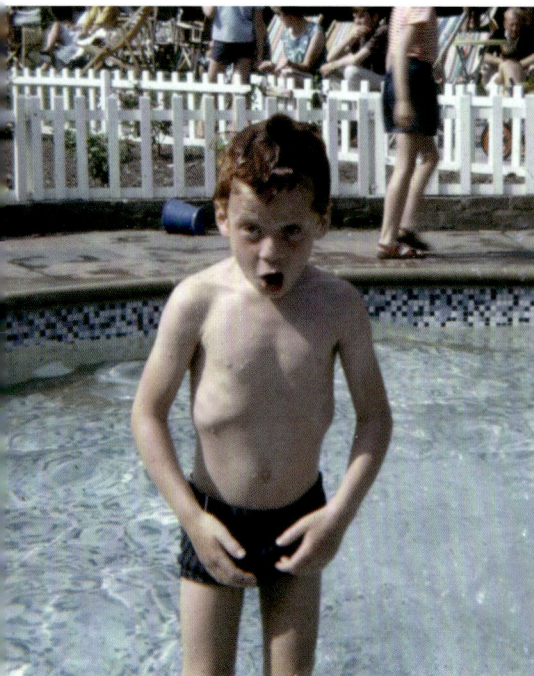

About to crack my head open...
Spain, 1966.

With Andy our first family dog
in 1966.

Ride a cock horse to
Banbury Cross... 1966.

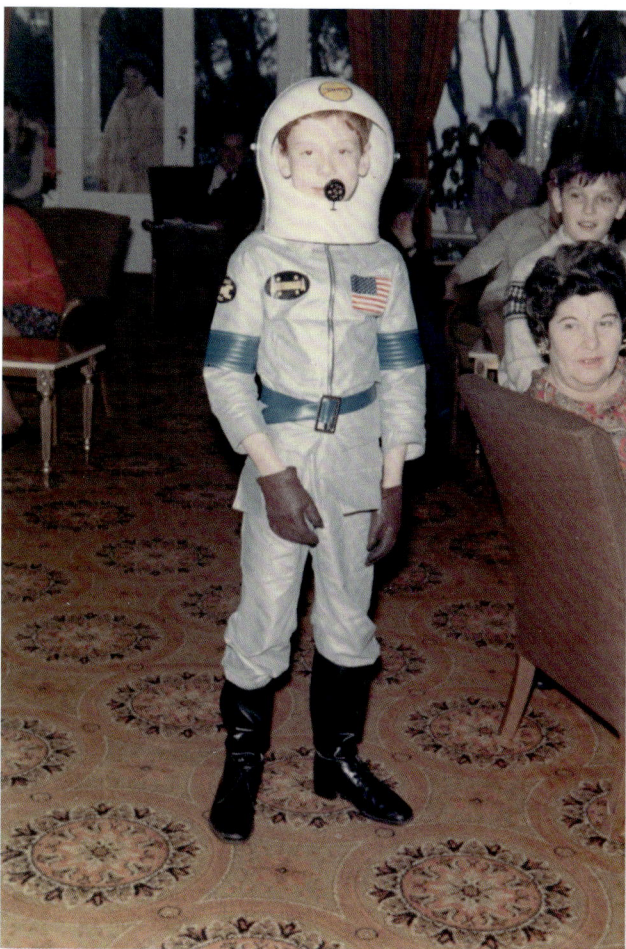

Above: Bobby Moore in Marbella 1968 (*me in the middle*).

Left: Fancy dress competition at the Sandbanks Hotel in Bournemouth in 1968.

Dad at Decca with Dick Rowe in the 1970s.

School football First XI 1978/79 season. My best pal Dave is fourth from the left on the back row. My hair is not dyed, by the way. Everyone thinks it is. That was my natural colour.

Dad in the studio with the Stylistics in London in 1978.

Seventeen years old in Greece during a month-long Interrail trip with friends.

They really did love each other so much.

My sister's wedding. My brother Nick and I as usual ruining the photo.

Left: Drowning Craze photo taken in London in 1980 by Ray Burmiston.

Below: 'Terry and June', 1981.

Dad with Frankie Vaughan on the *QE2* in 1985. They worked together a lot in the 1960s.

shooting us myself, so at least we had some natural-looking footage. The two films we made in the mid-'90s in conjunction with designers Dirk Van Dooren and Graham Wood – who took the raw shots and added *so* much more – finally got close to being visual accompaniments that we could truly stand behind. There were meant to be four videos all cut together for one twenty-minute short, but our new label Fontana thought it was a waste of money – thought *we* were a waste of money more like – and would only give us half the cash that we asked for.

Those two videos for the non-album versions of 'Rilkean Heart' and 'Half-Gifts' cost just five grand each. The huge pop stars of the '80s and '90s like Michael Jackson and Madonna were spending at least a cool million dollars on their promo videos and given their global sales, I doubt even that was much of a risk. But even bands who I figured weren't that well known had signed to majors and were spending upwards of 2 million on videos (Sisters of Mercy's 'Dominion' in 1988 – fact fans). This was a time when it was entirely 'normal' for labels to spend over 500 times what a whole album had cost to make on one video.

So, on the plus side, at least we never had that insane level of debt to recoup while we were signed to 4AD as they were never looking to make MTV-friendly videos to break their bands.

However, in early 1984, 4AD did ask us to make a video for our new single 'Pearly Dewdrops' Drops' which, very thoughtfully, was released on my birthday. I thought we were quite mad to be making a promo video at all. But I still felt like the new boy and didn't have my voice yet.

Quite appropriately, it was filmed in the abandoned Holloway Sanatorium in Virginia Water, mostly inside the chapel, and then all the outside locale stuff was shot in Virginia Water park in the same area. I think the director John Scarlett-Davis discussed it all with us and we trusted him to just get on with it, but on the day the reality kicked in. We figured he would be using the location for the atmosphere and vibes, but being filmed gliding (I'll be honest it wasn't really much of a 'glide', more of a 'skulk', but 'gliding' sounds more poetic, so I'm sticking with that) around moodily in that hallowed church setting felt just so 'goth'. It confirmed this existing stereotype that we felt wasn't us at all, so we were in the weird situation of not having made a promo video before and really *trying* to be enthused, but at the same time feeling uncomfortable, awkward and really unsure how to extricate ourselves from this predicament. A lot of effort had been made to put us here and we really didn't want to look precious. Ultimately, we just hoped that the final video would turn out OK in the end.

It didn't. Looking back I guess you *could* be polite and say the video was . . . 'a timepiece'.

Well, *YOU* could.

Me? No, I told you already. I thought we looked like a bunch of cunts.

The artwork for 'Pearly Dewdrops' Drops' and subsequently the LP *Treasure*, all within a few months of each other, sort of played into this whole Victoriana vibe that the label seemed keen to attach us to. Maybe they thought that we were so unfashionable and lacking in any style at all that we needed 'an image', any image, and this was what they came up with. I don't know if that's really what they thought because I was too busy being excited to be playing bass in this cool band and travelling around Europe in a little van with my new pals to dwell on stuff like that for too long.

But now that I have more time on my hands to laze about and write a book, I can look back and wonder. Initially we didn't really arrive with any ideas about how the sleeve art should look, or the direction or styling of videos. Our image or lack of it, and the absence of a band manifesto, seemed to cause issues for us over the years.

That created some problems because then folks were just guessing what we *might* like from listening to our music. That was a mistake. And of course there were certainly some people who thought we were full of shit, and that our 'we genuinely don't know why we sound like this' mantra was just a clever ruse and we were just fucking with them. There were others who thought we were three French girls and some who thought there were hidden messages in our songs. Nothing was very clear with us.

It's also highly likely that some people would have preferred us not to speak to the press at all, and they may have had a point. We weren't particularly good at it and I'm sure it left people with more questions than answers.[1]

---

[1] As fanciful as this all sounds, many years later when we too signed to a major label and had more access to funds we didn't need, we did employ Tim Pope to make a video, but on the eve of filming, Tim pulled out due to a personal matter he had to attend to. It was probably at this point that I decided that we should do it ourselves with my film cameras and just find some talented creative directors who could help us with the filming and editing. If you want to look at what we came up with, you can find a very low-quality version of the full nine-minute short film on YouTube. It's the only official film of us that exists that I really like.

Around the time Pat and I were eating our weight in Bolognese at the Chelsea Kitchen, Cocteau Twins also managed to fall out so badly with the BBC during a stormy 1984 that we didn't even have the pleasure or opportunity to fall out with them again until a full twelve years later in March 1996 when we found ourselves recording a radio session for lovely Radio 1 DJs Mark Radcliffe and Marc Riley.

Back in '84 they blacklisted us. Unofficially of course. Earmarked us as *trouble*.

Why? Well, tempers were so frayed when we played on the legendary TV show *The Old Grey Whistle Test* for the second time that it felt like blows were moments away from being traded. I had only been in the band five minutes, so I felt a little stunned that things had degenerated so quickly. And it wasn't even 9 a.m. yet.

Rewind.

From the genesis of the band back in Grangemouth in the last years of the 1970s, through to the end of the 1980s, after we had released the album *Blue Bell Knoll* on 4AD, Cocteau Twins had no manager. I can't think of one particular reason why we never found someone in that period, but my recollection is that maybe we didn't feel like we needed anyone. Or more likely we just didn't trust many people. Friends we had in bands who *did* have managers seemed to be constantly troubled and conflicted. And when the manager of the band is taking more drugs than the band themselves, not an uncommon state of affairs, it seems more than likely that it will all come crashing down at any moment. Add to that the pressure, explicit or otherwise, to succeed financially, when you have 'another mouth to feed' for *their* 20 per cent commission, and it just seemed like a recipe for disaster.

When you sign a record deal, you are putting your trust in those people, and the relationship with 4AD was certainly good for a time and they were always trying to help. Robin and Elizabeth's friend Colin Wallace, who moved to London at the same time, was *always* there, helping out with *anything* that was needed. A really great man is Colin, always with the band's best interests at heart. When the work we were able to give Colin dried up a bit, he started working at 4AD/Beggars and then later also managed artists including Elizabeth, but I would say of all the folks, he is the one permanent, positive constant throughout our time at the label. And maybe with Colin beside us, the need for a proper manager just wasn't there.

There is always the possibility that perhaps no one *wanted* to manage us. I don't know. We never really spoke about it and I assume if we had, then we would have realised we needed one. But looking back now, knowing what I know about managing these days, I do feel sad we didn't have anyone to help us navigate through some of these tricky moments, someone batting for our team. It felt quite a lonely place at times. Bands should know what's going on, but the busier you get, the harder it is to keep on top of everything, and a manager – well the good ones anyway – can take a lot of that pressure off. When we finally did get a manager after *Blue Bell Knoll*, I can't honestly say that anything got that much better. On the surface perhaps? But we did take our eye off the ball more, and ultimately that created even more problems for us.

The band's first big champions were John Peel at BBC Radio 1 and his producer John Walters – eccentrics both and yet for the most part avuncular and reassuring with the bands they encountered along the way. Once you arrived at the BBC, however, especially if Peel was not in situ himself that day, it was quite daunting. Everything had to be done *their* way. For a bunch of punk rock kids – and especially Robin who knew *exactly* how his band was meant to sound – there were some hurdles to overcome. The vibe back then whenever attending the BBC Maida Vale studios, Television Centre or Broadcasting House was quite different to the environment bands encounter now.

At this stage, I think it's important to make this point:

We didn't ever *ask* to be a special case. We didn't swan about feeling important, and we certainly didn't believe that our music required anything impossible from those whose job it was to record us. But for sure, I know that is how most people saw us during this time. We were perceived as difficult. If you have different ideas from the norm, you shouldn't be made to feel like you are a troublemaker, even if ultimately circumstance turns you into one.

Robin didn't want his band to sound like anyone else. And whilst walking into the studios to record the Peel sessions in the early '80s was a thrill, going into the control rooms to listen back to your performances was not encouraged. And you were certainly not allowed to touch the mixing desk. Something to do with union rules. Any attempts to add reverb to vocals or to balance the music in the way it was meant to be mixed was frowned upon. This occasionally caused some tension and conflict. It was always going to. Robin always stood up for his band, his belief in the sound in his head, and was just hoping for some respect. When he felt that wasn't forthcoming, and a collaboration wasn't going to be possible, he stood his ground, as he will have done hundreds of times growing up in a council estate. We became known as a 'difficult' band, which saddened me, because Robin developed his thick skin as a defence mechanism. People would always say to me, 'He's got a chip on both shoulders,' but he was just fighting for his band in the only way he knew how.

When we got the call about performing on the BBC show *Whistle Test* (formerly *The Old Grey Whistle Test*), there weren't many music shows on TV that featured live music. So while it wasn't always a consistent watch all the way through, some great bands had played on there and we felt we had every right to be on there too. We performed on *Whistle Test* twice. The first time aired on 24 February 1984, and the second on 15 January 1985.

The first time was a bit of a blur. It was only a month or so after we had finished recording the EP 'Pearly Dewdrops' Drops' / 'The Spangle Maker' and I don't recall much. Twenty-one years old and my first time performing on TV. I was probably too nervous, or too stoned, to take it all in. My memory of that show is hazy, but the second time – a month or so after our album *Treasure* had come out later that year – was when things really began to unravel.

This episode was fronted by new BBC wunderkind presenter Andy Kershaw. A protégé of the show's producer Trevor Dann, Kershaw didn't seem particularly interested in us when we arrived at Television Centre to film our two songs, and it was all over before it began.

Getting up before midday wasn't the norm for Cocteau Twins, so I can certainly attest to a likely residual grumpiness on our behalf as we arrived to set up around 8 a.m. that morning.

We were to perform two songs from *Treasure*. So those of you who are already seasoned fans of the band may by now be wondering why there is only *one* song from this session archived on YouTube.

Within twenty minutes of arriving, we were already in position, eager to have a few run-throughs before filming actually began. Our drums at the time were on a reel-to-reel tape machine that we always placed next to us on the stage. This was how we performed live. Whilst waiting, Robin and I had swapped instruments for fun. And as we were just jamming onstage, messing about like all bands do during such down time, the director walked to the front of the stage and instructed us to play through the song while they got their camera angles set up, and sorted out where the lights should be. Robin looked over at me and smiled as if to say, 'Come on, you know how to play it!', and pressed 'PLAY' on the tape machine. Luckily, I did know how to play it – it was only about three notes – and Robin was of course a very good bass player. So while staring around the room vacantly, watching in wonder as some of the crew were picking up what looked to be pretty heavy black cables that ran behind those huge BBC cameras, we concluded this most casual of run-throughs.

As the notes of my fuzzy guitar began to die away as the song concluded, the director shouted out to everyone:

'OK, that's great. Crew, please start setting up for the next song, let's go.'

Cue much shuffling around while we three remained onstage, puzzled and bemused.

'What do you mean? We haven't even played it properly yet. That was just for camera rehearsal you said?' Robin enquired in his soft-spoken Scottish brogue. The director ignored him as if he hadn't in fact heard a word of what he said. 'We haven't played the song yet,' he slowly repeated. 'We were just messing about, and weren't even playing the right instruments!', his voice rising with the indignation.

Responding as if he was talking to a child asking a daft question at school, the director chirped back, 'It's fine, Robin, we have got everything we need. It sounded and looked great. Let's move on please, we have lots to get through today.'

We refused to budge, incandescent that our art was being trivialised in this way. OK, so in the grand scheme of things, no one died, the song was performed competently and probably only three people noticed or cared that we weren't playing our correct instruments, but at the time this was not cool at all. It felt like a huge disrespectful snub. We weren't going to let it lie. A stand-up row followed, first with producer Trevor Dann – and Kershaw standing behind his boss – and then as the argument got more heated, Kershaw inched his way further forward, his voice aggressive and his tone condescending. It degenerated pretty fast. Whilst the phrases 'You'll never work in television again!' and 'You should be thankful you're even here!' weren't uttered exactly word for word, that was firmly the gist of young Andy's thrusting.

We were not a sideshow act, but if this was how 'TV' was going to be, I suppose we were probably not cut out for it. And we didn't know it then, but following this row with the producer and his cohorts, we were about to become a television footnote for more than a decade. In hindsight, I can now say that the next ten years were probably the most fruitful for us musically, so it does feel like the BBC really missed out on what some may describe as our 'golden period', simply because they didn't care to allow us three minutes to perform our song in the way it was intended. It's a shame because there is so little footage of the band performing live. But we didn't let it affect us negatively. In fact, I think it was incidents like this that drove us on.

I watched that performance back recently and the director's comment 'it looked great' is clearly way off the mark. One strip light is on above us, the extent of the 'production'. Very static, no shadows, no movement, no colour, just a big white static row of bulbs above our heads. Very uninspired. Compared to the previous performance less than a year ago, we felt like the sideshow. If Bob Harris had still been the presenter, I would have been able to make a little cultural joke there ('. . . we *were* the sideshow, Bob'). Oh well.

We left the scene, not at all triumphant, nor indeed deflated by it, just flummoxed at how quickly our morning had gone south. Robin, a smart, proud boy who no doubt had stood up to a lot worse in the playgrounds of his youth, was never going to back down, and I respected him for that. As I now move through life, perhaps like you, I can look back at some moments from my past, and feel I could have handled things better. But Robin was spot on here.

When it came to music, he had principles and integrity.

In 1984, 'Pearly Dewdrops' Drops' had entered the UK singles chart at number twenty-nine and an offer came in to 4AD for us to go and mime the song on *Top of the Pops*. We turned it down. I don't remember if the label were annoyed, but it seemed like an easy decision to make at the time. We were a strange, mostly static spectacle live, but miming on TV just felt wrong. We were quietly proud to have sold enough singles to even get into the UK charts and we didn't need to ruin it by chasing something we didn't want anyway. I know New Order did 'Blue Monday' 'live', but that wasn't an option that was ever discussed, most likely because they did sound awful. The week we would have been on, *TOTP* was presented by Mike Read and Steve Wright. The final song was 'Dancing Girls' by Nik Kershaw. I stand by the decision.

What I have noticed in writing this book and as a consequence of looking back at some of my photos and Super 8 films from the '80s is how great my hair was then. Even my publisher commented on what a prosperous decade the '80s would have been for Elnett hairspray when we were trawling through old press pics. I will only say this: I *never* used hairspray. Robin I think *did* – and he backcombed his too – but at one point I *did* use a combination of crimpers and Black & White pluko pomade. But that was it. I had a pair of barbers' clippers that I used to do the sides with and then I would just hack the top of my hair with a pair of old kitchen scissors. Karen, my girlfriend at the time, would help me with the back sometimes when I was feeling generous. I also had a pair of those hair-thinning scissors that I would use to chop into it when it got too thick.

I was lucky that my hair naturally stuck up and I did love fiddling with it, creating that 'just tumbled out of bed' au naturel look. *Although that wasn't actually a 'thing' in the '80s!* In the late '80s and early '90s, I did start to go to a proper barbers. Weirdly I signed an artist called Hilang Child a few years ago, to my label Bella Union, and it turned out that his dad used to be the barber that cut my hair all those years ago in Kensington Market. Mad.

I think all the crimping and fiddling about with my hair during this time must have done irreparable damage because in my late thirties, my lovely head of hair began to thin and I started to shave my head completely. Serves me right for being so vain I guess.

I should add that our personal style, and I think we did all have some, was not ever discussed or preconceived to aid our band or anything sordid like that. It was just who we were, and never about wanting to be someone. Sartorially, in the late '70s I was inspired by John Lydon's clothing choices, but it started and ended with him. Maybe the passage of time lends a different perspective to it, but we didn't see our 'look', whatever that was, as anything anyone was copying or marketing. What I wore during the day was what I wore onstage.

CHAPTER SEVEN

This Mortal Coil

Ivo Watts-Russell, the man behind 4AD, mentioned to me that he was going to be producing and creating an album under the name This Mortal Coil, which would have a floating cast, a collective of sorts, culled in part from his own 4AD stable and asked if I would be interested in contributing. Robin and Elizabeth, and Modern English, another early 4AD signing, had already worked on the 'Song to the Siren'/'16 Days' single, and the album was to be recorded at Blackwing Studios, within the deconsecrated building that was once All Hallows Church in Waterloo. It was owned by Eric Radcliffe who had worked with Daniel Miller on many of the early Mute bands including Depeche Mode. The engineer of *Speak & Spell*, Depeche Mode's debut album, John Fryer, was to be Ivo's control room partner in This Mortal Coil. Along with us musicians, he was the sonic genius who would try to turn non-musician Ivo's ideas into reality.

On the first day I arrived at the studio at 11 a.m. and my first 'job' was to listen to 'Kangaroo' by Big Star's Alex Chilton which Ivo wanted to cover. He wanted a minimal take. The main instrument was to be bass. Ivo may well have given me a cassette of it a few days in advance I am not sure, but I know I hadn't had a chance to listen to it until I arrived. I worked out an arrangement as quickly as I could and by lunchtime, while I can't say I was yet confident with it, I had recorded the bass part. I played an Ibanez Musician eight-string bass for the main part on this, the same bass I used that crucial day I invited Robin and Elizabeth to record at the little eight-track studio in Camden. Ivo wanted a little keyboard motif added so I played a Yamaha DX7 with a kinda flute sound. Martin McCarrick from Siouxsie and the Banshees added some lovely cello to finish off the music and, in the evening, singer Cindy Sharp (Gordon Sharp) performed their beautiful vocals on the track. Cinder (born in Linlithgow, six miles from Grangemouth, Scotland) had sung with Cocteau Twins before at live gigs and on a John Peel session for the BBC, both before I joined in late '83. Ivo invited them to be part of This Mortal Coil and we were both thrown in at the deep end. They were really lovely. It was special to have been part of this version of 'Kangaroo' with them.

The next day, Ivo and John had come up with a two-bar drumbeat and asked me to write a bass part over it. I could feel their desire to get things done quickly and that I'd maybe have half an hour to come up with something before I'd get a voice in the headphones – 'Sounds good, let's record it!' – but I enjoyed this pressure. Robin came in for an hour or so to add a signature guitar part and finally Ivo had me add some acoustic guitar and an e-bow solo thing to give it a finishing touch. This was entitled 'The Last Ray'.

While Ivo and John were doing their thing at the mixing desk, directing operations amid the constant departures and arrivals of singers and musicians like a pair of seasoned air traffic controllers, I would generally be messing about on one of the many instruments in the main studio room. On one such occasion I was sitting at the DX7 keyboard noodling around.

'Simon, we really like what you're doing. We'd like to record some of it?'

This track became 'Barramundi'.

I really liked it.

Everyone looked up to Ivo, respected him as a cultivated man of great taste and influence, and while we knew he was winging it to a great degree, at least there was no pretence. *We're all winging it, Ivo; it's OK!* So we all took on the challenge to help colour his blank pages in. He directed us the best he could, and by having us do cover versions of songs we mostly didn't know, our willingness to make him happy gave this first record a very unique sound.

The other piece that I co-wrote with Steve from Colourbox (RIP) was 'A Single Wish'. Steve had come up with this lovely piano part that Ivo and John recorded and they asked me to come up with some other stuff to flesh it out.

In 1979, Kevin Godley and Lol Creme from the band 10cc released a new device into the world called the Gizmotron (later amended to Gizmo). They invented it ten years before, inspired by their annoyance that they couldn't afford an orchestra for their records and imagined this guitar effect that would recreate something resembling violin sounds. They obtained a patent in 1975. I am guessing they were hoping for a similar success to the Mellotron which was developed back in 1963. It was a strange little box with small rubber/plastic wheels that fitted over the strings of a guitar with a button that, when pushed, would spin the wheels over each string and create a sound somewhere between the bowing of a violin or a cello. With your right hand you would move your fingers over the frets of single strings or, if you were very patient, chords. There were, however, a few inherent problems with it.

Firstly, the Gizmo unit had to be screwed on to the body at the base of the bridge. We didn't fancy doing that to one of our Fenders, so after Robin bought the Gizmotron – *of course he did* – he also purchased a cheap guitar where drilling two holes wasn't such an issue. The other pressing concern was that it wasn't very good. Design and manufacturing problems aside, if you played it exactly the same twenty times in a row, it would sound completely different twenty times. You had to have enormous patience and a light touch. I thankfully have both of those things, and if you listen to 'A Single Wish' on the first This Mortal Coil album *It'll End In Tears*, when you hear that cello *sound* playing that low melody throughout the track, *that* is my Gizmotron part.

Because I had to do one single take, rather than do it in sections, it took a lot longer than it would have done if they had just brought the exceptional cellist Martin McCarrick back in to play the part I'd written. But I do concede it *is* a cool sound and in hindsight I am thrilled to be in the company of some very fine musicians who have played this weird little gadget on record. Our number is very small and elite, largely because the unit never caught on in any serious way due to its faults. Even Kevin Godley admitted: 'Some days it sounded absolutely beautiful and other days it sounded like shit. Sometimes it was like a chainsaw, and sometimes it sounded like a cello and other times it varied between the two, so it was never a particularly stable piece of kit, but we persevered with it.'

I persevered with it. Ivo and John to their eternal credit did too, not giving up when it probably would have made more sense to. We finally managed to get one good take without horrid buzzing or some random dissonant harmonics coming out of nowhere.[1]

Creatively, this was a great album to be part of and I suspect that my commitment to it was the reason why they asked me to return for the 1986 follow-up *Filigree & Shadow*. The cast list of singers then was quite different, less from the 4AD family than on the first, but equally eclectic, a perfect representation of Ivo's elegant tastes.

Ivo Watts-Russell was older, smarter, way more sophisticated than me and with great taste in art, literature, architecture, film, fashion and, of course, music. I owe him a lot. He expanded my record collection considerably and introduced me to some of the greatest film-makers, and while I couldn't say we were *friends*, I

---

[1] The company that made it went bankrupt in 1981 and yet in 2014, with a complete technical and design overhaul at the hands of Aaron Kipness, a vintage keyboard specialist, it did return. I can report, following a recent purchase of both the guitar and bass version, that the initial promise of 'endless sustain' that Kevin Godley had thought possible back in 1969, now more than fifty years later, is fulfilled.

looked up to him for sure. His girlfriend Deborah, who was a talented and popular head of press at 4AD for a large part of the time we were there, was a delightful woman – kind, thoughtful and remarkably patient with the three of us, who let's face it didn't much care for all the photo sessions and interviews she was specifically employed to find.

In 1984, Ivo took us all to see a triple bill of Russian director Andrei Tarkovsky at the Curzon in Mayfair. The three films were *Mirror*, *Stalker* and the recently released *Nostalgia*. I can't pretend the twenty-one-year-old me fully grasped all the themes and meanings, and three in one night was quite a lot for my young hyperactive self to sit through. I nodded off for a bit during the final film as seven hours in the cinema was too much, but visually they all had a massive impact on me. I grew to become a huge fan of Tarkovsky and collected all his books and writings over the years. *Sculpting in Time* is an incredible read and whenever I am drawing a blank during a recording session or feeling stuck, I dip into that and I am always swiftly up and running. So inspiring. I can't recommend it highly enough. I gifted a copy to Dirty Three/Bad Seeds' Warren Ellis about fifteen years ago and he always mentions it when I see him.

On another occasion, Ivo bought tickets for us all to go to the Almeida Theatre in 1986 to see Estonian composer Arvo Pärt who was conducting choral and orchestra players performing his composition *Tabula Rasa*. It was transcendent, the first time I had seen or felt *anything* like this. This modest spiritual man stood humbly in front of his musicians inside the chapel, still dressed in the same long black overcoat he would have entered in from outside, his distinguished grey beard giving him the air of a much older man – he was just fifty at this point – reminding me of one of Roman Vishniac's portraits from his book *A Vanished World* that my dad bought me to help me understand the life that his parents would have seen in Eastern Europe. The next day I bought Arvo Pärt's *Tabula Rasa*, an album I must have purchased twenty times since for friends. This was on ECM Records, a German label that I eventually grew to love with a style not so far from 4AD and Factory, the work of the label boss Manfred Eicher. ECM is *another* recommendation from Ivo that I have to thank him for that I still cherish to this day.

*   *   *

On hearing I would be busy for a couple of weeks with This Mortal Coil's second LP, Robin and Elizabeth decided to go away and do some recording on their own, a few tracks, possibly an EP was the thinking. But when they came back with pretty much a whole album – which everyone loved – they asked me if I would mind if these recordings came out as a Cocteau Twins album, even though it was just the two of them. I loved it too and had no problem with it at all, but if I had known that its release would create a whole load of rumours that I had been kicked out of the band, then I might have not been quite as keen. But *Victorialand* simply *is* one of the most gorgeous records released under the band's name – light and airy, yet full of atmosphere and poetic beauty, the blissful soundtrack to early autumn mornings, the mist rising from the fields, the thick fog lying across the lakes. It was worth a few daft questions about my position in the group just to have this music out in the world. And bearing in mind we never really said anything to *anyone*, it was fair game that occasionally people would put two and two together and make five. You can't have it both ways.

As I readied myself for the next This Mortal Coil recording session with Ivo and John Fryer, away from music my dad was going through some health issues at home. I knew Mum was worried about him and even though she wouldn't tell me anything, I knew something was wrong. As her youngest, I think she still had that natural maternal instinct to want to protect me from the truth when she thought it might upset me, even though I was now a fully grown man. I had moved straight from boarding school into the room in Nick's flat in Kensington, so I guess part of her still thought of me as the wee boy in shorts she packed off to school thirteen years ago.

There were so many secrets hidden in our family, things I never knew about until I was so much older. I can hear Mum saying it again now: 'Oh, Simon, you did know all about it; you just don't remember!'

Once the baby, always the baby. *Oldest children are always smarter* I would be told, and *the youngest are always the favourites of the parents* was another thing the family would tell me.

The recording for *Filigree & Shadow* was split between Palladium, where we had recorded *Treasure*, and Blackwing, where *It'll End in Tears* was done. Palladium owner Jon Turner and I shared piano duties on this album; on the Judy Collins song 'My Father' sung so beautifully by Alison Limerick, I played piano and Jon those additional ethereal keyboards. I am sure Ivo couldn't have known Dad was ill or how I was feeling, but it really brought a lump to my throat whilst I was playing.

Dave Curtis and Richie Thomas from fellow 4AD band Dif Juz were also involved on the LP. Richie playing sax on a track I wrote for my mum and dad that afternoon called 'Ivy and Neet'.

Ivy was what my mum called Ivor and *Neet* was what my dad called Nita. I wasn't able to tell them in person how much I loved them, because I was such an emotionally cold fish incapable of expressing emotions verbally, but I wanted to think that this piece might do the trick.

It was another one of those out-of-the-blue tracks where Ivo and John were busying themselves in the control room and while I was waiting for them to let me know what they wanted me to do next, I would just sit at the gorgeous grand piano they had hired in and lose myself.

All the time I was writing and recording with Cocteau Twins, I never had an instrument at home. It probably wasn't until 2008 when I found an old baby grand piano on Gumtree for free.

It struck me that one of the main reasons I love being in the studio so much, and why I can be very productive very quickly, is *because* I don't really have any instruments in the home. So when I do find myself in a studio, I just get enormously excited and all the ideas and energy come flooding out the moment I sit at the piano, or pick up the bass or a guitar. Since I started the label, time is so precious and if I find three spare hours to be in the studio, I want to be sure to make the most of it. I don't take any ideas into the studio with me because I don't really have any until I get there. I don't think I always *chose* that method in the first few years, but bass guitar isn't an instrument you can really play easily at home – well, not without an amp, and with the kind of thin-walled flats I spent most of my twenties, thirties, forties and even fifties in, that wasn't an option. I have never owned an acoustic guitar either so that thing of sitting in a room strumming away has never transpired. I am never fed up with an instrument, never tired of playing, and every day recording with Cocteau Twins was always a thrill. This Mortal Coil was slightly different because mostly I was just a 'gun for hire' (though without the usual hire fee at the end), playing under direction. But those days where I am just enjoying the instruments in private, I have an inner peace. The outside noise diminishes, the internal dialogue dissipates and I can focus on me. I spent many years thinking that my lack of formal music education meant that I was not fit to wear Dad's shoes, but since I stopped comparing myself to him, I realised it's not a competition. He left me with a passion to experiment and to try anything, and while I can't play any one instrument particularly well, I can play a few decently and I know he left me with a genetic gift and the confidence to create. That feels like a good place to be.

CHAPTER EIGHT

Japan

'I have had a perfectly wonderful evening, but this wasn't it.'

Groucho Marx

Back in 1985 we were offered some shows in Japan, and nothing I had done before prepared me for the culture shock. It's certainly not as apparent these days but, back then, the difference in the body sizes of Westerners and Japanese meant that even walking along the street, at a very modest 6ft 1in, I towered over all the locals. And it was not only physical differences that literally stood out; pretty much *everything* felt fascinating and new, strange and exotic to my Western sensibilities. I found one beautiful temple there in Harajuku called Meiji Jingu, right slap bang in the middle of the hustle and bustle, where ornate rock pools surrounded by a dizzying array of colourful flowers were home to the most beautiful koi fish. The temple was within a huge forest of evergreen trees.

Such peace and serenity, an unusual – but welcome – sensation to feel while on tour.

When I had any spare time, I loved finding the vinyl shops and discovering as much new music as I could. There were some excellent noise and punk bands in Tokyo then and I was a little sad when I found out that I had missed a memorable gig by Hanatarash at the Tokyo Super Loft just a few weeks before we landed. The audience had been required to sign waivers before they were let in. While the band were known for their provocative shows, no one would have expected what eventually transpired. Frontman Yamantaka Eye, also known as Yamatsuka Eye (and later, a member of Boredoms), was onstage with the band when he suddenly disappeared. Ten minutes later, he re-entered the venue sitting astride a massive bulldozer as it smashed through the walls of the building, demolishing half of the club. He then prepared to throw a Molotov cocktail into the crowd but was stopped seconds from doing so.

Cocteau Twins shows may have been mild by comparison, but when we played at Nakano Sunplaza, we really thought *we* had bombed. Totally stunk the place out.

The hall is within the Nakano Sunplaza Hotel complex and has a capacity of 2,222 and as such it was a huge show for us. The venue itself was the equivalent of the Royal Festival Hall or any fancy concert hall around the world. The Cure had just played there, and the Police, Television, the Clash, PiL and many more household names of the time had all recently stood on these wooden boards looking out across the sea of fans on their red velvet seats.

But we weren't household at all. We were small potatoes.

When you perform live a lot, you quickly grow accustomed to things going very differently to how you might have expected them to, but when we walked out from behind the curtain to all those curious faces on 10 September 1985, the total silence that greeted us was unsettling. My shoes sounded *so* loud on the wooden floorboards as I walked self-consciously across the massive stage, like Godzilla with clogs on. Robin and I glanced at each other as we flanked Elizabeth, a little raised eyebrow in a shared 'yikes', as he pressed play on the tape machine for the first song to begin. The little tik-tik-tik-tik four count and then the drums and I come in together as we begin to play those first memorable bars of 'The Spangle Maker'. The song's underlying musical motif is a brooding bassline that uses repetition to build the tension as I pluck the top and the bottom strings together while the toms and the bass drum follow the rhythm. The changes are subtle but it grows into a gorgeous crescendo when Mellotron and snare are introduced under beautiful swooping guitars before the end and then it dies away with the choirs in their minor key fading out slowly. We opened with it a lot because it has a certain dark drama to it and has always been one of our most popular songs live. As the final notes disappear, I looked up into the audience for the first time in four minutes and there was . . . literally nothing. Terrifying, cataclysmic silence. I looked over at Elizabeth and then Robin. We were clearly in uncharted waters. Lots of things fly through your mind at times like these, but most of them are not very useful. Generally when I am very nervous, I like to think of the Marx Brothers. The humour often

helps deflate the absurdity of the situation. And I could definitely imagine Groucho reflecting on the performance in the bar
afterwards: 'Well, I didn't like the show, but then, I saw it under
adverse conditions . . . the curtain was up.'

Here's where it gets even more baffling.

The second song 'Dear Heart' began and a few bars in I was
already looking for the trapdoor in the stage floor hoping it
will magically open and we can all disappear. But just then, as
Elizabeth did one of her magical little trills in the song's chorus,
someone in the audience stood up from their seat and shouted
something and everyone started clapping and chanting. We were
only a minute or so into the second song. I was so disorientated.
Was this a good shout or a bad shout?

Did she perhaps shout out, 'Fuck me, guys, this is garbage!'
to which everyone agreed and they decided to join in with her?
Or was it a positive exclamation maybe? 'Oh yes! That was nice.
Thank you for coming to play for us!' The song finished, again
to dead air. Bizarre.

I wanted to leave but we couldn't rush through the set, and we
couldn't shorten it either.

The drums for all our songs were on a tape, and that tape
was wound on to two metal spools that were clamped on to the
front face of the machine which then ran across the tape heads.
The machine was sitting on the stage where a drummer might
be, so spontaneity or flexibility was pretty much out of the question. Today, four decades later, if you had no drummer now,
you would finish a song and if you felt like diversifying from the
planned setlist, a push of a button on a sampler or drum machine

would be all that was required to jump instantaneously ahead. Back in 1985, apart from winding the tape machine forward and hoping that when you pressed STOP it might miraculously be close to the song you now felt like playing, there was no easy way to make a change. We were a slave to the machine, and so we carried on, as did the erratic and unpredictable timing of the audience reactions. During 'Lorelei' we had some isolated jumping up and screaming, then more lengthy, loud but slow clapping halfway through 'Pink Orange Red'. By the end of the set, I was so traumatised and didn't know whether to laugh or cry.

Robin who was blunt and to the point said, 'Well that was a FUCKING disaster!'

Smash Corporation, the promoters who had brought us halfway round the world to play this show, were all standing by the curtain as we shuffled off this awful soil, no doubt ready to escort us out of the building in disguise.

'Why didn't they like us?!' Robin asked Masa from Smash.

Communication was always hard on these early trips; there was no translator and our Japanese was very limited and their English only a little better.

We were told and reassured constantly over the next few days that this kind of reaction by an audience is the very *biggest* compliment an artist can get. This is just how they showed their appreciation at all shows. I did think back to the bulldozer show at Tokyo Super Loft and how I bet the audience weren't fucking deadly silent then as that dirty big excavator crashed through the walls with Yamantaka Eye sitting astride it with a demonic stare and his little bomb in hand.

Silence really is so culturally and socially important in Japan. Maybe a little less so now than in 1985 but whether it be as part of certain Zen-influenced rituals like tea drinking, flower arranging or calligraphy, or with martial arts like karate or theatrical arts like kabuki, silence was both expected and desired. In business, silence was a strength, and even in public speaking, the orator would tend not to explain everything fully, and instead *intend* for the audience to just figure it all out. And in personal relationships when the matter at hand was maybe delicate or emotional even, silence was how it was dealt with.

In Western society we seem to have often been frightened of it, unable to deal with it. Silence is deemed a communication failure. But in the performing arts in Japan, including concerts such as ours at Nakano Sunplaza, during the silence at the end of each piece, the audience are not being disrespectful in any way at all, they are just focusing on acutely tuning into the emotions of the music. They look upon this unique *sharing* of silence as a kind of unification of the spiritual connection between us all. It really is quite beautiful when you think about it. But damn fuckin' weird the first time you witness it.

While we are talking Japanese translations, when *Treasure* was released here a year earlier in 1984 they included lyric sheets. We didn't find this out until we arrived in Japan for this tour and were handed a copy of the Japanese version. As there were *never* any published lyrics of Cocteau Twins songs, this was quite the surprise. They even decided they would subtitle the album *Treasure: The Woman Who the Gods Loved*. You think I am kidding, don't you? I am not. Here are some more *actual* lyric 'translations' from the Japanese album inserts.

114

'Let us rock you so / Rock you so good.'

'The wave of the earth has got me all fooled now.'

'Should have fixed it before it floated away.'

'Take this fish / Harder than roe / Who sauntered away.'

'Julianne was first called a genius / Julianne a genius too / Our song is framed by a genius / Suddenly she got up and turned it on.'

'I don't mend no fence.' (My personal favourite.)

And in the sleeve notes, it goes on to add that Cocteau Twins are three girls, that Robin sings all the backing vocals on the LP and that we are 'psychedelic but never freaky'.

Right on and far out.

CHAPTER NINE

Acton

After the This Mortal Coil sessions in 1985, I was excited to get back to working with my mates on the next Cocteau Twins recordings.

Victorialand had only come about because This Mortal Coil was taking up valuable time when *we* should have been making new music. I didn't realise it at the time, because Robin and, Elizabeth were too kind to tell me, but when it did finally dawn on me that it was my absence that had contributed to the whole situation, I returned to the fold like we had no time to lose.

Back in the 1980s, the twelve-inch 'extended play' format was one of the best things about releasing records. We loved them and, to fill the gaps between albums, we would often release several EPs in a year, usually with three to four brand-new tracks on each one. Pressing vinyl in the 1980s, while the quality was questionable, was at least quick and simple. Within just a few weeks of sending the music off, the record would be in the shops.[1]

Within the year following the *Treasure* album, we released the 'Aikea-Guinea' EP with four brand-new songs, a pair of EPs, 'Tiny Dynamine' *and* 'Echoes in a Shallow Bay' (which came out a fortnight apart, with a total of eight more new songs that we wrote and recorded in a room at the rear of William Orbit's house that we rented off him), and a further three-track EP of new music on 'Love's Easy Tears' (a fourth track 'Orange Appled' was added to the CD version and the US twelve-inch). So a total of sixteen brand-new songs, not to mention Elizabeth and Robin's *Victorialand* album and, to cap it all off, *The Moon and the Melodies* collaboration with Harold Budd.

I reckon that's thirty-three songs in a year.

This was us showing our commitment to each other, to experiment with our EPs and all the while to keep improving our writing. The higher purpose was to be ready to make an album that excited us. 4AD allowed us this room to grow, and with all these extended twelve-inch singles selling well – as this format often did in the '80s – it was also generating money for the label too.

---

[1] In this second decade of the twenty-first century, it takes anywhere between five and eleven months to get a record pressed here in Europe and has been slowly killing an already flailing industry. I should say that Dad told me that, in the 1960s, he would go into the studio in the morning to routine and rehearse the players/orchestras, record the album live to tape in the afternoon and the following week it would be in the shops and the charts.

Driving by Record & Tape Exchange in Notting Hill one afternoon on our way to the studio in January 1986 (there were actually two shops next to each other back then, one which housed second-hand vinyl, the other second-hand musical equipment), Robin and I spotted something striking in the window. Half an hour later, and £25 lighter, we walked out of there heaving an original Mellotron with the help of two strapping lads from the shop. It is a strange and wonderful contraption for sure, the Mellotron, and one that remains in our circle today, Elizabeth as its proud and current custodian. That makes me happy. I cannot explain why it was only £25, but I had no intention of over-examining the oral cavity of this particular gift horse.

They are very high-maintenance things and heavy as fuck. As you press a note on the keyboard, a thin strip of magnetic tape is pushed down on to a motor-driven spindle. Different sections of the tape can be 'played' to access alternative sounds. It's in essence a sampler with each sound recorded on to a separate piece of analogue tape. When you press a key on a piano or a digital keyboard, sound is immediate. On a Mellotron, however, there is a little delay before the key meets the head, and depending on how hard you press the key, the sound coming back will vary, so it does give a song a really unique feel. Listen to the Beatles' 'Strawberry Fields Forever' for a good example. Both John and Paul bought one, though producer George Martin always remained unconvinced by the instrument. 'It was as if a Neanderthal piano had impregnated a primitive electronic keyboard.'

There was a company we found called Streetly Electronics in Birmingham who still serviced Mellotrons and supplied spare parts, and found they would replace any old knackered racks of tapes with other combinations of sounds. I think if memory serves we had them replace ours with something like a rack of choirs and flutes sounds.

I did have another old Mellotron at some point in the late '90s. But around 2012, when I met my future wife and was travelling to Manhattan a lot to see her, I decided to sell it and buy a car for us to have in New York. So I was both sad and grateful to get a call from composer David Arnold who had seen my advert while he was at Air Studios recording the soundtrack to *Sherlock*. Within a few minutes, he had paid the asking price directly into my thirsty bank account and the next day I was waving goodbye to the vintage keyboard.

It was also in early 1986 that my family was rocked with the news that Phil Lynott of Thin Lizzy had died. Dad had played the Mellotron on the first Thin Lizzy album in 1971 at Decca Studios, on a beautiful Lynott composition called 'Honesty is No Excuse'. My brother Nick had also worked as a tape operator on subsequent Thin Lizzy recording sessions. I may only have been eleven or so when I first saw Phil Lynott on *Top of the Pops* on our black-and-white TV, but it stirred something in me.

(You are now scanning your Cocteau Twins bass lines aren't you, to find some spurious link between CT and Thin Lizzy? Trust me, it's a forlorn hope.)

Lynott was using this unusual Plexiglas bass on the song 'Whisky in the Jar', which I tried to find once I could afford a guitar of my own. Later, Phil used a Fender Precision Bass which became my go-to bass as well. His death was a terrible shock, but whenever I play the Mellotron now, I always think of Dad and Phil.

Around this time, Channel 4 approached Ivo about a new TV documentary music series they were planning, whereby two artists from different scenes would collaborate together and be filmed writing and recording together. Given our propensity for winging it and generally making shit up on the spot, Ivo suggested us alongside American composer and pianist Harold Budd. I had sold a few of Harold's albums when I worked at Our Price but I hadn't heard more than a few pieces. His signature low-key soft-pedal style heard on *The Pearl* (with Eno), *The Pavilion of Dreams* and *The Plateaux of Mirror* seemed a potentially good fit for us, and we agreed to do the TV show. Flights were booked for Harold to come over as we were just moving into our new studio in North Acton readying it for action.

We had recently grown tired of working in other people's studios where everything was on the clock, which really didn't suit our way of working. *And there were other people!*

We liked privacy and space and making our own hours. So after a few failed attempts to set up our slowly developing collection of gear (mostly a tape machine, pedals, guitars and a small mixing desk) in some very ill-fated spaces – an unused living room in William Orbit's lovely house in St John's Wood; a disgracefully damp and an unsafe shed in Poplar that I'm ashamed to say I found – we decided to rent a unit on an industrial estate in School Road, North Acton, West London and just build something ourselves from scratch. As highly adventurous as that sounds, we did have help at hand from the boys in Dif Juz, a band also on 4AD who we had become firm friends with. They were in the building trade and helped construct us a framed shell within the unit. They did all the plastering, the electrics and the soundproofing. Once finished, this is where we made our music with Harold Budd.

A few days before he was due to arrive, the production company making the series had gone bust, and the filming had been cancelled. It seemed too late to pull the plug on the whole thing, so we decided we would just go ahead anyway and welcome Harold into our world and just see what happened. He was such a lovely man, a laid-back Californian who treated every day with a child-like wonder. It was easy from the first day. Writing and socialising with him was a treat. We all loved him, but Robin and Harold got on particularly famously. I think Robin enjoyed that this revered ambient/minimalist musician really just liked to go to the pub and sit outside, drink beer and fart loudly, unashamedly. He was twenty-six years older than us but a kindred spirit, completely unpretentious and down to earth. He also liked ten-pin bowling, which Robin and I had already developed as our way to 'switch off' from music for a bit, so we were golden.

With our new pal, we recorded a whole album in two weeks.

It was decided, perhaps due to the confusion around me not playing on *Victorialand*, that this would not be a Cocteau Twins/ Harold Budd album and instead it came out under all our names in alphabetical order. For a record of improvisations that was certainly rough around the edges, it was a lovely surprise that, when *The Moon and the Melodies* came out in November 1986, it charted at number forty-five in the UK.[1]

After we finished the recording with Harold Budd, the three of us took a trip to 4AD in Wandsworth for a meeting. They said a film script had been sent over for us to look at, with a view to us writing songs for it. It sounded interesting.

The director's previous film *Dune* had been disappointing, I recall one reviewer said it was like an episode of *Doctor Who*, but from the new screenplay

```
B L U E   V E L V E T
A film by David Lynch
```

now in front of us at the 4AD offices, it was impossible to say too much about this one's potential. Scripts really are for actors and filmmakers, not young musicians, and we turned it down.

OK, so Dune *wasn't* great, but when *Blue Velvet* came out the next year to such acclaim, we did have to smile at making such a clanger. Angelo Badalamenti, though – I'm not sure we could have topped that anyway!

So, let me get this straight, first we rejected Brian Eno and *then* David Lynch? Do I see a pattern emerging?

* * *

---

[1] Between 2004 and 2020, Robin made three gorgeous albums with Harold, two of which were soundtracks for Gregg Araki films. Sadly, Harold died on 8 December 2020 of Covid-19 complications a month after suffering a stroke.

The Princess Victoria pub up the road in Shepherd's Bush was a few minutes' walk from my flat in Coningham Road, and a fifteen-minute drive from our studio on the industrial estate in North Acton.

Virgin's Richard Branson had bought the pub and was apparently turning it into a music venue. A couple of friends had popped around to visit Karen and me late one Saturday evening after I'd finished in the studio and, with 'last orders' about thirty minutes away, we decided we'd nip up the road for a swift pint before closing time and to see what Dicky was up to.

The pub was packed, though no Dicky in sight as I realised he wasn't the actual landlord, but we spotted a table for the four of us and headed towards it. There were some lads giving Karen some attention as we moved through the crowd. She had dreadlocks and for some reason they felt this worthy of their ridicule. Living in Shepherd's Bush, a multicultural and vibrant part of West London, this kind of bullshit was *not* normal. I loved the area so was pissed off when they started mouthing off. Karen turned and looked at me knowingly and whispered, 'Don't say anything; just ignore them.'

Once everyone was seated, I walked back through the crowd and up to the bar. As the group continued to shout their abuse at her, I walked up to them. I spoke quietly.

'Keep it down, lads, eh? We are just trying to have a nice drink,' and turned to the barman to order my drinks. In the blink of an eye, one of them picked up a straight pint glass and smashed it hard into my face.

I felt detached from my body for a few seconds, acutely aware of everything and then literally nothing. It was like time both sped up and slowed down. Initially I didn't feel any pain and remember being rushed into the toilets with the blood blotting my white T-shirt a deep red while I insisted, 'It's OK, I feel fine.' I remember sitting down on the loo seat and was starting to feel very dizzy when Karen ran in. I looked at her and could see by her face that it clearly *wasn't* OK. I asked to look in the mirror but everyone told me to just sit still until the ambulance came. As I was wheeled out of the bathroom in a chair they had strapped me into, I briefly turned my head to glance into the mirror on the way past. Basically the skin between my nose and my lips was just hanging down over my lips. I knew at that moment that my face would never be the same. I never had Mick Jagger or Ian McCulloch's lips but I was still quite attached to them. Well clearly *not* any more.

The surgeon at the hospital worked as fast as he could and put twelve stitches in, but it wasn't neat. It was zigzagged and lumpy. I think there was a bit *missing* so he'd overcompensated and pulled it too tight to try to smooth it out a bit. The surgeon said the only way to get it neater was with plastic surgery, but that just seemed daft. So I lay back and just scolded myself for being such an arse and not seeing that coming.

Within a few hours, I was back home, then had to talk to the police. It wasn't easy as it involved moving my mouth which was fucking agony and more likely to just open the wound up again. I just gently shook my head or nodded to their questions. I couldn't really identify anyone but they said they were sure the pub knew who they were because other eye witnesses said they'd seen the landlord usher them *through* the bar to an exit door round the back of the pub, so they could get away unnoticed. There had been a QPR vs Liverpool game up the road that afternoon and it was suggested that the lads were drowning their sorrows after the game. All I wanted was for the police to leave and to let me sleep.

I remember waking up the next day and seeing Mum and Dad standing at the end of my bed. They were upset and insisted that I help the police as best I could. The thing is, while I know they were reacting as any parent would, all I could think was that even if by some miracle I *could* identify the little fuck, he would probably only get community service or a month in jail and then Sod's law he would come out when I was on tour somewhere and find out where we lived and come over and beat Karen up too, and then I'd never forgive myself. While I couldn't help the police, I knew that the perpetrator would eventually get his comeuppance when he encountered someone with better reflexes or a bigger glass.

My mouth hurt for a good while and I had a big fat lip for a couple of weeks, but I eventually got used to the jagged scar, though it did totally change the shape of my mouth for evermore. I was told putting Vitamin E oil on it every day would help the scarring so I did that, but I was very self-conscious about it for a while and retreated even further back from the stage front during the shows. I was pissed off about it for a long time.

Didn't ever go into a pub again either.

* * *

After our run of stand-alone twelve-inch EP releases, several years of touring and the subsequent release of the Harold Budd collaboration, we decided we needed to make some changes to protect what we were building. Doing the same *'anything'* over and over is a sure-fire way to lose your enthusiasm for whatever it is, and while we hadn't stopped working since I joined, it was starting to bother us that since *Treasure* the three of us hadn't actually been able to get into the studio all together for a block of time to make a 'proper' Cocteau Twins studio album. In the years since I had joined, apart from that first month making *Treasure*, every session after that was just a few days here and there. It was a little hard to build any momentum. So the opportunity, when it finally came, to work solidly over a prolonged period in our new studio felt very special and exciting. I cannot stress the significance of having our own key to our own studio. It changed everything. I guess with the benefit of hindsight I can look back at all the twelve-inch EP releases and side projects of those last few years as a period of slowly growing and developing our writing and recording skills, to be ready for this exact moment.

We considered renting our studio out to friends when we were away on tour, but with the calendar now free for the next few months, and the storage cupboard freshly stocked to the ceiling with stacked boxes of Galaxy Ripples and more Walkers cheese and onion crisps than a thriving corner shop would sell in a year, it was time for Robin and I to start work. We had a few false starts. During that first week we'd find it very easy to arrive at the studio around 12 p.m., head to the café for an always unhealthy lunch, walk back into the studio feeling bloated and sleepy around

2 p.m., play Asteroids for a couple of hours, try to get motivated by eating too much chocolate, have a massive sugar crash as a consequence of eating too much chocolate, before finally deciding that today actually *wasn't* the day to start the album.

But from the very first day of recording *proper*, it felt like the shackles were off. For me, any insecurities I had felt in the first three years of being a Cocteau Twin, I left outside the studio. I was more confident in my playing, my ability to both create and collaborate, but the real breakthrough was in not repeating habits of the past and instead embracing the actual idea itself without thinking about whether it was good or bad. Robin was more relaxed. He was good to be with, to sit next to and write alongside. And our bowling skills were advancing too. As before, the two of us would create the music ourselves and then as we made progress, Elizabeth would start coming along. The energy between the three of us during these recording sessions was very pure. I can't speak for the others but I certainly felt a deeper connection with them than before. We didn't throw out everything we had developed over the last few years, but we found a new way of working together, with a sense of freedom that, whether we realised it or not, would help us create a sumptuous sounding album that sonically had little in common with anything we had recorded before.

Clearly having our own space that allowed us to take care over our work in our own time made a significant difference, maybe more than even I acknowledged at the time. We were all around twenty-five years old and simply weren't bothered about what others thought of our music. The only important thing was what we all thought of it. If we didn't like it, we deleted it, without any fear and started afresh the next day. The ten instrumentals Robin and I wrote sounded gorgeous as we recorded them; there was very little to be done during mixing. We were 'producing' *as* we were writing and recording. The balance of pianos, guitars and bass was simple and elegant. The reverbs, delays and effects were subtle and refined. The title track 'Blue Bell Knoll' was *always* going to be the album's opening song from the minute we finished it and it was one of those times where little discussion was needed when deciding what to do with a track, or where it would be sequenced. We all just *knew*.

I woke up every morning excited to get back into the studio and I was even a little disappointed when we finished the album.

It made me so happy to watch Elizabeth at work. She seemed to find the writing for this album quite joyful and whereas in the past I would worry that she was maybe stressed by the deadlines and subsequent pressure, I sensed that creating this brand-new language was something that brought her a lot of enjoyment. The titles were a delight. 'Cico Buff', 'Athol-Brose' (if memory serves I believe this is a Scottish porridge with whisky and honey), 'Ella Megalast Burls Forever' (inspired by Robin's mum, Ella), 'A Kissed Out Red Floatboat', 'For Phoebe Still A Baby' . . . what a wonderful imagination to come up with such ornate and idiosyncratic song titles.

Elizabeth's singing had moved to a new level too. She seemed to have found a higher register for this record that made the hairs on my neck stand up whenever she sang. Her melodies were warm and enchanting in one moment and exhilarating in the next. I never knew if she realised how good she was but she appeared to have more confidence, which may have been down in part to settling into the new studio we had built, and their new home just a few miles away. Certainly as was always the case, once Elizabeth came in to start her work, everything changed. Our initial instrumentals generally had a simple and even *traditional* song structure, but Elizabeth, whether by accident or design, would approach the creation of her vocal melodies by *feeling*, not by form. Where in *our* minds the chorus might begin, in hers it began where she *felt* it should, and this wholly unique way of working was, for sure, part of the reason our music may at times have seemed unconventional.

Robin clearly relished the time and space to develop *his* craft too, and there was a growing tenderness between them that seemed to inhabit these recordings. I just tried my best to pick up on these good vibrations and aid the whole process with any musicality and sensibility that I could. The trust was now there. We had known each other now for four years and in our new safe haven our improvisations sounded more natural and fluent and the doubts mostly disappeared.[2]

---

[2] After *Treasure*, *Blue Bell Knoll* felt like a quantum leap forward. I know I have trashed *Treasure* in the past in interviews but the passing of time has softened my views. The drum machines of the time had sounds that did swiftly become very dated, and our aim had always been to make music that was timeless. It felt like a half-finished record, because in a way it was. But we delivered it, we stood behind it, and people loved it, and those three things are incontestable! Listening to it now, forgetting the drum machine sounds for a second, it certainly doesn't sound like anything else, and for my first time working with Robin and Elizabeth, I can admire its boldness.

But after the constant touring that preceded *Blue Bell Knoll*, when we met 4AD to deliver the album, I think they were a bit flummoxed when we announced that we wouldn't be touring in support of this record.

In September 1989, almost one year to the day following the release of our new album, Elizabeth gave birth to Lucy Belle. 4AD would now of course understand.

*   *   *

For a band that was sometimes painted by the press as flitting through the ether on gossamer wings, the reality was of course quite the contrary. Like I would wager every band in the late '80s and '90s, (and '60s and '70s of course), we *were* often floating in space but it wasn't on any celestial cloud.

I hesitate to say it was all fun, fun, fun, because of what ended up happening to our band from the excesses that followed, but my inexperience was never an obstacle to my intrigue. My first acid trip was in 1990 with all our friends in a safe space, so it was for the most part incredible. Until it was a total nightmare.

After a beautiful if crazy night expanding our minds, Karen and I had to get a cab home around 7 a.m., which was only a couple of miles away, as we had the carpet fitters coming in at 8 a.m. Just getting into the cab felt so weird. As I opened the door, it felt like the tarmac was sticking to my feet, and the simple task of swinging my legs into the vehicle now meant I was dragging all this melted black oily tar up from the road onto *his* carpets. I was convinced he was going to see and freak out. The driver was a werewolf and, as he drove off, all the trees on either side of the road started dancing menacingly towards the car like the mushrooms in *Fantasia* (don't even *try* to tell me that movie wasn't written by someone on acid) and I was fucking terrified. The road looked like it went on forever and strange animals kept leaping on to the bonnet of the car. The journey was usually about ten minutes door to door, but I could swear it took at least an hour.

When we got home, the carpet fitters were due to arrive shortly, but instead of walking in, we crawled inside the flat on our hands and knees and lay on the tiles inside the front door, waiting for the buzzer to go. All I can remember after that is laughing hysterically as we tried to welcome them in and then falling asleep on the floor where I lay. When I finally woke up, it was pitch black. Evening had fallen and as I walked across the newly laid carpet into the bathroom to pee, I looked in the mirror to find my blurry face had a large red floral imprint of the tile pattern on my cheek. It remained there for two days. A useful reminder that I should most likely avoid acid for a bit.

When I later heard that a friend of a friend had died jumping off the roof of a Tesco while thinking he was a tropical bird, I told myself I would avoid it altogether.

CHAPTER TEN

The Greatest

Following my friendship with Pat Nevin, my sporting adventures continued in the late '80s and early '90s when music writer Steve Sutherland[1] asked me to play in the Music Business Sunday League. Steve Sutherland really liked Cocteau Twins records. He loved *Treasure* in particular so much that he wrote effusively about it, ending his review with the immortal line 'surely this band is the voice of God'. It's not often a writer would incur the wrath of a band with such an exultant claim, but Robin felt that having already made it to deity status, it was likely to be a downhill ride for us from there. Steve always seemed a decent enough chap to me and he just did what we all do – got a bit carried away in that first flush of love.

Thanks to Steve inviting me to play for the *Melody Maker*, I did take the field several times next to Chelsea fanatic Phil Daniels,

---

[1] Steve was deputy editor of *Melody Maker* up until 1992 when he 'did a Sol Campbell' and moved to the *NME* as editor.

the actor, who I must advise you is a fantastic player as well as a wonderful thespian. Steve made him captain and said of him, *'Usually brilliant except when he'd been out on a bender the night before with Ray Winstone.'* Other players who turned out ranged from Damon Albarn to Peter Perrett, another fine Spurs man.

Tim Roth and Gary Oldman are also superb in Mike Leigh's *Meantime*, but Daniels just played his role with such a simmering resentment it left a really indelible impression on me. I had a VHS copy taped off the TV that I took with me on every tour, hoping to find more fans within the band and crew. But I guess it's a pretty bleak film and has no Hollywood ending, or indeed any real ending at all, so maybe it wasn't really 'tour bus' appropriate. It rarely got played the whole way through. After a gig you just want to laugh. Well, after our gigs, we definitely needed one. You might imagine we were all sitting around watching Tarkovsky, but in the Cocteaus' tour bus VHS collection in the '80s, we rinsed *This is Spinal Tap*, *The Comic Strip Presents*, both Pee-wee Herman films, the *Airplane* movies, *The Jerk*, *The Man with Two Brains* (and then *anything* with Steve Martin), *Police Squad* TV shows, *The Young Ones*, anything with Richard Pryor or Gene Wilder and *The Godfather Parts I and II*. In the first half of the '90s, the tour bus VHS top ten included *Goodfellas*, *Clerks*, *Groundhog Day*, *Rab C Nesbitt*, *Wayne's World*, *Broadway Danny Rose*, *Zelig* and Bill Hicks's 'Relentless'.

Sorry to shatter any illusions, but a cerebral bunch of intellects we were not.

Steve and another excellent writer from the *Melody Maker*, David Stubbs, and I went to a few big boxing nights together over the years, but the day I will remember for ever is when the three of us met Muhammad Ali at John Gaustad's brilliant Sportspages bookshop in Caxton Walk, just off the Charing Cross Road.

I had been watching Ali fights since his first against Joe Frazier in 1971, and always with my dad who would get so animated whenever Ali was boxing. It was not something that I had seen in him before. Dad was generally very calm and sedate but man, he *loved* Ali. He said he was an artist in the ring.

It was half-term from school in October 1974, and on the evening after England beat Czechoslovakia 3–0 in manager Don Revie's first game in charge, Dad let me stay up and watch the delayed screening of the extraordinary 'Rumble in the Jungle' from Zaire. We were both sitting on the sofa, growing more anxious as the fight wore on. Foreman seemed so focused, determined to knock Ali out. By the end of round seven, it looked certain that Ali would be defeated by the weight of repeated crushing blows from Foreman. With sixty-eight KOs from his seventy-six wins, Dad said he was the hardest-hitting heavyweight of all time, and the commentators thought Ali's tactic of rocking back on the ropes while taking unbearable punishment round after round was foolhardy and sure to end in a sad loss. We had to agree; it was painful to watch. But the Greatest knew *exactly* what he was doing. He soaked up this barrage of punches knowing that Foreman couldn't possibly keep it up and would eventually tire. In round eight, Ali slipped away from the ropes and bewildered a tiring Foreman with a flurry of fast fists. Dad shifted his weight to the edge of the sofa, and I copied him. A left-right combination saw the reigning heavyweight champ's legs buckle under him and he collapsed in a heap on the floor. Dad and I leapt off the sofa and hugged for a few wonderful seconds. It was a lovely and unexpected feeling. I remember it now, the warmth of his body, the feel of his cashmere cardigan and the whiff of his Dior Eau Sauvage aftershave. Dad always smelled good, but this was the first moment I was truly aware of it. I always have a bottle of Eau Sauvage in my bathroom just to help me remember that moment. With only a few seconds of the eighth round remaining, what had seemed impossible only a few moments earlier would now go down in history as one of the greatest comebacks. Ali had snatched victory over George Foreman from the broken jaw of certain defeat, the unlikeliest of wins after nearly all the media had written him off. Given what had happened when he fought Ken Norton eighteen months prior, it is all the more remarkable. Harry Carpenter shouted over the crowd noise in a crackly voice, 'Oh my God, he's won the title back at thirty-two!' I turned to look at Dad who was in tears.

So, it was now 1991, Dad had been gone less than a year and Steve, David and I met up in town early to head to the bookshop where Muhammad Ali was due to be signing the new Thomas Hauser book *Ali: His Life and Times.* Can you even imagine that such a global icon would be coming to such a tiny independent shop? We couldn't believe it then and I can barely believe it now. It had the feeling of disciples waiting on the arrival of their spiritual leader.

The ravages of the Parkinson's Syndrome he had been diagnosed with in 1984 were clear to see in his shuffling walk and the frozen muscles in his face, but his eyes behind were bright and alert, and while it would be sad to see him this way after being such a supreme athlete and charismatic orator, just being in the same room as him was memorable.

Ali posed for everyone who wanted a photo taken (everyone) and even though he wasn't even yet fifty years old, with his condition it seemed like an exhausting day for him. But Steve, Stubbs and I left feeling blessed, all proudly carrying our signed books.

That one is for you, Dad.

CHAPTER ELEVEN

September Sound

I knew when I started to think about this book that I wanted to try and give some understanding as to why Cocteau Twins' music sounds the way it does. It's the question I get asked the most about the band. And I don't necessarily mean which pedals did we use, or 'is that a guitar or a piano?' But rather something *deeper*.

Back in that little eight-track studio in Camden in 1983, Robin and I had written this piece of music out of nowhere in an hour, and then Elizabeth added her beautiful creations on top of it the next day. *That* really is the simple template for every piece of music we wrote together from that day forth.

However, we did have some clear golden rules that got us to this point:

NO demos made – ever

We were all aware of that dreaded 'demo-itis' often discussed by bands. It can have two meanings:

i. when you play your demo to a label person, manager, friend etc., because they are 'fans' of what you do, *they* listen to it over and over and over and all the little weird hiss, fuck-ups and nuances of it become part of their attachment to it – to the point where any future version will *never* equal it in their eyes.

ii. as a musician, when you listen back to your original demo once you have recorded it 'properly', it is often apparent that the new version has LOST something. It's usually 'energy' and I don't mean volume or too much technique vs not enough personality. It is often hard to even describe in words what it has lost, but we have all been there. Many times.

Cocteau Twins, from the day I joined anyway, *never* made a demo.

Somewhere along the evolutionary chain, our ancestors had limited language capabilities yet substantial emotions that music allowed them to express. Meaning from music came to us long before meaning via words.

NO songs ever written in advance of any recording session

The classic 'pop' songwriting style that most of us grew up witnessing is of a musician sitting with an acoustic guitar or piano and for a melody to be set to some chords, and either some mumbled words being uttered just to get the melody ingrained. Now there are a ton of variations on this, and that *is* a simplistic view of songwriting, but it serves a purpose to explain how maybe without even realising it, we were doing things a little differently, and how that also created some of the misconceptions about us as a band. Again, none of it was wilful, it was simply what felt right and authentic to us.

Our method, or rather *lack* of method, was to start with a sound and go from there. Robin would often say, 'If you just plug a guitar into an amp, or straight into a mixing desk, it just sounds boring, and like everyone else.'

So whether it was messing around with some pedals, or some new effects unit, he would hope to make the instrument *not* sound like itself. Also, as important as the 'sound' was the *beat*. Using drum machines and samplers as we did all through our albums, the beat always had to come first – a two-bar pattern, almost like a metronome to play along to. Once we had a beat (*our* drummer) and a guitar sound, then the 'songs' would usually come together within an hour or two. I don't like the word 'improvised' because that suggests a level of technical ability, and we were quite honest and open about our *lack* of technical ability. But maybe what we lacked there, we made up for in the imagination department.

When we had the arrangement vaguely worked out, we would record the bass, and the guitars, then maybe add some piano or additional guitars.

At this point, even though Robin and I would call them 'songs', they were really just instrumental backing tracks that we would give names to.

NO songs left over at the end of any album session

This baffled lots of my friends.

'You must have tons of stuff that was never released!'

The main reason we didn't is because we already *knew* after recording the bass and the basic guitar on top of our drum 'loop' whether the track was going to be any good or not. And it would never progress beyond that to even be considered a contender. If we weren't sure and thought it *might* have some potential, we would ask Elizabeth to come in and take a listen. After all, these were just relatively blank canvases for her to paint on top of.

So for an album we wrote ten songs and then we stopped. Ten songs in our world was usually between thirty-five and thirty-eight minutes, the perfect length for us and the listener – five songs on each side. The symmetry was appealing. We didn't write fifteen and then choose the best ten. This worked for us. The only issue we had is that once we had finished the album mixes and delivered it all, discussions would start about singles and then we realised we had no B-sides. So we would have to go *back* in and write and record a B-side. Now traditionally, B-sides are the not-so-good spare tracks that didn't make the album, but well . . . we didn't have any spares. And nor could we just go in and knock out a not-so-good sounding track. Our method was just the same and in 1990 after finishing the album *Heaven or Las Vegas*, for its first single 'Iceblink Luck' we had to go back in a few weeks later and write two new songs. Now this is all subjective of course, but one of these new songs 'Watchlar' turned out to be one of my favourite Cocteau Twins songs *of all time*. And it's the third track on the B-side of the single.

If we had written that a month or two earlier, I am certain it would have made the album.

But let's not get too far ahead of ourselves . . .

* * *

After we had released *Blue Bell Knoll*, we wondered if we had outgrown our small studio a bit; it felt like we could do with a bit more space. One day in the cafeteria near our unit we saw an ad in *Music Week*.

'Riverside Studio space in Richmond looking for an active and successful band who would be interested in becoming a full-time tenant, using part of the building for their own projects.'

Miraculously, we really fitted the brief.

We drove over to the address and soon found ourselves chatting with owner Pete Townshend who showed us around the building, a boathouse on the banks of the River Thames. I had to pinch myself. It seemed too good to be true. Within a month we signed a lease.

We started our new tenancy by renting the upstairs part of the building with Pete retaining the ground floor. That was more than enough for our needs. But after a few years, Townshend found he didn't want to be there at all, in any part of the building, and offered to rent us the whole thing. It was enormous downstairs as you might imagine, a place where there was a lot of rock history. It was sorely tempting, though I think we all had our concerns about taking on such a huge responsibility.

Even though we were only renting the space, Pete was more than happy for us to completely renovate it, and we did. I'll take you on a little tour. As you walked upstairs, we had an office on the left where we had a couple of desks with telephones, a fax machine, a storage cupboard for all the tapes, and a photocopier. The next room on the left was a maintenance room where Lincoln Fong worked, repairing and preparing equipment for the studio and for our tours, and then at the end of the corridor was the kitchen that had a small door leading out on to the large terrace. We painted the whole place in really bright colours – the walls were mostly a deep orange and we loved that it was becoming *our* place rather than adapting to someone else's taste that we couldn't feel wholly comfortable in.

After Lincoln's maintenance room, you would find yourself in a lovely big living room where we had a TV and big blue sofa and a dining table where we would do interviews and eat when we remembered, and this room had floor-to-ceiling sliding glass windows that also opened out on to the massive terrace overlooking the River Thames. There were three studio rooms, a large control room (also with floor-to-ceiling sliding windows to the terrace/river, where Robin and I wrote and recorded all the music), a small recording room next door where Elizabeth would record all her vocals, and a large porthole window between the two rooms so we could 'see' each other. There was one further soundproofed space which we called the 'programming room'. Robin planned the layout of all the equipment and Lincoln installed and set it all up. It probably took a good few months for us to be ready to record, but this was an exciting time. Lincoln was an exceptional engineer and for pretty much all of our time in the new space, he was indispensable. Lincoln was also a great musician and he and his brother Russell had a band called Critical Mass. Russell Fong also made guitars as well as playing them, and he made a custom guitar for Robin and two beautiful five-string basses for me, one of which is now owned by the actor Jason Lee, who won it in a charity auction and gifted it to his daughter!

* * *

Via our friendship with Lush, a fellow 4AD band, we bonded with another wonderful band of the time called Moose. Russell and Lincoln both started playing with them as had Richie Thomas, drummer of Dif Juz. We took both Dif Juz and Moose on tour with us, the former in 1984, the latter in 1996, and to round it all off, in 2017, some twenty years after Cocteau Twins called it a day, I started a new band with Richie called Lost Horizons.

The singer of Moose – *also* called Russell – together with the former drummer of Moose, Mig Morland, set up a radio and TV promotions company called Cool Badge in 1997, the same year we started Bella Union. We have worked with them for every one of our twenty-five years as a label and still do to this day. The Lush/4AD/Moose connections do not end there either. Singer Miki and drummer Chris Acland lived near me in Camberwell and they used to cat-sit for us. When we could, we would all go to Spurs together. Together with Russell and Mig from Moose, and Chris and Miki from Lush, we all celebrated Spurs' famous victory over Arsenal in the 1991 FA Cup semi-final by having a few drinks at our studio September Sound where we all 'wrote' the awesome – but slightly petty – track 'And David Seaman Will Be Very Disappointed About That . . .' under the band name the Lillies (Spurs' nickname is the Lilywhites). It eventually appeared on a flexi disc for a fanzine we supported called *The Spur*. The 'song' itself took no more than a few hours to write and record. I nicked commentator Barry Davies's line from *Match of the Day* by recording it off the TV on to my VHS player at the moment Paul Gascoigne scored a 35-yard screamer of a free-kick, and then we finished it off with Miki singing a chorus of her chanting '3–1' (the final score) over and over. It was a lot of fun.

*   *   *

Back in the mid-'80s on our first mind-expanding trips to Japan, we would travel to Shibuya, Shinjuku or Ochanomizu to look and drool at all the new gadgets and technology that weren't on sale in the UK yet. We bought a lot of Roland gear over the years – drum machines, effects, keyboards – expensive though it could all be, and they are for sure a part of the story of our sound. But in 1989, the Swiss-German Uli Behringer, frustrated at the prices himself, founded Behringer to develop alternative audio equipment and sell it for a fraction of the price, enabling more young bands to access this equipment.

One day back in December 1986 before our show at Korakuen Hall in Tokyo, we came across the Ishibashi music store where Robin found some of his favourite Ernie Ball plectrums which he needed for the show. The sales assistant was sweet, spoke not one word of English but managed to communicate with us nonetheless. He and Robin connected over some new Boss guitar pedals that weren't available in Europe yet, and a mutual respect was clearly formed through knowing glances and admiring nods. Silence again winning the day.

After that trip, we wouldn't return to Japan for a long time, but three years later in September 1989 as we were now settling into life at our lovely new studio, the doorbell rang. I went downstairs and opened the door. A shy Japanese boy mumbled some words. He tried again slowly. 'Want. Be. With. You.' My dad co-wrote 'I Only Want To Be With You' but I was pretty sure this wasn't a singing telegram. If it was, it was brilliant!

'Want. Be. With. You,' he repeated. His demeanour was kind, apologetic, a little scared maybe, but he seemed determined to get his message over.

Robin came downstairs. He recognised him immediately.

'Ishibashi!'

The shy boy smiled.

'What are you doing here?' Robin asked.

He repeated, 'Want. Be. With. You.'

Those really were his only four words, but we brought him inside and well . . . Mitsuo Tate – Tate-san – didn't leave for the next sixteen years.

I could probably write at least three chapters about this fine and curious gentleman and his extraordinary attributes as a human, but I will start at the beginning.

Language was clearly a huge issue and progress wasn't so much slow as non-existent. He slept at the studio for a while and we tried to involve him as much as we could in our social lives, but without any basic English, it was a struggle. What we did know about him was that he had left Tokyo to come and be with us. That was fine for now.

Over the next few months, he found himself a job at Shogun restaurant, one of the premier Japanese restaurants within the Britannia Hotel in Mayfair in London and when he did come to hang out at the studio, he would prepare the most beautifully ornate fruit and vegetable dishes, so in his own way, he was thanking us for taking him in.

Around this time we had begun discussing taking some additional musicians on tour with us next time and I had placed an ad in the *NME*, for a second guitarist. We managed to whittle the interested parties down to a shortlist of about fifteen and it was decided that I would meet any possible candidates at the White Horse pub down in Richmond to see if they were a good personal fit with us. I found one guitarist, Ben Blakeman. He was a good man. Robin and Elizabeth liked him and after a successful, hastily arranged audition, we offered him the tour.

The following week as we entered the studio to start work on some new music, Robin and I climbed the stairs to the familiar sound of 'Pearly Dewdrops' Drops' drifting out from one of the studios, except without the vocals. Curious. As we walked past the smaller 'programming' room, the door was slightly ajar and as we peeked inside, there was Mitsuo with a guitar playing Robin's part for the song with the exact same sound as on the record. Robin and I looked at each other.

We continued to hover silently outside the door as the song finished. A few seconds later, an instrumental version of 'Pink

Orange Red' started playing and once again Mitsuo performed the guitar parts and sounds with frightening accuracy.

It turned out our next guitarist had actually been sitting here silently all along. While he couldn't communicate in words to us that he could play or indeed would be interested in the job, he did an even more remarkable thing and learned the whole canon of songs, note perfect. It wasn't so much learning the notes that was impressive – although it was – but rather his meticulous attention to recreating the sounds, with all their subtle nuance.

As we had already offered the job to Ben, we decided we'd just take them both on tour.

We named our new studio September Sound and this place is of course hugely significant in the story of Cocteau Twins, as our last three albums were made there, but it also plays a part in our downfall. Originally named Oceanic, apparently because it is an anagram of cocaine, back in the 1960s it was an actual boat-house. Pete Townshend loved it because he could commute there by boat after he was disqualified from driving. In 1981 it became a commercial recording studio where bands such as Thin Lizzy, Siouxsie and the Banshees and A-ha all recorded, as well as the Who of course. Pete had called it 'Eel Pie Studios' due to its close proximity to Eel Pie Island. We changed it to September Sound.

With Robin and Elizabeth's daughter being born in September, my son Stan being born in September, and *Blue Bell Knoll* and *Heaven or Las Vegas* both being released in September, it won't come as much of a surprise to you that this month had some significance for us.

CHAPTER TWELVE

Birth, Death and Vegas

I read somewhere that Robin thought that it was *because* of the drugs that our work was getting better. I don't know if he *actually* said that, but *I* believe it was because we were just dedicating so much time to the music, cared about it obsessively and had gradually developed such an intuitive way of working that seemed to suit us all.

The problems increased when we moved out of the North Acton studio to our September Sound studio in 1989. Cocaine hadn't just entered the bloodstream though; it had begun to slowly poison everything. I either didn't realise it or chose to ignore it.

We began recording *Heaven or Las Vegas* as soon as the studio was installed and while I don't believe the record would have been any different without coke, it just might have taken longer. Cocaine does make your heart beat faster. But while it made me temporarily chattier and briefly more confident, after a while

I found myself becoming agitated and very depressed. I was constantly feeling negative about everything and everyone. It made me argumentative and arrogant, not traits I liked in other people. So when I noticed it in myself, I remember staring at myself in the mirror one night after getting home very late, and tears were just streaming down my face.

'I really hate who you are becoming.'

I said it out loud. It shocked me to have verbalised it but at least I knew I had to find the strength to stop.

As it turns out, I found stopping easier than quitting smoking, that's for sure. The depression certainly did eventually lift, but the greatest damage seemed to be to my relationship with Robin. Creatively, things on the surface were the same. Our writing was still strong. But I know he thought I was judging him every time I said, 'No, thanks' – that I was taking a superior stance by not partaking.

Nothing was further from the truth. For my own sanity, I just couldn't do the drugs any more.

The studio wasn't just a place we recorded; it had become a second home. And a phenomenal place for a party. On the bank of the River Thames by Richmond Lock, 'The Boathouse' was idyllic both inside and looking out. A dysfunctional band, renting a million-dollar property from the guitarist from the Who, in leafy suburbia and close enough to London to be there in fifteen minutes from Hammersmith meant that the studio was a magnet to anyone who knew us, and plenty who didn't.

As time wore on and Robin's addiction was starting to have serious repercussions on us as a band, and in his personal life,

I hoped he would want to be able to stop – for his health *and* for his relationship – but I could also see that there was a small group of people coalescing around him that weren't interested in either. Thankfully, even though we weren't doing the drugs together any more, our musical relationship was still progressing. That got me through the times when I felt so conflicted. I do have a lot of regrets, though – the worst being that I didn't have the strength or foresight to work out how to help Elizabeth when she probably needed a friend.

The recording of *Heaven or Las Vegas* came at a time in our creative lives where we were all thankfully tuned in to the same sonic wavelengths at the same time. Notes just seemed to present themselves and when this occurred we didn't ever question it, because it *is* a bit of a mystery when you think about it too much. So we didn't. The approach was always to play with open hearts and minds. I think by this point in our work together, ego played no part in the way Robin and I wrote. It was all about what was best for the song. On these sessions, as we were recording, most days we *did* feel that something special was developing. We would try to have Elizabeth come in and listen as soon as possible, all proud of our efforts like children seeking approval for a good drawing, whilst at the same time trying to totally downplay it, hoping she would love them as much as we did. So nonchalantly, we said:

'Yeah, so no big deal, we just finished this one, thought you might want to have a listen,' *really* meaning, 'LIZ, LIZ, LIZ, LIZ. Come in here quick. You HAVE to hear this! You're going to flip out!'

Such outbursts of exuberance at our own work were not something we usually indulged in, even privately.

Elizabeth's vocals on '50–50 Clown' in particular were of course stunning and to this day it remains one of my favourite songs of ours. Prince ended up using that intro section as a sample just ten months after the *Heaven or Las Vegas* LP release on his 1991 production of a Martika track he wrote called 'Love Thy Will Be Done'. We all loved Prince so that was a *lovely* thing to discover. To subsequently read that he listened to our music a lot with Wendy and Lisa, and his girlfriend Cat, always brings warm fuzzy feelings.

* * *

Mum called me up one Sunday in May to say Dad wasn't feeling well and may have to go into hospital for a few days, but not to worry. On the contrary, this was *very* worrying. Mum wasn't one for sharing bad news unless she absolutely had to, so I know the fact that she called at all wasn't a good sign. I went into the studio on Monday thinking about him whilst throwing myself into the music, working on some ideas on a new keyboard we'd recently bought.

While ninety-nine times out of a hundred on Cocteau Twins songs you think you're listening to synths, you're not. They're guitars. But on *this* new composition, what you hear is a synth. The song is called 'I Wear Your Ring', and without doubt is another of my favourite songs that we ever wrote together, in part due to the fact that it is so inextricably linked with thoughts of my dad. Music as therapy.

When I came back in the next day, I couldn't believe how good it was sounding. Robin had already added the drums. I would doubt anyone could believe this wasn't a real drummer playing, and while his innovations on guitar and production are rightly why he is held in such high regard, his abilities stretched way beyond that and the drum parts and sounds on *Heaven or Las Vegas* in particular should get a special mention.

When I got back home in the evening, I called Mum. Her voice soft and trembling, she explained that Dad had been complaining to his doctor that he was getting terrible pains in the months prior, but all the tests and examinations found nothing. A week or so would go by and then he'd be hit with another bout of excruciating pains in his body, and again the doctors sent him back home, diagnosis inconclusive.

When he couldn't stand the pain any more, he told his doctor to get an ambulance and by the evening they had found cancer in his kidney. A bout of radiotherapy seemed to be working and Mum had hopes he would recover. The next day I went to see him. He tried to put on a brave face when I walked in, but he looked like a ghost. By the next day, the cancer had come back and spread to his liver, and less than a week later he had a pulmonary artery aneurysm and was dead. Sixty-three years old.

At the funeral, everyone said he was a special kind of man. I thought about those rare moments we had together, on the sofa watching Ali, driving up to White Hart Lane to watch our beloved Spurs, listening to him talk about his early life, the war and busking on the streets of East London. I replay them over and over in my mind even now and hold on to them dearly. At

Christmas around the piano as he sang songs for the family and on holidays in Spain, he would be the life and soul of the party, and yet I am left feeling like I barely knew him. Researching his life's work over these last twenty-odd years has been a wonderful way for me to get closer to him. But that is only as a musician, not as a man. In my childhood years, he was rarely home due to all his varied jobs as musician, producer and arranger, and even on the rare moments when he was, he wasn't hanging out in my room! When I was older and his career was slowing down and mine was taking off, I didn't spend as much time going to see him and Mum as I should have. When I did, he would always ask me about the band and the touring and when I'd updated him, he would smile gently and nod. He was happy for me I knew that, but I could also sense some sadness behind his deep, dark mahogany eyes. He was still hurting that he wasn't as in demand as he had once been. The synthesiser had all but killed off string arrangers in the '80s.

When he died, I didn't know what to do with myself. None of us did. I didn't know how to comfort Mum for which I still have some regret. I retreated deep into music, *Heaven or Las Vegas* being the grateful receptacle.

I wrote the music for 'Frou-Frou Foxes in Midsummer Fires', the final song on the record, the day after Dad's funeral. I had come into the studio early as I couldn't sleep. The piano was set up in the control room where Robin and I always wrote together, so I sat down and subconsciously began to play, looking out across the river as a light summer rain began to fall from the skies. My heart was heavy. I played what I felt.

I didn't notice Robin come in at first but when I did, I stopped playing. 'Don't stop,' he said as he gently placed a new reel of two-inch tape on the machine. 'Keep playing and working it out and I'll come back in a bit and we can record it.'

He never actually *said* he liked it as that wasn't really his way, but I believe he did. And so much of being in a band seems to be about building towers of illusion, that in my fragile state I *needed* to believe it.

I finished working out the arrangement and after Robin recorded me playing it, he added those exquisite guitars. It remained this melancholic instrumental piece only for a few days, until Elizabeth came into the studio to record her haunting vocal to the verses. The ending she wrote is just euphoric and quite uplifting. To me it felt like the perfect eulogy to Dad. All three of our fathers died young, and the empathy they both showed me then meant a lot. It still does.

It's hard for me to listen to that song now because it is just so sad, but I know how much it means to a lot of people and that's all that matters once you've written something.

The *Heaven or Las Vegas* record is also filled with love, joy and heartbreak, the balance of emotions across the ten tracks was just about perfect.

Elizabeth had given birth to Lucy Belle in September 1989, and my dad suddenly died in June 1990.

As Lou Reed once said, 'There's a bit of magic in everything, and some loss to even things out.'

The high highs and the low lows.

* * *

We needed to get to work on the sleeve. Vaughan Oliver at 23 Envelope, the in-house 4AD designer, hadn't been on board with us for a while as Robin wanted to move away from his unique style to something he felt better represented the music in a more abstract way. The designer Paul West, who as a student was actually a huge fan of Vaughan's, had been brought on board to design the previous album's sleeve for *Blue Bell Knoll*, working with photos taken by Juergen Teller. He also designed the logo for September Sound. With time running out and having already tried a few things that we had rejected, Paul managed to hastily arrange a shoot with photographer Andy Rumball in his kitchen where he was going to try to capture something abstract and 'other-worldly'.

The kitchen session Paul and Andy had set up was going on long into the early hours and they had used sparklers, colour fades, even clothes to try to get a textural feel to it. Remember this is before the arrival of digital cameras so they had no idea how these experiments would turn out for a few days as the film had to be sent off to be processed. Before they packed up for the night, they tried one last idea and waved a string of Christmas lights back and forth on a long exposure in front of red and blue colour backdrops with an orange fluorescent plastic rose held up close to the camera lens.

Once the film was processed, Paul would have less than twelve hours to present the sleeve images to us as we needed to make a final decision. Negatives came back and photos were printed and cropped, and a provisional album font was then hand-painted on to an acetate overlay to create a mock-up for us to look at.

I remember walking into the room, seeing these pictures and feeling a wave of emotion sweep over me. A big lump formed in my throat as it just hit me that my dad would never get to see this beautiful cover or hear the music it housed. Or indeed that I was never going to see him again.

Thirty-two years on, this album continues to find new fans and that is a beautiful thing. I know Robin always wanted to make a record that sounded 'timeless' and I think we got close with this.

* * *

Going to Las Vegas on the *Heaven or Las Vegas* tour seemed like the perfect end to a long run of shows and would see us get home in time for Christmas, hopefully with a small wad of cash for some presents.

I had been into a few casinos over the years – usually just the naff ones on ferries – but I still thought I had some 'magic in me' when I was at the roulette table. I had read a couple of books on gambling and figured I was way ahead of everyone in there.

I also thought this about golf once, when I went round a nine-hole course in just forty shots, just one day after lying in the bath devouring page after page of *So You Want to Play Golf*, Peter Alliss's book on technique. I've cracked it!

The next round I played, a few days later, I scored a dreadful sixty-three. And after that I lost interest a bit as I realised golf must be truly impossible and took far too long.

I was such a massive twat sometimes.

But as Karen's dad would always say, 'Golf is just a walk, spoilt.'

There were a load of journalists out with us at this point. The lure of Vegas! It was also the final headline show of the tour and I guess, being a band who had already been on the front covers of the music papers a few times already, they figured there was probably the chance of a decent story in there somewhere, alongside an all-expenses-paid jolly to the desert. Robin had this reputation for drug excess, and Vegas was the *capital* of excess, so you can see the headline writers rubbing their hands with glee. 'Beer and Loathing in Las Vegas', 'Gear and Loathing . . .' etc., etc. Take your pick. Plus the last person to play the Aladdin casino before us was Elvis Presley, so we had a *lot* of excess to live up to.

As it turned out, there were no great surprises: the band did what the band did, the writers got their story, we made the front cover and everyone went on to the final date. Except *me*. I stayed, convinced in my deep delusion that I was a character in a Scorsese movie. The sleeper bus would roll out of Vegas as normal but I wouldn't be on it. I told the tour manager I would meet up with them again in Phoenix for this small festival we were playing the following afternoon before we flew home.

I had $1,500 in cash, my whole wages for the tour basically. We always made sure we paid ourselves something for touring, because generally all the money we made we ploughed back into the recording studio. The tour manager, Scott, being kind and smart, and with my best interests at heart, had recommended caution and said he would get out half the total $750. But I insisted on the full $1,500. He reluctantly handed it over.

He went on to manage Paul McCartney. I told you he was smart.

I had no luggage, just a Tesco carrier bag with clean socks, a shirt and underwear, and I checked into my room at the MGM Grand which was, like everything in Vegas, just massive, and totally unnecessary for one person. I quickly showered, got dressed back into my suit – a slightly too-big black Oxfam pin-stripe which I wore most days anyway – and my pointed creepers. A quick glance in the mirror just to reassure myself one final time that I had the air of someone who knew what he was doing. So deluded.

I put $200 in my left inside suit jacket pocket, an emergency fund basically to ensure that *if* it all went pear-shaped, I would at least be able to get out of there and get a flight to meet up with the tour bus in Phoenix the next day.

When, not *if*.

I walked briskly past the slot machines where bespectacled, bejewelled and well-heeled besozzled pensioners were sitting, in a zombie trance, feeding the machines like those gold mechanical cats that you can see in every window in every Chinatown, with the arm that moves slowly up and down without pause, with the same frozen smile.

I stopped briefly to watch a poker game when a middle-aged man with a comb-over, even more ridiculous than the one Spurs' Ralph Coates sported in the 1970s, stood up in an agitated and animated fashion, realising he had just folded with a better hand than the winner of the pot who only had a pair of sixes. *Ooh yeah. I feel yer pain, Ralph, feel yer pain!*

I reckoned I should stay away from poker as I wasn't confident in my 'face', certain I was probably easier to read than Spot the Dog.

The odds at winning on roulette are the highest of all the 'games' in the casino; in other words, it is the least likely to bear fruit. Of course, that was to be where I chose to spend most of the evening. I had a system. This system had worked the first time I played roulette for fifteen minutes on a ferry to France, so why would I possibly change?

I handed over $200 in cash and the croupier pushed all my chips over to where I stood. I put about half my chips on the numbers and edges of 25–36 only – THE SYSTEM – and won immediately. If you haven't played roulette before, if you put chips directly on the number and win, you get thirty-five times your stake. For example, putting $100 on one number pays out $3,500 if the wee ball lands on that number, and if you then put additional chips on the edges, sides and corners of that number too you will also get a further payout of seventeen times or eight times. To win big you have to bet big and just be incredibly lucky. Sometimes, just to mix it up, I put a few chips on '0' which sits in its own big green box at the other end of the table. Within the first hour – or it could have been the first five minutes, it's hard to tell as I am sure they pump some kind of mild hallucinogenic spray through the vents to keep everyone entranced and unaware of time – I had about $6,000 in chips on the table. A very tidy profit of $4,500.

I should also mention that in the casinos you don't pay for your booze. I did *not* know this when I walked in. These days, the free-drink rule is reserved for the high rollers. In 1990, maybe it was for high rock 'n' rollers.

When I had money in a bar on tour and back when I was drinking, I would order Jack Daniel's and Coke, because it was basically sweet and tasted like a soft drink.[1] I didn't really like the taste of beer, wine or spirits that much, so drinking was always a challenge to find something that did the business, but without me having to grimace every time I took a sip. I didn't realise it was free initially, but after about the fourth time that a waitress asked me if I wanted a drink, she added, ' You know the drinks are all on the house right, honey?'

'Actually, you know what, I *will* have a drink, thank you! Jack Daniel's and Coke, please.'

Free booze. Count me in.

Another part of my clearly foolproof roulette system was never to outstay your welcome at a table. The second you feel that your luck is running out, move to a different table, watch for a few minutes, and then join in. I was informed from my extensive 'How to Gamble . . .' tour bus reading that numbers fall in patterns and if none of those numbers 25–36 have appeared for a good while, you just have to ride it out and wait, and then join

---

[1] Side note: I used to love those Smirnoff Ice bottles when they first came out in 1999 because they tasted more like a soft drink too and had me drunk in no time at all. But I didn't realise until many years later that it isn't even vodka, it's made of malt, which explains why I always felt rotten afterwards as I am allergic to malt. Indeed it was this Ice habit (not the crystal meth one) that precipitated me quitting alcohol altogether a couple of years later, and I am happily more than twenty years sober now.

the table at the right moment. And of course always 'quit while you're ahead'.

Some of these theories may well be true, but when you are seven or eight Jack Daniel's and Cokes in, all the theory in the world ain't gonna help you. Fortunately, alcohol never made me belligerent, aggressive or argumentative, but *unfortunately* it did make me incredibly stupid, show poor levels of judgement and be incapable of sensible logic and reason – four things that ideally you will be fully in possession of in a casino.

So I am drunk and ignoring The System and yet I am not quite at that stage where I am *aware* that I am drunk. That's a dangerous point to be when you feel you're invincible and winning. Any sane – or sober – observer can see the folly in this state of mind.

There is no time as such in a casino, because there are no windows and no clocks, and they don't want you to be thinking of time, and well . . . I don't wear a watch, and mobile phones don't exist yet, so *my* concept of how the passage of time moves is dependent on three things i) how well things are going; when time will appear to slow or ii) how badly they are going; when time appears to be moving uncomfortably fast and iii) how drunk I now am.

The third thing does unsurprisingly affect i) and ii), but it also affects my ability to recognise the difference between i) and ii).

I am drunk enough to still think I can win $10,000, but not drunk enough to fall over and be carried up to bed without losing my underpants. *Oh how I wish I could have lost my underpants.*

So my winning streak on roulette has now been over for a time, the length of which I cannot quite fathom, but I am now not following The System *and* have been at the same table for too long.

But thankfully – and fearing losing it all – I cash my chips in and put the remaining $3,000 left in my inside suit pocket and slug back the last of my eighth free drink and head for the lift. *Not a disaster.*

These casinos are long and deep and the lifts just seem soooo far away. There is *so* much happening between here and there. So much to look at!

More poker tables.

Sober, I cannot really play poker with any degree of skill, and therefore I do not play. Drunk, I may as well just save everyone's time and hand over my entire wad to the casino now.

However, drink doesn't enhance my self-awareness. It inhibits and distorts all my rationale and I make totally incomprehensible decisions. *Yep.*

I was nearly at the lift, but got distracted by some whooping as a poker hand ended with someone cleaning up with a massive payout I would estimate at $100,000. People were cheering and clapping and the gentleman thanked everyone and walked off with his box of chips to cash in. Next thing I know, I am sitting down at a poker table and it was just me. Me and the croupier.

'I'll show *you!*' I thought. Sitting there all clever and smug with your new deck of cards and your silly red waistcoat.

Within a minute I had lost the entire $3,000 that was in my right-hand inner pocket. So I reached into my left-hand inner pocket for the emergency $200 fund and then in the blink of an eye that was gone also.

I felt sick. And not just from the bottle of Jack Daniel's I had consumed.

I had a credit card with which I intended to pay for the hotel room but when I went to the ATM it was already maxed out.

I slowly went back up to the room and considered the next move. The digital alarm clock beside the bed said 4.50 a.m. and I knew I couldn't 'check out' in the normal way. I was sobering up very quickly and had a shower to aid the process.

As I didn't have any luggage, I knew I could probably exit the lobby without drawing any attention to myself, but how would I get to the airport? On my way out of the lift, I casually picked up one of those little maps of Vegas tourist spots and the Strip, and nonchalantly went over to the little table where there was a free pot of coffee and paper cups. I drank two cups and then sat down in one of the large armchairs and studied the map through my tired and bloodshot eyes.

My flight was due to leave at 9.30 a.m., and it was now about 6.15 a.m. so with a plan so loose it needed a belt, I walked through the exit, which was, at this particular moment in Vegas's history, a huge lion's mouth. Seemed appropriate. About seven years later, they removed the lion's mouth entrance after many complaints, mostly from Chinese gamblers who refused to enter the jaws of a lion to come inside, considering it 'bad luck'.

The airport was about two and a half miles by my calculations, and if I could walk it in under two hours, I should be OK. It was hot in Vegas but at this time of day it was still cool enough and the walk wasn't too arduous, though brothel creepers were probably not made with power walks in mind. I did, however, make it in good time for check-in. What was bothering me the whole way there though, was how I was going to pay for the flight, with no cash left and a maxed-out credit card. I had one forlorn hope.

Electronic card machines had been introduced some time before, but I knew that a lot of places still used the carbon-copy imprint machines, if not exclusively then often as a back-up.

I got lucky, which after my recent bad streak on the tables seemed unlikely in the extreme. When I arrived at the desk, the electronic card machine wasn't working and the guy apologised and ran my card through the carbon copy imprinter and handed me a copy for my records, before printing out my boarding card. Somehow, against all odds, I was on my way. I had no idea how I was going to get to the actual festival, which I'd been told was forty miles from Phoenix airport, but I would worry about that later. This was a minor victory for now and I was going to take it.

The flight from Vegas to Phoenix was only seventy-five minutes, but just long enough for me to fall asleep for half an hour or so and when I opened my eyes again, we had landed and were ready to disembark.

As I stood outside Phoenix airport, just where the taxis were picking up passengers arriving back home, I drew hard on my last cigarette and considered how I was going to conjure up my next magic trick of teleporting to the festival site.

It was sunny and hot, and a pinstripe suit was not the right attire for this climate. I was sweating inside and out.

I walked a few metres away from the general hubbub and sat on the kerb out of the sun. After twenty minutes or so staring blankly at a grey wall, I was considering hitching when a red open truck drove past me with a couple of passengers on board, and then slowed. They reversed back towards me.

'SIMON? SIMON RAYMONDE??!!! We are going to the festival to see you! Need a ride??'

Miraculously, they were fans of the band, and were more than happy to give me a ride to the festival. So not only did I arrive in good time, before the rest of the band even, but when checking in at the entrance, I was given food and drink tickets for the artist catering backstage and then driven on to site in a golf buggy.

I am not sure if there is a moral to this story, but my adventure with gambling was almost over and my Vegas adventure remains simply as one of those lessons that I *did* learn something from. I used up all my luck that day.

When I arrived back home in England, I called the MGM Grand to sort out my unpaid bill to ensure that I would not be arrested the next time I flew into the US.

CHAPTER THIRTEEN

A Bit of Old Wood

I have so many great memories of the times at September Sound, but when I discovered that my lovely 1958 Fender precision bass had vanished from the studios sometime during the making of *Milk & Kisses* a few years later, I started to think that maybe our open-door policy needed looking at a bit. I first realised it was missing when we went to begin rehearsals for the tour and grabbed everything we needed from the loft. It wasn't there. Months of searching and asking around if someone had borrowed it proved fruitless, and for the longest time I mourned that bass like a dearly departed family dog. That may seem a little sentimental but I love dogs more than most people, so the analogy isn't as loose as it sounds.

An old guitar like that is an antique, and truly a work of art. When I bought my first old Fender, so began a deeper connection with the bass that still lives with me today.

The wood they used on these old basses was alder for the body and maple for the neck. Alder is part of the birch family and for centuries these beautiful trees have been mostly found around swamps and rivers, thriving in the damp conditions. The 'live' wood is a pale colour, but after it's been cut it turns a lovely dark orange. It was also nicknamed 'Scots mahogany' which I liked, given that I was in a band with two Scots. I bought this three-colour sunburst Precision from Andy's in Denmark Street for around £800 in the '80s, which was a fortune back then, but it just played so beautifully and contained all the history of the tree whence it came. All those ancient held secrets would then somehow emerge magically as music when it was played. I felt that. I should add I am not a tree-hugger but definitely feel a connection with the earth and the natural world, through wooden objects like old guitars and pianos. Even my ancient violin, though I grew to hate playing it, I still have.

Losing this antique piece was painful.

I wondered for years who might have stolen it, because as wild as some of our parties were, walking out of the property with a big old bass guitar in a big old flight case was quite the high-risk move, given the human traffic that came in and out of our studios most hours of the day and night. We were in leafy Richmond-upon-Thames down the end of a quiet road beside the river, but we may as well have been in Soho for the amount of people who seemed to turn up unannounced day or night. The lure of free cocaine was attractive to some of the late-night visitors up until 1993, but after that, when we were drug-free, the parties tended to end a bit earlier with less debris, less fallout. So the loss of this lovely slice of alder hit me hard.

It is 2013 and I'm driving through London when my mobile phone rings.

'Hello, is this Simon Raymonde?'

'Yes, who is this?'

'Simon, my name is John. You don't know me but I work in a guitar shop called Rock Around the Clock in Crouch End. Did you ever have a '58 Precision bass?'

'Yes.'

'I think I might have it here.'

Silence.

'Simon, are you there??'

'Hold on, John. I am going to pull over and park up. OK. Please start at the beginning.'

John then proceeded to tell me a barely plausible story about a sketchy-looking chap in a black hoodie who came into his shop a few weeks ago with a dustbin bag full of bits of old crap.

'How much will you give me for this?' he had mumbled at John without once looking up at him, his hood pulled up and over his bowed head.

John looked quickly into the bin bag where there was a load of old guitar-related crap, just as he had suggested. A dirty, mouldy neck, some rusty strings, and various other filthy guitar body parts which he didn't think amounted to much.

'£100?' offered John.

The sketchy gent hurriedly accepted the £100 and he shuffled out of the shop. John was busy and popped the bag into the doorway of his workshop out back and promptly forgot about it.

A few weeks later, he had a day off from being on the shop floor and decided to work on some repairs in the back and emptied the contents of the bin bag out on to his desk.

He put the radio on and began absent-mindedly cleaning each piece one by one. It took a while as it was all caked in some sticky black residue, but by the mid-afternoon he felt the neck was actually looking like quite a decent piece of wood and the headstock decal suggested that it was once from quite an old guitar. By the end of the day, things had taken quite a turn. The main body, which he hadn't even recognised in the bag, was now showing as a beautiful two-colour sunburst and matched the neck perfectly. The next day, he cleaned up all the other bits, the electronics and the volume and tone pots which had been just blocks of dirt, screwed it all together and gave it a lovely final polish. He typed the serial number into his Fender database and up came the news. It was a 1958 Precision. He was gobsmacked.

He told his boss, who did some research on current values and told him to put it in the shop window next week for £15,000.

That night, John slipped into bed next to his wife, but he couldn't get to sleep. He tossed and turned, thinking about this peculiar chain of events, the sketchy guy, the bin bag of dirty clutter, and the wonderful, surprising denouement.

None of it added up and he wasn't going to sleep until he had more answers. John quietly got back out of bed, popped downstairs and went on to his computer. He typed the serial number into his search engine, and a tiny thumbnail photo popped up of a musician playing that bass.

Back in the day (that *day* being the 1980s) – ironically a 'day' that returned in 2020 post-Brexit – bands had to complete a 'carnet', a full detailed list of every single thing that would go out on tour with them. Pedals, cables, guitars, keyboards, amps, flight cases, the lot, and of course all the serial numbers.

Somehow one of those lists must have been uploaded in a database of one of the cargo companies and found its way on to Google. And the picture of the musician playing the bass at the Royal Festival Hall was, of course, me.

John continued down the internet rabbit hole and, over the next few days and after a few calls and emails, found my mobile number.

'So, I'm thrilled I found you, but are you able to prove it was yours, Simon, just because my boss is going to flip out when I tell him I can't sell it?'

'Yes, of course, John!'

'And sorry to ask, but do you think you can give me anything for it?'

'£101 OK? Then you're a pound up on the deal!' I joked. *'John, look, I don't have much and it is mine, so I'm not going to be able to get close to what your boss values it at, but I am so stunned right now having not considered ever seeing that guitar again. I will get out a grand for you right now and drive over to you and collect it. Is that OK?'*

He agreed, and the next morning I was finally, unbelievably reunited with my lost guitar almost twenty years after it went for a walk from our studio. It hasn't left my home since this day. *Ladies and Gentlemen, if we could give awards for Best Customer Service Ethics Ever, it would go to John O'Connell from Rock Around the Clock – now Edgware Music – in Crouch End, London. Thank you, John.*

CHAPTER FOURTEEN

Trouble at Mill

Like my father before me, at times the work consumed me and I wasn't around for my young children as much as I wish I could have been. The band became more successful after they were both born – Stan in 1991, Will in 1993 – and with that came longer touring and inevitably more pressure on Karen stuck at home.

We weren't going into this blind of course, but having to bring up two boys pretty much single-handedly for several years, while I was away gallivanting around the world, was no fun for her.

Karen had worked in graphic design for several years when we first moved in together, but was yearning to break free of the office routine and workplace politics and was accepted onto the fine art degree course at Goldsmiths as a 'mature student' (she was still *only* twenty-five!) and was in the same year as Damien Hirst. Her work was daring and original, but Damien was already the darling of the art world before he was even finished with his degree, and it would have been hard to compete with that. After she graduated, she felt rightly proud that she had done it, and was ready for whatever the world had waiting for her.

We were now living in Camberwell in South-East London as we had moved there to be closer to Goldsmiths. The journey for me to get over to the studio in Richmond, West London each day was exhausting during the sessions for *Heaven or Las Vegas*, but I did it until after our second son Will came along. The week after he was born at King's College Hospital in Denmark Hill, I left for a tour and then I didn't see him again until he was seven months old.

That was no fun for any of us – mostly no fun for a young mother stuck at home with two young boys. I certainly didn't feel great about it, but this was the life Karen and I had known might happen. So we dealt with it. Well, she did. I just felt guilty.

Once we moved to a place in Twickenham much nearer to the studio and the boys started school there, on the surface things seemed to be going OK. But seeking some sort of equilibrium, some life balance, was proving tough for me. Sure, being in a three-piece where the other two are a couple with their own stuff going on is always going to have its challenges, but mostly we got along well, and certainly the 'work' was always a joy. 'Time management' I think they would call it now, but I did find that balance of home life and band life – and all the pressures that it seemed to create – difficult to deal with, and it was something I struggled with enormously. I was never good at sharing my worries with anyone and would rather try and solve them myself or ignore them until they hopefully went away. Of course they never did. The band was doing OK but we seemed to be just paying ourselves the bare minimum, and after we moved I got into severe debt, with about ten credit cards and was juggling my finances day by day, just trying somehow to make sure I had enough for the kids and for the mortgage each month. Bailiffs were turning up at the house and eventually something had to give. When it all began to implode, I went to see the bank.

While my own finances were spiralling out of control, the band was having troubles too with 4AD that had been brewing a while. Again, mostly about money, our lack of it specifically, and I wondered if the writing was on the wall. Finally, our good friend Marc Geiger, who was our US booking agent for many years, recommended someone he knew to be our manager, a man who he felt could help us with some of the big issues we were dealing with. There were even more pressing issues looming on the horizon but, for now, the attraction of someone helping extricate us from this fractious, increasingly bitter battle with 4AD was tempting, and preliminary meetings were positive.

Robin, Elizabeth and I were all members of what we called the Dead Dad Club, so the man we were talking to about becoming our manager, I subconsciously saw as a bit of a 'Dad' substitute. He seemed like he would help take the heat out of the equation and either resolve the issue with the label, or if he had to as a last resort, find a new home for us. I didn't think for a second we *would* actually leave 4AD. I was sure that our terms would be met and having a third party 'middleman' involved would de-personalise it all a bit and help us navigate through these recently choppy waters. Ray came on board to manage us in 1992. No doubt he tried to do his best, but maybe we were just beyond help by that point.

These situations can resemble a high-stakes poker game, where all of a sudden, on the turn of one card, a strong hand suddenly seems a bit more vulnerable. As you feel good about your ability to bluff your way through, you carry on – 'all in' – before barely a minute later you lose everything.

I had been wrong about things working out with 4AD, and all of a sudden, we were out. Ivo hadn't wanted this to happen either I am sure, but he didn't see eye to eye with Ray at all and let us go from our one remaining album.

I have been asked numerous times over the years how 4AD inspired me, both as an artist but more importantly as a label person myself.

I certainly would never deny the cultural significance and musical influence 4AD had. It's been a fantastic label for many, many years and continues to be so, but I have never been trying to emulate it. The owner of the company now, Martin Mills, is a shrewd and canny entrepreneur who understands business, market trends and where the intrinsic value is better than most. He employs great people and he controls a large catalogue with longevity. And in the case of Cocteau Twins, to put it bluntly, he owns our shit for evermore.

I have a lot of respect for him, and within the parameters of our deal, a deal I should add we did not sign with a gun to our head, he has always been very fair with me. I know what he has done fighting for the independent label community over the years, and while we have very different approaches, I would never even compare my label Bella Union to 4AD or to any other record company for that matter. There is space for us all. I have fewer than ten staff, Martin has more than 120. Martin has built an empire. Mine is more like a house of cards, but I don't believe one is better than the other; I don't think my approach is better or worse than anyone else's.

To explain the difference between labels, it is maybe simpler to look at the kind of deals they are offering. Labels like 4AD own your masters *in perpetuity*, meaning for ever and ever. This is where the value lies to them. They will pay a premium for those rights.

I wouldn't want to own anyone's anything, because that is just how I am. I'll *borrow* your stuff off you, invest in you over an agreed period of time (Bella Union have done deals of between seven and fifteen years in length), but at the end of that period, the *artist* retains those rights, not the label.

I do have some issues with the deals we signed back in the early '80s, because they were not in my opinion fair. But that's easier to say with hindsight and experience. They should have been drastically improved over the forty years since and while new circumstances *have* created some opportunities for artists from that period to fight for their copyrights and often win, we were not advised well at a time when we didn't know who to ask for advice. Do I believe there was a wilful effort to deceive us into signing deals that we shouldn't have? No, I don't think so. But I *do* feel that we were all let down by those who courted us and whom we looked up to for guidance.

There's *doing something naively because you truly don't know better*, as we surely did as a label ourselves in the early years, and then there's *knowing something is not quite right about it but choosing not to do anything*.

As young musicians with no income, you already feel like second-class citizens in society as it is, so the deal you sign as a naive teenager can have a huge impact on your future. And as for the remuneration for your live work, well that hasn't really changed in the forty-plus years I have been doing this. In the 1980s, a support band might get £50 to play before the headliner at, say, a 300-capacity room. In 2024, the £50 fee is unbelievably *still* the same, despite that same £50 being worth about £250 today.

Most young bands I know, and we were no different, just want a fair deal; if and when things go well and the band are selling hundreds of thousands of records, then reward them with an updated deal or a sales bonus etc. But *business* and *fair play* are not comfortable bedfellows. I was naive to believe that contracts reflected the outward personalities of the people running the labels. Having seen what a recording contract looked like back in the 1980s right through to what it looks like now, I can say hardly anything has changed. And while technology moved at a lightning pace, the terms of deals did not keep up.

I performed on twelve different This Mortal Coil tracks across two albums, wrote several of the songs myself, but didn't ever bring up 'money' once. That's not ever why I do things. But later on I did think, given how successful those records were around the globe, that perhaps *something* might have been appropriate even as a gesture of gratitude. I realise that 'Song to the Siren' was the breadwinner in that relationship and have no idea what Elizabeth and Robin were compensated with as that isn't any of my business, but while Ivo did buy me a teapot and some lovely mugs as a thank you for all my contributions, sweet though that was, I was twenty-two years old and had no money at all. I was still signing on and a few quid would have been nice. I've no idea if anyone else in TMC got anything, because no one talked about money because it felt wrong and a bit sordid. The inference back then was always that if you asked or spoke about money then your heart wasn't really in it, you were just a bread head and I felt guilty enough just asking for a fiver for a cab to be honest.

I should have known better. I should have asked for advice. Shouldn't have just signed the first piece of paper that was slid under my nose. Not having a manager was our decision, no one else's, so to use that as an excuse is not something I can do. But by the time we worked out what was going on, it was already way too late. It took ages for us to realise that Warner Brothers were paying 4AD to put out those records in the United States, but we never saw a penny of it. Our heads were elsewhere and our hearts were most certainly only focused on one thing.

CHAPTER FIFTEEN

Fish out of Water

While it felt strange leaving 4AD, we were so sharply focused on making the next album that we figured we would just find a different label. The thinking, as I recall it, was that being friendly with our label had ended painfully with hurt on all sides, so we would be better advised to try and find a label with slightly deeper pockets than 4AD, and simply have a transactional relationship, one with no friendships to get in the way if they went wrong. The choices were all major labels or subsidiaries of the majors. I'm laughing now at this marvellously naïve idea, almost charming in its utter stupidity.

Once the news was out, we had a first offer come in from Warners-backed East West. The boss flew out to Brazil to try to sign us where we were playing. He was very nice but I could never work out why he just didn't wait a week until we were back. They made what I would assume was a good offer, but because it was the first one we really hadn't a clue how it stacked up, so we met some more labels more conventionally over lunches in Soho before settling on Fontana. It wasn't like they shone out over the others particularly; they were all offering similar amounts of money.

For me it was simply because they had signed Scott Walker.

Ray improved a lot of things, but we were so distracted trying to make music, running a studio and expanding our live band – while also being young parents – that we occasionally took our eyes off the ball and found ourselves in uncharted territory. The money we received from Fontana – part of the Universal conglomerate – helped fund the rent of the recording studio space, and while it was no lottery win, having had ten years of nothing and then suddenly having more money than we were used to, I think it messed our heads up a bit. We invested a large slice of it into the studio equipment we wanted, which made sense at the time, except it wasn't *our* studio; we didn't own the building, just the gear inside. And it's like buying a car – the moment you purchase a mixing desk or a tape machine, it's worth half what you paid for it the minute you walk out of the shop.

When you take your eye off the ball for a moment, which was inevitable during the time when all our personal lives were such staggering messes, decisions were being made that I am sure wouldn't have been made if that major-label money hadn't come into play. The pressure to tour relentlessly weighed heavy and I think deep down we knew something was wrong about this new version of *us*. But we just didn't have the tools or the nous to do anything about it, until it was too late.

After *Heaven or Las Vegas*, Robin's drug dependency got a lot worse before it got better. There were protracted efforts over a year or so to get him help, then the awful talks of intervention and all that guff, but it did finally end up with Robin agreeing to enter a rehab facility *outside* of the UK (the idea being to help avoid the problems he'd had before of being too close to temptation) and surprisingly he asked me to go with him as a 'family member'.

I had thought I was going to this rehab place to understand *his* problems, but once the first introductory session ended the morning we arrived, it became quickly apparent that I was there for *me*. We were separated on entry, and he went off to his part of the centre, and me to another part. What I learned in rehab was that unbeknownst to me, I was enabling the problem, exacerbating it even. My thinking was skewed. I justified things by saying to myself I was just trying to be his friend and keep this album on track, so when I'd get to the studio in the morning and Robin hadn't been home yet from the night before, he would ask me to go and buy him some white wine. Even though it was 10 a.m. I didn't have the courage to say no, so would just go and get it and then hate myself afterwards, but he would still be my friend and we could maybe do some music together. Enabling.

So hearing that I was actually making his addictions worse was mortifying, and two weeks later I returned to England duly chastened and humbled at my own part in the whole sorry mess.

The rehab place was renowned and he stayed the course – I think around eight weeks – and even seeing him before I came home I had a lot of hope for his recovery. He was always a lovely bloke really, underneath all the drama that seemed to constantly follow us around. *That* had just got lost deep in the mire. I was just glad he was going to be OK.

Making music again after coming back 'to work' was initially a struggle for Robin and he went away to France for a while to try and get some ideas going on his own. His relationship with Elizabeth was now over but they were trying so hard to make something work for the sake of their beautiful young daughter, and if the band could somehow continue then that would be a bonus. This was new territory for us all I guess, and I was just hopeful and cautiously excited for the future, one in which Robin continued to get well, and he and I could hopefully claw back some of the friendship that seemed to have been lost in the purple haze, and one in which Elizabeth could blossom.

I rate our next album *Four-Calendar Café* highly. It signalled a massive change of course, with Elizabeth and her writing. It was the first record where they were no longer a couple. Maybe with the LP being on a 'major label' this distorted the view of it initially, but I always said at the time that this felt like an album that people won't probably appreciate for years to come. Maybe that's what all artists say when your new record isn't liked as much as the last . . .

I find the songs to be both incredibly sad and profound. It's not a typical break-up record at all; to my ears it was about soul salvation and taking steps to avoid a breakdown. Life lessons being written and sung in real time. I felt it was about recovery and starting again. The honesty and truth of Elizabeth's words was emotional for me to hear. That is raw power right there.

Music as therapy. Again. I remember being very confused hearing that the album wasn't well received in the press. It seemed like the change in record label and our departure from 4AD were more significant to some than the seismic change within our band's personal lives. After years of debate about Elizabeth's lyrics, now and arguably for the first time she was singing words that were entirely *easy* to understand, and no one much seemed to care. That upset me and still does.

With the artwork, the style was different, the fonts were quite a change too, but it was something Robin and Elizabeth seemed thrilled about as it was inspired by a children's book they loved, so I kept my opinions on the design to myself. I was just thankful that somehow our band was still going and that we were still making beautiful, brave music that moved me. A year earlier, I couldn't imagine that we would have reached this point at all.

Ray was left to deal with Fontana once the record release was approaching as we had backed away from all contact with them a few weeks earlier. This whopping sixty-page contract that our lawyers had constructed to protect us from every possible eventuality had quickly turned out to be a massive waste of their time and our money.

When we sent the album to the label, we shared what the first single should be: 'Evangeline'. A beautiful ballad that sounded like nothing else at the time. It was about growing up. Again.

It has some stunning lines about childhood. Whether this is Elizabeth's own childhood I cannot confirm as she never spoke about it to me, but I always heard it that way.

As the lyrics were never made public, this is only *my* interpretation:

I had to fantasise
I was a princess, Mum and Dad were queen and king

And later about life as an adult:

I was a famous artist
Everybody took me seriously,
Even those who did not understand
I had to fantasise
Just to survive.

There is a key change at 3:42 – those things are often corny as fuck aren't they? – but you have to choose your moments and this is one rare occasion we used it, and emotionally it took the song up another notch. Robin's crystalline guitars in this section are a match for anything on *Heaven or Las Vegas*.

And Fontana didn't fucking get it at all.

Word came back that they didn't want to go with 'Evangeline'. We put our size-thirteen foot down, silently waving our contract that said we had 'creative control', but we learned pretty swiftly that 'creative control' is worthless if no one at the label is driving it all forward. They weren't even picking up the phone.

From that day forth, the relationship was probably over. We went from being a priority to being a footnote. This was *before* our first music with them had even come out.

But we had signed a deal and spent some of the money so we honoured the contract, closed our eyes and stumbled blindly through it. Well that was what Ray tried to make happen.

In 1996, we released *Milk & Kisses*, our second and last album for Fontana. It had been surprisingly enjoyable to make.

Because it was once again on a major label and our switch from the much-loved independent label 4AD was still seen by many as a desertion and a mutiny, the press again didn't give it much attention. Generally the reaction from everyone was lukewarm.

I certainly loved all of the songs and was really proud of our performances. I was enjoying the writing and it seemed like I had unwittingly developed a new bass-playing style in this last period. During my early years with the band, I was playing a lot of strummy chords and melodies, driving the song, but not really many low root notes like bass players are often expected to adhere to. By the time of *Four-Calendar Café*, and scared of just repeating myself, I began to feel that 'less was more' and moved to a dubbier, low-end style leaving more 'space' for other things. But on *Milk & Kisses*, I decided to work out a way of combining both. It meant that in the studio I would usually have two or three bass parts on one song. I could almost hear Robin's eyebrows raising when I plugged in yet another bass.

So a low dubby part to start, as the anchor, and then a high melody bass over the top. When we played live, I had to work out a hybrid bass part that incorporated both or all three of my lines, but with my trusty five-string bass made by Russell Fong on hand, this was just a case of practice. It *felt* like a new energy

was coming. A few years had passed now since Robin and Elizabeth had split as a couple and both seemed happier. They were
building new connections, both in healthier relationships, so
maybe this was all going to work out after all. Although I felt
the final mixes weren't as good as I wished they had been, I also
conceded that Robin was far more talented than me in the sonics
department and, looking to avoid any confrontations with him,
I let it go.

Away from the music, Karen and I were trying our best. Our
two boys Stan and Will were growing up fast, but I was still away
from home too much for a healthy relationship to blossom, and
I wasn't sure how to fix it.

*   *   *

I had begun writing some music on my own over the past year or
two. The studio wasn't always busy and I was keen to not be so
reliant on others. I had recorded some instrumentals in the tried
and tested manner but needed some vocalists.

When you're in a band with one of the greatest singers of all
time, the idea of stepping out in front of a mic doesn't even enter
your head. I didn't really know many people back then. We were
so far removed from the music community and so private that
the only people we knew were some of the bands we took on tour
or friends from the 4AD stable. So when I asked our manager
if he could ask Patti Smith if she'd like to sing on the album, I
could tell from his response that I was setting the bar way too
high and that just wasn't going to happen. So one night in late

1996, I was in the studio wondering what the hell I was going to do with this album of instrumentals I had created. I rolled a big joint, and ensuring there was no one around – *literally* no one within the building – I tried to sing myself. Terrifying. While my voice is *OK*, it's just a mildly pleasant sound rather than a particularly affecting or interesting one. But I had this idea, because I could harmonise well, that I might be able to at least mask the inadequacies of my lead voice by having tons of backing vocals behind it, a sort of 'thug squad safety in numbers' who would protect me. I just needed to do *something* with all this stuff in my head from the past few years.

I had tried to keep it quiet and away from Elizabeth and Robin, but when you're all sharing the same studio, it's not that easy and somehow they had both heard most of it by the time I was about three-quarters of the way through. I'd press STOP on the tape machine anytime they came in the room, but after a while that just seemed ridiculous and they made me play the songs while they sat at the back of the room. They were very kind and encouraging and I was buoyed by that. Robin played guitar on a track called 'Muscle and Want', the lyrics of which were written by friend and Cocteau Twins' fan club moderator Leesa Beales.[1] She was a fine poet and any chance *not* to have

---

[1] Leesa was a lovely woman and all of the Cocteau fan community were devastated when on 20 March 2010, aged just forty-one, she succumbed to an aggressive cancer, leaving behind three beautiful young sons. I am glad she is still remembered fondly by so many people who have remained fans of the band in great part due to the connections she encouraged through the websites and the Cocteaufest she instigated in 2003

to write another set of lyrics was attractive. Plus I actually found singing someone else's lyrics far easier than singing my own.

I found it impossible to ask Elizabeth as I really didn't want her to feel like she had to say 'yes' just because we were in the same band. But then out of the blue she said she'd love to sing on this track 'Worship Me' that her new partner Damon Reece had played drums on, and that of course elevated that track enormously.

A young arranger Andrew Skeet, whom I had met through our manager's assistant Fiona, offered to do something for the record. I must have been feeling very pleased with myself because for some reason I decided to cover Scott Walker's 'It's Raining Today' with an ensemble Andrew was developing. I had convinced myself on numerous car journeys that I could sing that song well, but as we all know, there are some singers you should *not* cover on record anyway. Scott is one of them. Elizabeth is another of course.

*   *   *

Following the release of Cocteau Twins' *Milk & Kisses*, we played more than' thirty shows around the UK, Europe and the

---

in Boston. Every year since it has moved to a different location and twenty years on it has been held in Los Angeles, Toronto, Manchester, New York, London, Muskoka, São Paulo, Paris, San Francisco, Santiago and Berlin. The band's fans care so deeply about the music and Leesa's torch-bearing for the band has been carried and held by so many wonderful people the world over. We are nothing without this.

US with an expanded band including lovely Sheffield musician Dave Palfreyman on percussion and good vibes, who was a really positive presence on tour. With a recovering addict in the band, we had to make the tour as safe and clean as we could and that meant having as many good people around as possible, who would respect the situation. It wasn't like being on tour with Morrissey where no one in his entourage can eat meat; folks could drink and enjoy themselves but just thoughtfully!

When it came to where we would play in London, we gave in to the pressure to play the Royal Albert Hall, but only on the proviso that we could do a second night at Ministry of Sound. I loved drum and bass and as a huge fan of his debut *So Far* LP, I'd invited Alex Reece to do a DJ set as our 'support'. Paul Oakenfold was due to play a set at the Albert Hall show the night before but didn't turn up for some reason I was never party to or have just forgotten in the ravages of time.

Maybe a nightclub like MoS was surprising to some, but we did champion a lot of eclectic dance music of the time, no doubt influenced by the early days of the ecstasy explosion. We couldn't just listen to Swans and Einstürzende Neubauten for ever.

The tour was strange. The shows were some of the best we played, but something wasn't quite right. For my physical well-being, I knew I had to just look after myself better on these dates. And for my own sanity and mental health, I had to find a positive way of getting through the day until show time. In the US, we were on a sleeper bus, and always drove through the night. As soon as I woke up, I'd get off the bus and find something to do in whatever city it was. Museums, cinemas, galleries, any culture

I could soak up. I don't think I'd have made it through without those daily adventures.

Just because of all the stuff we'd each been through in the past, everyone was doing their own thing and avoiding possible tension points. I think we did a great job in a pretty impossible situation. We came through, as Scott Walker would have said.

When all is said and done, Cocteau Twins may not be a band that most people would associate with the mainstream rock festival circuit. I think we played only five or so festival sets in our entire career, most of which were fairly unremarkable.

Roskilde in Denmark *was* extraordinary, but only because before our set I had sat on the floor at the side of the stage watching two of my favourite musicians in the world at that point, Patti Smith and Television's guitarist Tom Verlaine, who was part of her band. I hadn't seen Television before and the last time I'd seen Patti Smith was at the Rainbow in 1978 so this was a massive treat. I met her afterwards. And when I say 'met', I went up to her as she wandered barefoot through the backstage area, shook her hand and mumbled.[2]

Phoenix Festival in 1996 was only notable in that it turned out to be our last-ever live UK performance on a bill that also included David Bowie. I didn't have an opportunity to meet him

---

[2] I still pinch myself now that through my label I have released four albums of her poetry and spoken word performances alongside Soundwalk Collective, and got to meet her properly in 2022 at the Pompidou Centre in our twenty-fifth anniversary year when we released a magnificent limited box-set of her work. She was, of course, a delight, as was her dressing-room friend, Michael Stipe. OK, I name-dropped. What are you going to do about it? It's my memoir for God's sake.

again sadly, and my mood wasn't great as I thought our performance was limp at best. We probably shouldn't have played those kind of enormo-festivals as our sound really didn't suit the conditions. No soundchecks, wind, to name a couple.

The T In the Park festival in breezy Strathclyde Park in Lanarkshire, Scotland was where I bumped into a senior 'player' from our US label Capitol Records who was over as a guest of headliners Radiohead. He was vaguely coherent, three sheets to the westerly wind. I'd only ever encountered him previously when he was warm and welcoming – but he was serious and hard-working. All about business. He insisted I walk with him from one stage to another as he had something he needed to tell me. Ooh. I was excited. I was usually the last to know everything so was I about to get a scoop? Was he going to take me back to meet Thom, Phil, Colin, Ed and Jonny? Did they want to take us out on tour? Did Thom want to duet with Elizabeth, or Robin to produce the next Radiohead album? He put his arm around me I think more to stop himself from falling over than out of friendship, and hissed into my ear, 'Sorry to have to tell you but your manager is an absolute cunt.'

Oh.

Lollapalooza Festival started in the early '90s after Jane's Addiction singer Perry Farrell and Marc Geiger (our long-time US booking agent) were both over in the UK and standing side by side at Reading Festival watching Pixies play, while tens of thousands of their fans chanted 'Debaser!' in glorious union. They hatched the idea there and then that the time was nigh for them to team up and create a festival of their own in the US with so-called 'alternative rock' bands. It would be a touring festival. Farrell came up with the name Lollapalooza. He said later that he heard it in a Three Stooges sketch, but to date no one has found any evidence to prove that to be the case. For the most part, like many festivals of this time, it was pretty white. And for the first five years, around 90 per cent of the bands were male.

In 1996, after five years building it up, Perry Farrell decided he'd had enough. Marc's feeling was that the 'alternative rock' scene in the US was pretty much dead or close to it, the bands just regurgitating the same old clichés, and so he resolved to throw some big hairy cats amongst the skinny pale pigeons. For his next bill, he chose Metallica to headline, a bold move as they were a colossal mainstream band. No one would bat an eyelid now but back then, it did create some waves. Among the other main stage acts were Rancid, the Ramones and Soundgarden.

The band Metallica, in particular their guitarist Kirk Hammett, were fans of Cocteau Twins and requested that we join the tour. I'll be honest, I'd never heard a Metallica song in my life at this point, nor a Rancid song, nor anything by Soundgarden, and maybe that was our clue that the majority of the audience turning up to watch these very well-known bands in the heavy guitar world might struggle to enjoy what *we* were doing. But we didn't really know for sure. Plus, our singer was female. I figured if nothing else, it would be interesting.

We first encountered Marc Geiger in the early 1980s when he had flown to the UK, a time when very few American booking agents were remotely interested in British bands. His bosses all thought he was mad. When he returned to LA, having signed us,

New Order and several others up to the Triad Agency, the bosses were still certain their initial scepticism was entirely justified. A few years later, when that first wave of British bands began to break in the US, the naysayers all conceded that they had been too hasty to judge. Marc was now regarded as quite the visionary.

Marc just wouldn't let it lie. Every week he would come back and ask us to reconsider. I am sure he was genuinely convinced that this band he came to the UK to find in the early '80s, that he loved so much, could cut through and affect swathes of people who may not have been exposed to the music we made.

He was good at his job and also annoyingly persuasive. After we turned down his offer to play Lollapalooza for a fourth time, he said:

'OK, how about you just play one show? ONE! The opening date on the tour and then you're done. Just one show! Metallica really want you to do it, this isn't just me . . .'

'OK, Marc, OK! Just to shut you up for five minutes we'll do it. One show though.'

So, in June 1996, after another headline tour across the States, we headed to Longview Lake in Kansas City for the opening day of Lollapalooza '96. Once we had settled in, I decided to have a wander out into the grounds to get a flavour of the festival. I had my old Super 8 camera with me and filmed bits of Rancid and the Ramones. I had loved the Ramones ever since I heard 'Sheena is a Punk Rocker' on the radio.

I couldn't believe that they were on *before* us.

It was all very strange, and the more I walked around and soaked in the atmosphere under this intensely hot sun, the worse

I felt. Was it fear? The heat? Or just the usual pre-gig nerves? I used to dry retch before some of the bigger shows ('dry' and 'retch' are two words I don't enjoy writing down next to each other as I can almost feel my throat contracting at the sight of them), but this was different. I began to have a very empty feeling in the pit of my stomach, which was *not* satisfied by eating.

The last three bands of the day would be us, then Soundgarden and then Metallica, on the main stage and playing to around 40,000 people, certainly the biggest crowd I'd ever played in front of. I never feel particularly at home onstage. I feel self-conscious and insecure, but thankfully my bass playing doesn't allow me any time to really think about anything other than what I'm doing, so I usually just lose the nerves as soon as I start playing, and it's fine. But I was feeling queasy.

As our set time approached, Metallica's Kirk Hammett came into our trailer and asked if we minded if he could say a few words before we went out. We'd never met him before, or anyone else in the band nor any of the other bands on the bill. We definitely felt a bit out of place and our trailer wasn't near to anyone else's, which may have contributed to us feeling isolated. So we all walked down together, stood on the side of the stage and as soon as he appeared, the crowd went crazy. These were *his* fans. He picked up a microphone and went to the front and said:

'Hey, everyone, how you all doing? This is exciting for me. So listen up, I want to introduce you to my favourite fucking band in the whole world. Ladies and gentlemen, I give you . . . COCTEAU TWINS.'

Screams and cheering welcomed us on to the huge stage as Kirk exited it the all-conquering hero.

What a nice bloke!

You could *see* the crowd working it out.

'OK, I've never heard of whatever that was he said but if Kirk loves 'em, then man SO DO I!'

He had whipped them up into a mini-frenzy and now we just needed to put a cherry on it. This was going to be great!

We started up our first song while the wild applause and whooping was dying down, and we played it well. At the end of the second song, the endorsement of Metallica's famed guitarist was still clearly ringing in some ears, but I could tell many were looking a bit puzzled. The next song 'Half-Gifts' was more of a ballad, and as I went and sat down at the piano, I had a bad feeling about it. In hindsight we should have dropped all songs with the piano for a rock festival set. Rock festival lesson number one: unless you're Elton John, Coldplay or Billy Joel, *ditch the piano!* We had lost pretty much the whole crowd by the time we finished it. As we started the next track 'Rilkean Heart', there was a loud electrical bang and all the power onstage went out. A divine intervention? We stood there feeling like a bunch of right plums waiting for the technical crew to sort it but nothing happened. And fairly swiftly the crowd began to turn.

'Fuck you!'

'You suck! Get off the stage!'

Then the mud pies started.

Weirdly, Robin got hit on the leg by a cassette, mud balls landed at my feet and I saw Ben in his summery dress and Doc Martens nimbly dodge out of the way as a dry dirt bomb headed towards his torso. As the power was restored, and we quickly started another song, the loud booing continued. And as Elizabeth did her very best to soldier on, she got hit square between the eyes by another sizeable dry mud pie. I was standing next to her and even with all the noise, I could hear the *thwack* as it landed. It was even louder than the nearby snare drum.

That was enough. She calmly leaned into the mic and said, 'Thank you and goodbye,' and she turned and went offstage. Graceful and classy, Kirk Hammett came into the trailer within seconds, profusely apologetic for the crowd's reaction and bless him, he was genuinely upset.

I think we were onstage about sixteen minutes. And an hour later we were gone from the festival site altogether. It was almost like we were never there.

CHAPTER SIXTEEN

'Let's Start a Label'

On returning to September Sound after the touring finished, talks began about the next album and finally setting up this label to release our own music, something we had first discussed a few years before.

With enormous help from Fiona Glyn-Jones, whom we were dealing with more and more on the management side, and Nina Jackson who ran the studio, we started the label Bella Union in 1997. Pete Townshend had moved out of the larger downstairs studios and we now had the run of the whole place. We all put a little bit of our personal money in to kick things off with our new label, but the plan was that the label would *just* release Cocteau Twins music and whatever solo or collaborative projects any of us wanted to put out. With this beautiful studio space, and all of us now living nearby, it seemed like a plan that *could* work. Elizabeth had made it clear that she wanted to be more involved in the musical side of things this time rather than just coming in at the end to sing. I for one loved that idea, and was excited about the new dynamic and how that could generate something unique.

Progress was slow but several tracks were under way and while it was hard to see where it would end up, it felt good to at least be moving forward, even if we weren't all moving at the same speed.

On 29 May 1997, Elizabeth's dear friend Jeff Buckley died tragically in the Mississippi River after going swimming.

I only met Jeff a few times. He was introduced to us when he was just a young teenager having come to one of our shows at the Zenith in Paris. We were all thrilled to meet him. It was especially poignant I am sure for Elizabeth and Robin who had recorded that beautifully sparse and atmospheric version of his father's 'Song to the Siren' for This Mortal Coil a few years prior.

In March 1994, when we were on tour in the US promoting our new album *Four-Calendar Café*, Jeff came to see us play at the Roxy in Atlanta. He invited us to come and see him play a late-night set at Omage, a bar that was close by, so Elizabeth and I decided we would go. The show was breathtaking. I had no expectation but recall being very conscious that my mouth was wide open and that I was drooling. His voice was astonishing enough, but his guitar playing was phenomenal. Coming from a punk background, I've never been one for fussy playing – Tom Verlaine being the exception as he was a genius, of course – and for a while, at least until my mid-twenties, was allergic to anything resembling a guitar solo that extended beyond a few seconds.

But seeing both Prince in 1988 and Jeff at Omage six years later opened my eyes and ears to just how beautiful a solo *can* be in soulful hands. After his set was finished, Jeff came out to meet us both and suggested we come with him to a party he was going to at a friend's house. We had a few days off before our next show at Lisner Auditorium in Washington, so we jumped into Jeff's friend's old convertible and sped off into the night. What struck me about Jeff that evening, apart from his extraordinary gifts, was his voracious appetite for music. He really was like a student *and* a scholar. On the journey out to the party, Jeff sat in the front passenger seat, holding his trusty ghetto blaster to his ear, blaring out his favourites – Aretha Franklin, Nusrat Fateh Ali Khan and Led Zeppelin. I had never heard of Nusrat before and am ashamed to say at the time I wasn't even familiar with either the Aretha or the Led Zeppelin songs he played. Jeff's passion was infectious. And from the way people gravitated towards him that night, it was clear he had a rare magnetism. I don't remember the party really; I don't think I lasted too long. But not drinking or taking drugs any more, I hadn't yet reached that point where I felt comfortable in social situations without being wasted, so quietly left and went back to the hotel.

I didn't see Jeff again until sometime later when he came to our studio back in Richmond, with a plan to record something with Elizabeth on a day when the studio was empty and quiet. I had two young sons at home at this point and had to leave at dinner time, but I remember setting up a microphone and a cymbal for them in the vocal booth. That night they recorded a song that they were working on together called 'All Flowers in Time

Bend Toward the Sun', essentially at this point just an acoustic guitar and a few lines of vocals. It sounded like it could have been really beautiful. What happened to the recording after that is somewhat of a mystery as several years later a different version was leaked online. *Different* as in more developed. I know someone *must* have gone into the studio and copied the tapes but I don't know who or how. That must have been upsetting for Elizabeth – a private recording in nascent state, now out in the public domain and, to make matters worse, having been clearly interfered with. The two-inch tape that contains the original recordings is still in storage along with all the tapes from September Sound studios, but since 2002 when the studio went bust, those tapes have been only accessible by trusted. How a demo that had so little music and vocals on it suddenly appeared almost fully adorned with additional instrumentation and vocals is really beyond me. I am sure someone will come forward one day and explain how that happened, but so many things went 'walkies' from that studio, including two of my prized basses, it shouldn't be such a surprise I guess. We *really* should have had some cameras installed.

While she never spoke to me in any detail about her feelings, I knew that Elizabeth had cared deeply for Jeff as interviews with her since will testify. I can't say for sure if this tragedy directly influenced her decision, but Elizabeth called me some time after and said that she couldn't continue with the band any longer.

In truth I was only surprised she had lasted this long, given that her and Robin had broken up five years ago after *Heaven or Las*

Vegas. I've thought long and hard about this in the intervening years. I imagine there is more than one reason why it happened then, but sometimes I guess with the weight of it all, you wake up and you just *know*. That's it.

Since 1992, I too was gradually finding it harder and harder to keep it all together. Watching people you care about fall apart is a painful experience. I deeply regret not having the vision or capacity to have reached out more to Liz when she needed it. Communication for us had never been simple, but I should have done more. Fourteen years writing together, touring together and seeing each other most days is a lot. Things didn't go wrong overnight, they had been going wrong for a long time, but we were all spinning so many different plates that every now and then some would smash into little pieces, until eventually, five years later, there weren't any plates left at all.

When Elizabeth did call me to say that she couldn't continue, I was standing outside the studio on the raised driveway. Because of the close proximity to the river and the Richmond lock, the road flooded at least once a week and all the parked cars that had forgotten to move would be fully underwater. As she spoke, I looked out at the submerged vehicles and it felt like all the air in my chest was being sucked out.

Although I was reeling, I could also understand exactly why she had reached this decision. The more we talked, the more I realised that this dynamic wasn't really sustainable. Although I had known this deep down for a while now, accepting it wasn't easy. Our whole lives were so wrapped up in this beautiful crazy mess of a band.

Looking back now, I have no idea how we actually survived leaving 4AD, the drug problems, the break-ups, running a commercial studio, the last two albums, mortgages and young families. The odds were surely stacked against us, our band life a constant flurry of near-fatal wounds, both self-inflicted and otherwise.

I knew that whoever got to work with Elizabeth next would be the luckiest band on the planet. And a year later, when Massive Attack released 'Teardrop' featuring her sublime, haunting vocal, I couldn't help shed a tear or two; maybe one of pride in her, and one of sadness of what I'd lost.

A few years later in an interview with Dave Simpson in the *Guardian*, while talking about Jeff Buckley she mentioned that the 'song was kind of about him'.

Of course we made some mistakes, but they were all honest ones. Even the ones I regretted immediately afterwards, like the 1996 performance on the music show *Hotel Babylon*. But you know what?

There is so little footage of us performing that even the crap stuff now seems a delight.

It is heart-warming that for all those people born *after* we broke up who are unable to see us, at least some footage is there for us to see Elizabeth Fraser sing. There should be more, but we will take what we can get.

*　*　*

Following Elizabeth's call, instead of moping, I sprang into action. We had just started Bella Union and had staff to consider at the studio *and* the label, so I figured I should finish this solo thing and get that out as the first release. It seemed like a plan. And right now, *any* plan felt good. I was frightened of inertia, of becoming rudderless, so with my friends to help steer, we weighed anchor and started to sail off into the unknown.

And it really *was* the unknown. I didn't really know what I was doing. But neither did anyone else with me. We worked it out, slowly at times, and for sure certain releases would suffer from our lack of experience and knowledge. Last week I was a bass player. This week, I'm running a record label. A bricklayer can't become an architect overnight. But they can at least *try*.

We knew how to make records, but not much else. We knew how *not* to make videos, how *not* to take photos, how *not* to do interviews, but people said that you learned more by your mistakes than getting things right. I don't know if I really believed any of that at the time, but it sounded like a positive spin on how to navigate a business we only knew from one side.

Our own erratic relationships with the two labels we had worked with as a band did at least confirm early on that we definitely didn't really want to be like either of them. Fostering strong relationships with the bands was my sole initial intention.

Robin, being so technically gifted and a brilliant problem-solver, found his own way of coping with his beloved band being no more. He set up everyone's computers, creating email accounts and generally being a one-man IT department for the studio and the label at a time when a new burgeoning online world was knocking at the door. I reckon this was *his* version of my obsession with cleaning during grief.

He threw himself into production and music-making but the first years were tough for all of us.

We made as many bad choices and decisions as we made good ones.

Robin had bumped into Dirty Three at the Phoenix Festival where Cocteau Twins had performed what proved to be our last-ever show. By some small miracle, they were looking for a new label and swiftly joined Bella Union. Shortly afterwards, I signed the Czars from Denver. With these two bands on board, it felt like the start of something special. Well certainly *something*.

With Nina Jackson running our studios and Fiona Glyn-Jones now helping to run the label, a small team was coming together. Fiona had been working with us for a few years as our manager's assistant, and then in early '97 she joined the label. She was very smart as well as kind and thoughtful, and when we didn't know how to do something, Fiona would often find the solution. The idea with the label (version 2.0 i.e. minus Cocteau Twins) was that we could create albums made for 'free' in our own studios. We had the staff costs of course and our crazy ass rent to pay, but we wouldn't charge the bands anything. So, a bit expensive for us, but free to them. Bloody *ridiculous* if you think about it. And if that wasn't mad enough, we also rented a cottage in Twickenham near the studio for two years just so the bands could stay there for free when they came to the studio. Another hare-brained scheme of losing more money hand over fist.

As far as what our artist contracts would look like, this developed a bit over the first few years. But one thing Robin and I were certain about was that we would never own anyone's masters in perpetuity.

Back in 1983 aged twenty, when I signed my first contract with 4AD on joining Cocteau Twins, I didn't have a lawyer look at it. As it was only two pages long, I just signed it. I received another piece of paper from a publisher and signed that too. I didn't really understand any of it, and to be honest, I wasn't very interested. Long paragraphs with no punctuation. But all the 4AD people seemed really *nice*, I'd known them for a few years, so why wouldn't I sign it? Robin and Elizabeth had the same deal so of course it was all going to be fine. In time I would come to realise that the terms we had agreed were far from great and this would define how we approached signing bands to Bella Union.

The Czars' singer John Grant had mailed me his band's first demo in 1997 from his home in Denver. Sent directly to September Sound studios, it was just a few songs on a DAT (a digital audio tape format that the industry curiously adopted as an alternative to reels of 1/4 or 1/2 inch tape for masters) with a hand-written note.

The demo wasn't perfect but John had something and I encouraged him in my reply to write more and to keep sending me stuff. Over the course of the next few months, the songs kept coming and kept getting better, as did his voice.

One day, a new audio tape arrived from John. The band was still sounding a bit rough around the edges but everything had gone up a level or two. If I could somehow get them to come to September Sound and we could take the time to get a great performance of each song on to tape, then John could make this band something very special. I was convinced that John was a horse worth backing. I just wasn't sure how we'd afford it.

My solo record, the first-ever release on Bella Union, had sold well enough to bring a few grand into the coffers, so I scraped the money together and flew the Czars over from Denver to the UK to record their first album for the label.

It wasn't the easiest session. Once we got going, we realised that the band probably weren't quite ready yet to record all of these songs. And maybe John knew this too. We didn't have the luxury of sending them away to practise some more, so I helped as best as I could, playing bass on a few tracks, some slide guitar here and there, and slowly but surely the album came together. Bringing Paula Frazer from Tarnation over to record some vocals with John was a master stroke. We were both such fans, it really was a major boost to the session.

John was insanely talented but had very little confidence in himself at that point, and I knew well that if Giles – my co-producer – and I could just help a little bit here and there, he would blossom. It can be intimidating being in a studio when you're new to it, and even a few kind words can go a long way.

But it's also often about what you *don't* say, as much as what you do.

Over the last years of Cocteau Twins after her relationship with Robin had ended, Elizabeth would often ask me to record her vocals. I learned *so* much. With Elizabeth, after another staggering vocal take where I would be discreetly wiping the tears from my eyes in the control room, I knew that showing my emotion or giving my thoughts wasn't what she needed. She didn't need *my* opinion. Play it back to her and let her tell you what *she* wants to do, whether to keep it or redo it. Once I'd worked that bit out, it was easy. Keep it simple and work fast. Don't fanny about.

With John, it was more a case of him feeling relaxed and being able to hear what he was doing. Once he had confidence, he could articulate what he needed and he began to get it every time. The more you do anything, the better you get.

After the Czars album was done, Warren Ellis, Mick Turner and Jim White of Dirty Three came into the studios to record *Whatever You Love, You Are*, simply the best-sounding album they ever made.

You can put that down to at least four things: the band being on great form; not having to rush like they would have had to in the past; the studio and the equipment being of a high standard; and Lincoln Fong being a brilliant engineer who loved the band and who just recorded everything *so* well. That we continue to work with both Dirty Three and John Grant twenty-seven years after we initially signed them is a dizzying fact, and one that makes me very happy!

One of our next releases was Robin's own new band Violet Indiana. Sadly, they didn't set the world on fire. And then when another artist he'd been developing didn't take off either, his curious assumption was probably that this must be all *my* fault. It would have hurt him that coming from such an acclaimed band as Cocteau Twins, his new music with Violet Indiana was not heralded in the way he would have wanted.

When his solo instrumental album – which was of course utterly lovely – also didn't get the press it deserved, I think Robin just mentally left the building. I was left to run things, whether I wanted to or not. At this point I didn't know *what* I wanted. I was just trying to create something worthwhile, and clearly failing miserably. Our lack of experience with contracts and accounts, our lack of finance, and a general excess of *lack* in every aspect of running the label meant that if we carried on in this fashion, our vessel of tunes was soon to be running aground.

I have never been under any illusion about my place in the Cocteau Twins story.

I was not there at the beginning, did not form the band, was therefore not an 'original' member and despite being in the band for fourteen years, it will always be rightly known by most people because of the extraordinary voice of Elizabeth Fraser and the shimmering guitars and masterful production skills of Robin Guthrie. The band is nothing without those two. One without the other is significant but together, well . . . you can hear the results on their *Victorialand* LP, *Head over Heels* and on This Mortal Coil's atmospheric cover of Tim Buckley's 'Song to the Siren'. Both are outstanding talents, and it was a privilege to have been a significant part of this band for such a large slice of my life. So while this book isn't really about setting the record straight about my time and contribution to the band, I am happy to confirm reports that I *was* in the band from 1984 to 1997 and *did* write the music *with* Robin, in *our* studio.

Elizabeth and Robin were a couple when I met them and would remain so until a year or so after *Heaven or Las Vegas* came out. After they broke up, I figured the band would follow suit. Indeed, at the time, I couldn't see any way in which we could continue, but over the next six years, we made two more albums together, both of which may not be the fans' favourites but have some wonderful moments on them. I am proud of us all for working through the pain.

For sure, the period after I joined saw the band reach new levels of success, but I know that probably would have happened anyway, with someone different, or with no one else.

Reading interviews Robin has done since things unravelled – with the band first and then subsequently between him and me and our label Bella Union – you'd be forgiven for thinking I had never been in Cocteau Twins or been an equal partner in the studio. That makes me a bit sad. But no doubt he will feel it was *his* band not mine, and maybe he wants to diminish my part in it. He said recently his favourite albums were *Head over Heels* and *Victorialand*, which I was not part of. Maybe he sees these times as the most romantic or perhaps they were when he had the easiest time in the studio without worrying about anyone else's input on the musical side. That's fine.

Writing me out of his history does seem a little extreme, given the amount of years we worked together and the beautiful music that we wrote together in *our* studios. I have made my peace with it now, so the pain is, if not entirely gone, mostly dissipated. Robin's previous issues with drugs have been covered enough in the music press that I have little to add to what I mentioned earlier, partly because really no one cares about it, and also it is massively boring. I already gave up enough of my life dealing with it, being there with him and for him during and after his rehab in the US, that further re-examination of this part of the band's story is not one I am keen to dwell on. We all know too well that drug addiction, *any* addiction, will be destructive to all the relationships around it, and that was firmly the case here. Robin's much-publicised issues with drugs, and how that played out, weren't insignificant, and affected us all of course. But that is *his* story not mine.

CHAPTER SEVENTEEN

UPS

In the autumn of 1999, after finishing the Czars' debut album, I was back at September Sound producing Welsh singer Anthony Reynolds' band Jack, for an EP on a Spanish label called Acuarela Productions.

We had one of those video phone things like a '90s version of the Ring system, whereby any visitors or deliveries would walk up the drive to the front door, press a buzzer and a low-quality image of them would come up on a little screen. We could speak to them and buzz them in if we recognised them.

One morning I was in early and making some coffee and scrambled eggs in the kitchen when the doorbell rang and I walked over to the nearest phone. Seeing that instantly recognisable UPS uniform and cap, I lifted the phone and said, 'Come on in!' pressed the button to allow entry, and went back to making my breakfast.

'Hello?' a voice called out from the corridor.

'Oh hi, sorry. If you could just leave the package in the office there that would be wonderful, thank you!!' I shouted back.

'I'm not a courier,' a quiet voice responded.

I took my eggs off the hob and popped my head out into the hall.

He repeated, 'I'm not a courier, I'm David Sylvian. I'm here to meet Robin Guthrie. Is he in?'

Fuck me, so it is. Beautiful, elegant, debonair David Sylvian, whose Japan albums and Sylvian and Sakamoto releases had been gracing my turntables for many years, standing not four foot from me, dressed in lovely brown slacks, a smart brown shirt and brown cap, looking EXACTLY like a fucking UPS man.

Fuck. Fuck. Fuck. Fuck.

There really is no recovery strategy applicable here. So I nervously laughed and tried to make light of it, but I was already six foot under.

In my head it would have gone more like this:

'Hi, David, how lovely to meet you. Can I make you a coffee, and would you like one of these croissants? They're just fresh out of the oven.'

'Yes? OK, great. Why don't you come into the kitchen with me so we can talk while I sort that for you.'

'Oh, thanks, yes it is so beautiful here isn't it?'

'Yeah (laughing), oh, almost ten years now. Feel very blessed to be here.'

'Let's take the coffees into the living room.'

'Oh, on the balcony? Yes of course, it's lovely outside; we can sit out there.'

'So what are you up to right now? Are you working on something new?
Dead Bees on a Cake? *Right, well I will make sure to pick that up!'*

'Can I show you around the studio until Robin gets in?'

'Yes, I would love to play on the next album! Thank you for asking!'

'David, if it doesn't sound too creepy, can I say I've been a fan of your music since the late '70s, with Japan and then the solo records Brilliant Trees and then Secrets of the Beehive with its gorgeous Vaughan Oliver sleeve? They are both just sublime. Oh yeah, and those two records you did with Holger Czukay, I LOVED those.'

'Oh really is he? I figured as much. Hahaha.'

'I'm guessing you've Googled "Can" and "Japan" haven't you? Yeah, Freddie said the same thing about Queen! Such a nightmare, right?'

CHAPTER EIGHTEEN

Mexico City

I had no intention at all of playing live shows as a solo artist. I had an album to promote but I had no 'band' as such and just didn't see myself as a singer or a frontman. I always felt happier in studios and in the background.

A couple of years later, I found myself back in the United States, producing the Los Angeles band the Autumns' second album. The studio – Prairie Sun – was located in Cotati, California in the beautiful Napa Valley. I received an email from a promoter in Mexico who was a fan (*the* fan) of my solo record, enquiring if I would be interested in performing a couple of shows in Mexico City. The boys from the Autumns were with me when I read it, and as I was about to answer a polite 'thanks but no', Matthew, the band's gifted singer, said, 'We could be your band!'

I had never been to Mexico City and just before Cocteau Twins finished, talks were apparently under way about us performing there, so on the spur of the moment and buoyed by the Autumns' enthusiasm for the idea, I replied to the promoter and said 'yes'.

So in September 1999 I flew to Los Angeles with the Autumns and with barely any rehearsals we performed one warm-up show at Café Bleu before jetting off to Mexico City to play our first show at Cine Bella Época.

We were collected at the airport by the promoter Eduardo who drove us around for the next couple of days. He spoke just enough English to explain the dos and don'ts for bands in Mexico City.

The gist of it was:

Don't go anywhere without me.

Don't take cabs anywhere.

Stay close to the hotel or the venue.

If you need to go anywhere – to eat, drink, shop – just call me and I'll come and pick you up in the van.

Got it.

The crime wave in Mexico City back then was, as ever, partly linked to the economic crisis, but the justice system was also in a terrific mess. Crime was just another career path that simply competed with many others. It was lucrative of course but popular too because punishment of any kind was so remote. The rumours that members of the police were not just corrupt but currently the main organisers of crime were *not* exaggerated, Eduardo said, adding that if you were out driving and got stopped by police, they *would* plant drugs on you and then bribe you to avoid you being arrested. Happened to everyone, he said.

The show day came along and Eduardo collected us in his van mid-afternoon from our hotel in the heart of the Zona Rosa and drove us the short distance to the venue in the city's Condesa neighbourhood to set up for our soundcheck. On the way there, he told us that our second show in Guadalajara tomorrow was now in jeopardy as the police had declined the permit and were now asking for an additional deposit of $20,000 for a new one. He said this too was commonplace but it was a *lot* of money. He was going to try and raise it somehow, but as the show was meant to be in twenty-four hours, I was pretty sure that was unlikely.

Undeterred, we started to load in and set up on the stage at Cine Bella Época, a grand art deco building designed by a modernist American architect called Charles Lee back in 1942. Eduardo said that he had designed more than 400 theatres in California and Mexico during the '30s and '40s, including the majestic Los Angeles Theatre in 1931.

All was beginning to sound good inside this gorgeous building, but I had forgotten to bring a CD that had some drum samples on it that I needed for the show. I knew exactly where it was in my hotel room, so we finished up the soundcheck and I told the boys I'd get Eduardo to drop me back to the hotel to pick it up. I'd be back in plenty of time for doors opening.

I looked around for him for about twenty minutes but to no avail. So I wandered out to the front of the venue to have a cigarette. All taxis in Mexico City at the time were bright green VW Beetles with a white roof and while Eduardo's earlier warnings had been clear enough, they just looked *so* cute and I figured that

I was pretty streetwise, that I had been in enough rough spots around the world and that a ten-minute ride back to my hotel was going to be fine.

Several taxis were waiting in the street by the nearby university and I signalled to the first in line.

These lovely Beetles are two-door cars with no front passenger seat so when you open the door you climb straight into the back seat of the cab. My taxi driver doesn't turn around to look at me but I see him in his rear-view mirror. I ask him to take me to Hotel Century in Zona Rosa, but he doesn't seem to hear. He puts the car into gear and drives off regardless.

'*Hotel Century. Zona Rosa, por favor,*' I repeat.

Again, no recognition or response. I reach into my suit jacket and pull out my long wooden hotel key. It had the hotel address engraved into the wooden part of the key. I hold the key up so he can see it in the rear-view mirror. 'Hotel Century?' I repeat. Driver looks at me briefly but then suddenly reaches around and grabs the key off me.

Rude.

Well, I guess now he has the key and that *has* got the address on it, so it's all good. He now knows where I want to go.

I exhale slowly and settle back in my seat and look out of the window as we make our way through the rush-hour traffic, and while certain that we are going in completely the opposite direction to the way we should be, I realise the driver knows I am 'un turista' and is just going to take the long way round, to get some extra pesos. I am fine with that. It's a beautiful city and I don't mind being taken for a little detour. After twenty minutes though, I don't yet recognise any of the landmarks

I had clocked on the way here. Surely now he is starting to take the piss.

'*HOTEL CENTURY, si?*' I said slowly and loudly, looking into his rear-view mirror for a reaction.

For the first time, I could see his eyes clearly, and now I was apprehensive. The penny was slowly dropping. He wasn't just after a bigger fare or a tourists' tip.

He had a cold expressionless face, a man who was doing what *he* had to do to survive. He was small, squat but looked powerful enough. Oiled black hair, several days of stubble, a white vest under his shirt.

We were not going to the hotel. I could see that now.

Why the fuck didn't you listen to Eduardo? Why do you always think you're right about everything? You're not.

After forty minutes, we pass a sign for Iztapalapa and seem to be heading out of the city altogether and this is really bad. I'd heard one or two tales of tourist kidnapping, but I never thought for a second it was going to happen to me. All I can think of now is the eerily prophetic phone call from my mum a few weeks before I left for Mexico. 'Eat well when you're out there. Remember the more you weigh, the harder you are to kidnap.' She was only joking but I'm not laughing now.

Now there were hardly any shops and the street lights were fewer and further between. All I could hear is the roar of the Beetle and the thump of my racing heartbeat.

We were almost out of the main city, and that would be the end of that.

I'm going to be driven into the middle of nowhere and handed over to a gang and have my throat cut if I don't get out of here. That's how I saw this playing out. I was glad that fear of death didn't bring on a panic attack. On the contrary, it seemed to have clarified my thought.

A set of traffic lights up ahead went red and my driver came to a halt with at least two cars in front of him. I had a quick glance over my shoulder and could see several cars stopped behind his. In a split second and with reactions I had no idea that I possessed, I lurched forward into the space where the passenger seat would have been and yanked down the lever to open the door. I jumped out on to the pavement and began sprinting back towards the city in the opposite direction the cab was going. I knew he couldn't move for a minute or two at least because he was wedged in between all those cars on a red light. I ran down a side street, turned right again and zigzagged a couple more times so even if he did manage to turn around he wouldn't know which way I'd gone. I didn't stop running for about forty-five minutes in the intense city heat, with my black pinstripe suit and brothel creepers on. *Escaping* felt very good but running in *that* get-up in *that* heat deserves way more credit.

Eventually when I was pretty sure I wasn't being followed, I slowed to catch my breath. Several hundred yards ahead of me, I could see some people, and as I got closer saw that it was a young couple holding hands standing outside what looked like a hostel. I approached them and asked in English if they knew where Zona Rosa was. To my great relief and surprise they were Australian, super-friendly and said they thought it was a few more miles but that the centre of the city was 'definitely that way'. Two hours after I had left the venue for a simple detour to my hotel, I was finally approaching it, sweating profusely, blisters on my feet and chafed thighs. I asked at reception if I could use the phone and called Eduardo. He answered immediately, frantic with worry. I briefly explained what had happened and he drove straight over to pick me up.

'What did I tell you *not* to do?'

'Not now, Eduardo. I am sorry but you need to find me another hotel room because he has my room key, and I do not want to go back there tonight and find him hiding in the wardrobe with a knife to slit my throat.'

The hotel receptionist picked up the CD from my room for me as there was no way I was going into that room, then Eduardo drove me to the venue and walked on to the stage before me to explain to the audience in Spanish why I was two hours late for the show.

The second show in Guadalajara never happened. I returned home with all my parts intact but a peg or two shorter. I didn't perform again live in any shape or form for more than ten years.

CHAPTER NINETEEN

2001: Aerospace Oddity

Back home, thanks to all the hard work Nina Jackson had been putting in, the studio was becoming busier than ever, with artists like Beth Orton, Hope Sandoval, Nick Cave,[1] Mark Hollis, Mark Owen and Nick Lowe all coming in to use it. There was so much to be positive about but as always, round the next bend, a juggernaut was heading our way without any brakes.

---

[1] Nick Cave was in the studio downstairs one day with Dirty Three's Warren Ellis, working on something with Jim White on drums and Susan Stenger from Band of Susans on bass. Mid-afternoon, and Giles, one of our house engineers, poked his head round the door and whispered to me, 'Nick and Warren want you to come and play bass; Susan had to leave.' I felt the blood drain from my face. I just remember shaking my head and saying, 'No, I can't. I can't.' I've thought about that moment a lot since then, the pointless 'what if' syndrome. I even had a vivid dream the other night that our new soundtrack was about to come out. Cave–Ellis–Raymonde. That's a rabbit hole that I would rather skip over. Would never have worked anyway. I have too much flesh and not enough hair to be in their band.

With no Cocteaus album advances incoming to cover the rental of the property, the purchasing of new equipment or even maintenance of the *existing* gear, we had been running on empty for a while. The money we were getting in from the bookings at the studio wasn't enough to cover the rent, rates and staff costs. We had buried our heads in the sand for too long, hoping things would improve in the studio business or that one of the bands we signed would take off. But neither happened.

A few months previously in early 2000, I had watched Denton-based trio Lift to Experience perform in a fierce thunderstorm at a Taco Shack in Austin. The ferocious power and celestial beauty that they managed to achieve in such apocalyptic weather conditions shook me to my core. As it turned out, it was a portent. I offered to release their debut record almost the second they had walked offstage, and so began a manic twelve months for me and the band. I offered to help with the mixing of the record which had been recorded in Denton. When I got home, still unaware of the precarious financial storm that was brewing for me, I put aside time to mix. It was difficult without the band being there with me, but we barely had enough money to pay the bills so I couldn't bring them over, even though I would have loved to.

And then, out of the blue, the accountant called us. We owed more than £120,000 to HMRC and the VAT man. The receivers were going to be called in. I don't recall the exact chronology of events, as I tend to start doing the washing-up when things get a bit too stressful, but this phone call simply accelerated us from a slow, painful death to a quick execution. Clearly we couldn't afford to be paying the fancy West End firm of accountants, and we were starting to fall out with Ray around this time, so it was time to put the big boy pants on and accept the inevitable.

Fuck.

I decided I had to start the mixing of the album now and just hoped that I could finish before the heavy mob turned up. They usually only give you a few hours' notice before they arrive, I assume to make sure you don't sell it yourself and pocket the cash. And true to form, at 3 p.m. the following Monday, there was a knock at the door.

The day the receivers started to rip the studio apart, I had stayed up until 4 a.m. the previous night mixing the final track on the debut Lift to Experience album *The Texas-Jerusalem Crossroads*.

Four hours later, however, and I was back watching as the remaining mixing desks, tape machines, ADATs, amps, speakers and racks and racks of all the outboard gear I had used to finish the Lift to Experience mixes were being loaded on to a large van.

Everything.

Fifteen years of *stuff.*

Thankfully I had a couple of my bass guitars in a repair shop but everything else went. And within a couple of weeks, it was all on sale with the studio broker Don Larking for a fraction of the price we paid for it.

Now it really *was* all over.

It was heartbreaking, but if you think about stuff like that for longer than a few minutes, you will torture yourself into an early grave. So while I *hated* that we were declared bankrupt, felt like a total failure, despaired that everyone like Nina, Giles, Lincoln,

Fiona and Mitsuo who had worked so hard for us were now without their livelihoods, there was literally nothing I could do any more. I needed to get away for a few days to get my head straight, and a month or so after the summer 2001 release of Lift to Experience's album, I decided I would buy a cheap flight to New York for the annual music conference CMJ, a great place to see bands and meet fellow label folks. I figured I might even find a US booking agent for Lift to Experience there.

So I flew into New York on 10 September, a few days before CMJ started, and checked into my room. Dirk van Dooren and Graham Wood, two marvellous film-makers and designers who we had worked with in 1996 for our short film for the EP 'Twinlights', were the directors of Tomato Films and the company leased this lovely apartment in Washington Place in the heart of Greenwich Village. They kindly let me stay there for free. After the collapse of our beautiful studio back home, it felt good to get away for a couple of days.

I woke up early around 6 a.m. the next morning and walked down to Hudson River Park to see Pier 90 where the *Queen Mary* had docked back in the 1950s when Dad played in his jazz trio on board. The weather was good, the skies cloudless and the pale sun had just begun to rise as I sat on a bench by the river's edge, thinking of Dad being right here half a century ago, and how this city was really the start of his big adventure in music. Walking back in search of a coffee, I found an internet café on the street just a few doors down from the apartment and wandered in. It was only 8.30 a.m. but I sat down at the computer with my coffee and croissant and wrote an email to Tony Kiewel at Sub Pop

Records. Tony had emailed me after reading the five-star *Uncut* review of Lift to Experience's album and I was hopeful he might want to sign them to Sub Pop for the US.

Suddenly a woman came running in from the street screaming.

'Call 911! A plane has just crashed into the World Trade Center!'

She turned and ran back out.

I got off my stool and went out into the street. The World Trade Center was essentially at the bottom of the long road I stood on, no more than a mile and a quarter away. And there, sticking out of the north face of the North Tower, was an aeroplane. From where I stood, it looked like a small plane, not a commercial passenger flight. I went back into the internet café. The owner had turned on the news on the TV above the counter. Initial reports were coming in and at this point it was all quite vague. I sat back down at my computer and over the next hour, Tony Kiewel and I exchanged an incredible set of emails as in real time we bonded indelibly in response to the dreadful events the world was waking up to. Being there was surreal of course. I returned to the apartment around 9.30 a.m. after the south face of the South Tower was hit and turned on CNN. I tried to call Karen and the boys who I knew would be seeing this either at school or as they were getting home, but I couldn't get any signal. I watched on the TV as the South Tower buckled and fell around 10 a.m.

I really didn't know what to do with myself, but thought I should go back to the internet café and at least send an email to let them all know I was OK. As I approached the café's door, I stood for a moment in the street along with hundreds of other shell-shocked faces looking down at the one remaining tower. Seconds later, I watched in disbelief as the North Tower collapsed in front of my eyes. For a building that stretched up 1,400 feet high into the sky, it was razed to the ground in a matter of some ten seconds. It was a *shocking* thing to actually witness. I felt helpless but went back into the café and sat down to compose an email that I would send to Karen and my mum as I knew they would be worried. I noticed that there was quite a commotion outside and turned towards the window to see hordes of people running up the street away from downtown, towards Manhattan. Young families dragging suitcases and children in buggies. With nowhere to go, for the next few hours I wandered up and down the street, the awful smell hanging in the air. Metal, fuel, death and despair. And what seemed like snow was falling on the pavement and resting on my coat. It wasn't snow of course. It was ash. Debris from the twin towers. Throughout the afternoon, I saw fire engines pull up on the sidewalk by the café, the firefighters' faces grey from the ash and the shock, sitting numb on the pavement for a moment just enough to catch their breath before returning downtown to pull more bodies from the scene. Incredible human beings. I bought some bottles of water from the café and walked over to where a few of the firefighters were sitting, silent. I placed the water beside them and walked back to the café.

Later, I returned to the apartment with a box of painkillers. My back was killing me. I lay down on the floor with the news channel on. For the next twenty-four hours, I didn't leave my room. And I didn't sleep a wink for the pain, hallucinating at the horror on the TV. I managed to get through to Karen on the phone the next day and told her that with CMJ now cancelled, I would try to get home as soon as I could. The tension around the world was of course pretty intense at this point and trying to find flights out of New York was impossible. I did manage to find a chiropractor nearby though who had said I could come and see him at 4 p.m. The clinic was probably 100 yards from the apartment but it took me about thirty minutes to walk there. My back and legs just wouldn't move. He tried a few things but nothing much worked. I told him I absolutely *had* to get home for my son Stan's tenth birthday on the 15th and he explained there was no way I should be sitting on a plane in this condition and, besides, he couldn't see how I was going to make it given the situation in New York. He kindly gave me a prescription for Valium and said only to take it if things were desperate and I did manage to get a flight.

I spent the next day and a half trying to get out of New York. Just when I was about to give up, I managed to find a Greyhound bus to Toronto – around eleven hours – and then a flight from Toronto to London. It was a journey and a half, but it *could* get me home around 11.30 p.m. on the 15th. I popped the Valium as I walked up to the Greyhound bus and don't remember another thing until someone shook me awake in Toronto. I slept the whole way there. I headed to the airport and boarded my plane to London.

I walked back in the door at home with half an hour of Stan's birthday to spare. I hugged him and his brother Will tightly. I knew they must have been worried watching all this stuff on television where the edges of reality can be very blurry, especially for a ten-year-old and an eight-year-old. Watching first-hand how a city deals with mass trauma and destruction showed me that my own crisis was trifling by comparison. I had so much to be thankful for.[2,3]

---

[2] Tony K from Sub Pop and I are forever linked because of that day. I am glad that something beautiful came out of a week of my life that I won't ever forget.

[3] Sixteen years later, Lift to Experience singer Josh T Pearson would say in the press that the mix I did was awful, that he had always hated it, always hated the sleeve; hated everything we did. He had the album remixed and rereleased it on Mute in 2017. Not quite sure why he bothered adding the original album to the double vinyl package if he hated it so much.

But it is an incredible album, and any shortcomings I may have had as a mixer were thankfully not highlighted by the press acclaim that heralded its release in 2001. I sent it to Allan Jones at *Uncut* and he flipped out and gave it a glowing five-star review, the like of which none of us could have dreamed of. This debut end-of-times concept album with Texas as the promised land enthralled me. It was so perfectly and pains-takingly put together across its ninety minutes. It managed to be funny, self-aware and profound. That *Uncut* piece sparked an interest in the band I had been trying to ignite for a year, and finally gave me the reason I needed to pay for them to come over. In addition, I found Pearson a very lucrative publishing deal (that I took no commission on, I should add) and set the band up with a top-notch booking agent. After a personal tragedy beset the band on their fourth trip over, they had to fly home before they had even played a note. They never played again until a reunion show for mega-fan Guy Garvey at his Meltdown in 2016.

While some had wondered if they were being serious when they sang 'So all you haircut bands, doing headstands, thinking you'll turn the world upside down, put your guitars up over your shoulders, a new sort of experience is taking over, cos we're simply the best band in the whole damn land and Texas is the Reason' on 'These are the Days', or were simply just pompous and pretentious, the first time I brought them to the UK for the release in 2001 (I had seen them in Texas in March), people here

Following the terror attack on the World Trade Center, alone in New York, my thoughts were dark. I was wandering aimlessly around a broken city, picturing my boys at home thousands of miles away, and thinking of the father I never really knew, and I knew I had a big hole I needed to start filling if I was to really move on. I knew New York had been significant in Dad's career, and while it had been more than ten years since he died, it was in this moment as I stood there in Greenwich Village, looking down the street in shock at the rubble beneath the ghostly towers, that I decided I would begin in earnest a thorough research into my father's work – to find out who this man was, what my own life in music was all about and how it might all be intertwined somehow. As soon as I got back home after 9/11, I went down to visit my mum.

---

in Europe understood it immediately. One of the most important releases on Bella Union up to that point, and one of the most important live bands I had ever seen, but I can't lie and say I feel the same way any more since those interviews Pearson gave in 2017. It soured it.

The remixed album is great, of course, but if I mixed it today in a fully functioning recording studio it would be too.

HALFWAY TO PARADISE

The Ballad of Ivor Raymonde

Prelude

As mad as it sounds, I never had a proper deep chat with my dad about music. Indeed, we never really had a proper chat about anything. He wasn't around much when I was a child. Then as a teenager I was away at boarding school and rarely saw him and even when I *did*, I was itching to get away as quickly as I could. Once I was in a band, *I* wasn't around much.

And then, he was dead.

The only time he came to see Cocteau Twins play was at the Royal Festival Hall in 1984 and when I asked him what he thought, he commented that 'it was interesting!'

Which as we all know means he didn't really get it.

Whether it was because of my own distant relationship with him, or in spite of it, I was determined that this would not be how it would be with my own sons, and even though I was away a lot, I made sure I spent as much time with them as I could, reading to them, talking to them, listening to music with them and ensuring that they knew how much I loved them.

As the melodramas of my own life began to unfurl, I realised I had a lot of unresolved feelings about Ivor dying young and my own inability to have a meaningful conversation with him while he was alive. There is a real guilt there that I didn't acknowledge until recently. I cling to those rare moments of intimacy that we shared – a couple of games at Spurs in the '60s, and watching the Ali fights. I think back to when I had been sent to my room for forging Mum's signature on my school report aged eight. It was of course easily detected by the headmaster because this mastermind here wrote it as '*Mrs* Nita Raymonde' in a shaky flourish, clearly unaware that signatures do not come with a prefix. Mum was incandescent with rage, maybe accelerated by her embarrassment that she had a son *that* stupid, and sent me up to bed without tea, with the threat that 'your father will come and give you the slipper when he gets home'.

When he did come to my room, he closed the door behind him, walked over to the edge of the bed, winked at me and whispered, 'Don't worry, I'm not going to do anything.' He proceeded just to thwack the slipper down on to the mattress nowhere near my backside. I looked up at him like Jimmy Olsen looked at Superman. I guess he figured the sound of leather on blanket was, when heard downstairs in the kitchen, not discernible from leather on bottom.

But such memories are few and far between and I probably grant them more significance than they merit.

For years, strange as it may seem, I didn't see the parallels in our lives.

Apart from all his musical work, which I have devoured, the tapes of him looking back on his life and telling his own story – which my mum studiously recorded and transcribed – are all I have left to help me make sense of his world.

(I)

It was during the war that Dad's tastes began to develop and he would absorb all the music of the day: Glenn Miller, Artie Shaw, Teddy Wilson, Benny Goodman, Count Basie, Duke Ellington. His ear was forever glued to the radio and he spent any spare money he had on records.

It was an incredibly exciting time for jazz and swing addicts and he began experimenting, copying the sounds and styles of these great musicians. He felt he had found his true vocation. He would become a jazz pianist. At his local boys' club, there were several others with similar ambitions and they would form trios or quartets, most of which lasted no more than a few weeks, but all of which gave him valuable experience.

His father Hirsch's hopes of seeing his son turn into a classical virtuoso were fading fast. On leaving school at sixteen, he took a daytime clerical job with John Line, the wallpaper company, and combined this with playing piano for various semi-pro bands at night and at weekends.

By 1945, he was already starting to play piano most nights across the wartime dive bars in London. To find work, he hung about in Archer Street, just behind Piccadilly, and just next to the stage door of the Windmill Theatre. These were the main meeting places for musicians looking for work or for those with a job to offer. Most of the musicians were either very young or unfit in some way for the armed forces. Whilst there was a real shortage of musicians, there was no shortage of gigs. These were offered, accepted, swapped or passed on. From around 11 a.m. each morning, small groups would form, chatting and fixing their deals. Money was never openly discussed. Instead, a kind of sign language operated. An average fee for a gig at that time was about three pounds.

'How much?' Three fingers would be placed against the lapel.

'Three pounds, ten shillings?' and you would get three fingers and one finger bent in half.

His older brother, my uncle Len, was a barber, but at the outbreak of war joined the army and was promoted into the air-raid division posted to various secret locations around the UK. Len's twin, my Aunt Gertie, who was born with a severe disability, had to wear a leg brace and disability boot and was of course exempt from joining the armed forces. When Dad was seventeen and old enough for National Service, he was conscripted as a Bevin Boy and worked down the mines in Nottingham and Doncaster. Bevin Boys were named after Ernest Bevin, Minister of Labour and National Service during the wartime coalition, who devised a plan to increase coal production which had heavily dwindled because of the war. The operation ran from 1943 to 1948.

After four weeks' training at Ollerton Colliery, he began the job proper and while in Nottingham had a nasty accident. When moving some steel pit props from one place to another, he let them slip from his grasp and one came crashing down, crushing the fourth finger of his right hand underneath. He was taken up in the cage immediately and rushed to hospital where his finger had already turned completely black. As a pianist, he feared the worst, but before he had a chance to protest, the doctor stuck a long needle into the tip of the black finger and drew out about a pint of blood. He was sent home to recover in London for seventy-two hours, but liked being back so much that he stayed. He went AWOL for more than a week, playing a few shows in London with his nine good fingers before returning to Nottingham to take his punishment.

He remained down the mines until he developed trouble with his lungs and the sickness that followed got the better of him, and he was conscripted out. His health recovering in London, he continued to play as many evening gigs as he could and sometimes helped pay his way by busking on the streets of the East End during the day with a piano accordion he bought from Jennings in Charing Cross Road. Both he and his dance-crazy sister Lillian soon decided that if they were to get more work, they should change their name to a more 'entertainment-friendly' one. Their great-uncle was called Morris Raymond, which they both thought was a perfect showbiz name. They both officially changed their surnames from Pomerance to Raymond while Lillian also joined ENSA.[1]

Dad later added the 'e' to his surname as he thought that looked better written down.

With his new name and health restored, he continued playing every gig he could get, and one morning found himself auditioning for the bandleader Geraldo who was putting together some jazz trios to perform on the *Queen Mary* which sailed from Southampton to New York and back every two weeks. This was very significant for Ivor.

One of his most vivid wartime memories was when a bomb partly demolished Peter Robinson, the department store on Oxford Street, in September 1940, not far from where he lived with his mum and dad.[2]

The front and the sides of the huge display window looking out on to Oxford Street were completely blown out, leaving only the back of the shop and the floor wide open to the elements. The very next day, Geraldo and his full orchestra arrived unannounced, set themselves up inside the shop, sitting in the gaping hole in the middle, and playing all the latest hit songs for all

---

[1] The Entertainments National Service Association was created to provide some musical and comedic distractions to the British armed services. The spread of decent entertainers had become pretty thin as the war progressed and the anacronym was unofficially amended to Every Night Something Awful.

[2] Peter Robinson went on to create the Topshop brand in 1964.

those passing by. It must have been such a morale booster, seeing and hearing that as you walked past on your way to pick up your rations. Dad always loved Geraldo for that defiant gesture, so this really was an important audition for him to get.

Dad was obsessed with jazz, and the opportunity to get to the US where all his idols were was too good to be true!

He got the job.

Playing in a jazz trio on the *Queen Mary* in 1949 must have seemed like a dream come true for a young man hoping to make his way as a musician – and for someone who only a few years previous had been down the pits mining coal.

There were three cabin classes on the ship, and two jazz bands to cover all bases. In the first-class cabin, they would often find themselves playing to some of the biggest celebrities of the day. Dad saw Hedy Lamarr, the beautiful Hollywood film star (he said he dreamed about her every night after) stood next to Bob Hope in the men's urinals, and recalled comedian Jack Benny leaving them a huge tip after one set.

While his night-time dreams may well have focused on Ms Lamarr, in the daytime his thoughts were centred entirely on getting to New York and seeing Erroll Garner, Art Tatum, Miles Davis and Charlie Parker, but most of all Lennie Tristano, his own particular idol. Tristano was a highly innovative avant-garde pianist who had fascinated and puzzled him enormously for some time. Dad had a couple of imports of the Tristano Sextet, on Capitol Records, but he'd found the structure of their music more than just complicated. It was unfathomable. One of his prime objectives on reaching New York was to see him perform and, if possible, learn more about his techniques.

To be plunged into the utter luxury of the *Queen Mary* after the austerity of post-war Britain was bewildering. They had gone without everything but the bare essentials for so long, and even *after* the war, the shortages had continued. From a weekly allowance of a couple of ounces of meat, an egg and a knob of butter, they were suddenly confronted with this abundant extravaganza of food. It was quite overwhelming. The breakfasts were the best; cereals galore with cream instead of milk, and, wonder of wonders, ham and eggs. He was just glad none of his family could see him as he tucked into enormous platefuls of hitherto forbidden delights.

Back home, his mother had always kept a kosher house and bacon was banned. Although Dad had eaten and been rather partial to the odd cheeky rasher when working away from home, he'd kept pretty quiet about it. The sight of those breakfasts on the *Queen Mary*, after years of food rationing, would have turned a more resolute head than his. They all ate themselves stupid. Massive steaks, roast beef and lamb, asparagus, corned beef hash, followed by mountainous desserts smothered in whipped cream, strawberries, waffles with maple syrup; if such things had ever existed before the war, he'd certainly never seen or tasted them.

When the ship finally docked in New York at 5 a.m. that first morning at Pier 90, he walked down the gangplank, got on his knees and kissed the ground. The beautiful Manhattan skyline veiled in mist must have been awe-inspiring.

During their thirty-six-hour stay, the band would continue to live and sleep on the ship. That was the arrangement, but the reality was quite different. *Time enough for sleep on the return trip.*

The plan was to stock up with everything they could lay their hands on and visit every jazz club in the vicinity. They'd heard all about the clothes you could buy; flashy socks and ties, Humphrey Bogart-style trench coats, string vests and, of course, nylon stockings for their girls back home. After five years of clothes rationing, this was their own American dream, and they intended to take advantage of every opportunity. The all-American tough-guy image was much envied in England at the time, and they knew that whatever they could buy now would be snapped up back home. They would kit themselves out, and then sell the rest, thus financing their nights out on Broadway next time round.

But that first night, they headed for what was eventually to become the Mecca of all the jazz clubs in the world: Birdland, which was opening for the first time the very night they arrived, 15 December 1949.

Almost every major jazz artist they'd heard of was playing that evening: Charlie (Bird) Parker, after whom the club was named, Dizzy Gillespie, Bud Powell, Lester Young, Lee Konitz, Stan Getz, the list was endless. And – the act who really set Dad's heart racing – the Lennie Tristano Quintet were also said to be appearing. When they arrived, they found a queue about a mile long around the block. It seemed like the whole of New York had turned out. With formidable bravado, they walked straight up to the entrance, fronted by a neon sign that read 'Birdland, Jazz Corner of the World', and spoke to the doorman. They told him they were musicians from England, playing aboard the *Queen Mary* and only in New York for one night.

Incredibly, he hustled them through and they were taken inside and given a table.

There was only one thing spoiling this unique experience. The crowd at a table just a little way down from their own who were talking, laughing and apparently paying no attention whatsoever to all these geniuses up there onstage.

Dad grabbed the attention of a waiter.

'Excuse me,' he said very politely. 'Do you think you could ask the people at that table to hold the noise down a little?'

The waiter looked at Dad pityingly.

'Are you kidding? Do you know who those cats are? That's Billy Eckstine and Sarah Vaughan.'[3]

Dad said he could have died from embarrassment.

Docking at Pier 90 meant that they were just a few yards from 52nd Street. This is where all the coolest clubs were situated in the basements or cellars of the brownstone buildings which lined both sides of the street. The best place to sit was usually at the bar. A beer cost less than fifty cents and they could make a couple last all night, soaking up the music until they could hardly keep their eyes open any longer and headed back to their bunks aboard the *Queen Mary*.

On their second trip to New York in early 1950, one of the band had got hold of the phone number of Dad's hero Lennie Tristano and rang him, explaining who they were and why they

---

[3] Billy Eckstine wrote 'As Time Goes By', as immortalised by Dooley Wilson in *Casablanca*, and Sarah Vaughan sang such classics as 'Lullaby of Birdland'.

were in New York. Kindly, he invited them up to his apartment. There, they talked, met his wife and also Lee Konitz, the brilliant alto sax player who was then part of his Sextet. It was agreed that they would call Lennie up each time they reached New York, and he would give them an hour's instruction in the art of improvisation.

Before Dad studied with Lennie, he believed that to improvise in jazz, as in any other form of music, one always first took the key, time signatures and the chord sequences as a basis. The Tristano Sextet had completely dispensed with structure and *their* starting point was purely spontaneous. The music developed through the interaction of one another's ideas. The result was strangely esoteric, with no recognisable form or pattern. Many people found the style unmelodic and discordant, dismissing it as too way out. During these 'sit-ins' with Lennie, they would often experiment with new methods of piano composition, using some well-known tune as a basis on which to extemporise. It became not an arrangement, a variation, or an adaptation of the original, but a completely new composition. The experience of working with Lennie Tristano was invaluable and it was, in its way, like a master class. Lennie had enjoyed a classical training himself, gaining all sorts of honours and degrees, but chose to ignore all this and go his own way.

On his fingering technique, Dad said that some of the things he did he wouldn't have believed possible had he not actually seen it for himself. He played all the usual scales, but used only one finger, and far faster than Dad or any of his band could while using all five. He could do this with every finger and in every key, which as anyone who can play the piano even a little will understand is unbelievably difficult. Another of his tricks was to play different time signatures with each hand, simultaneously. Most good jazz pianists can do that, of course, but not like Tristano. No combination was beyond him and he was never off tempo by as much as a split second. They would time him on a metronome. He was always completely on the money.[4]

Although Dad's career ultimately took a totally different turn, everything that happened during those trips to New York had a profound effect on him. It widened his overall understanding of improvisational techniques, and influenced the things he did later on.

But I think he'd already begun to realise he probably lacked the real hard-core dedication needed to become a top-flight jazz musician. He was a far better reader than most, but this was not the prime consideration for a jazz player. What mattered was natural flow and feel. The music came from inside their heads and hearts and into their fingers; a combination of intellect and emotion. He could hear it, feel it, and understand it, but somehow couldn't express it in the way they did. He said his approach was too simplistic. Jazz would always be his favourite kind of

---

[4] Researching this book, I bought the 1946 Tristano album *Abstraction & Improvisation*, which he had mentioned, and I played it for days while listening to all Dad's reminiscences about meeting and working with Lennie. It was remarkably evocative and made these stories really come to life – like a soundtrack to my dad's movie. Oh, and he hadn't mentioned that Lennie was also blind.

music, but as Ronnie Scott once remarked, 'Jazz musicians live to play; they don't play to live.'

Whenever they could, he and the band would eat in the many diners spread around New York. They were cheap and served fantastic fast food. They couldn't get over how clean these places were, with a glass of iced water and a napkin placed in front of you the moment you sat down, even in the most modest snack bar. Taken for granted now, but back then it was such a pleasant surprise. Cheap cafés in London were always sleazy, but in New York, the standards were on a different level.

As ever, high on the list of priorities for the band on these brief trips was the purchase of as much American clothing as they could afford. The shops on Broadway were open all night. You could get your suit dry-cleaned, your shoes shined, buy a complete wardrobe, or eat almost anything you fancied at three o'clock in the morning. It was a wonderland to kids who not long ago were having bombs dropped on their heads.

It must have been lovely for the returning musicians to treat their families thanks to those New York trips. Ivor's mother Sarah nearly fainted at the sight of a catering-sized tin of fruit salad he walked in with, and on the next trip he came back with a complete china dinner service that he'd bought for a ridiculously tidy sum.

To Ivor – from a Britain blacked out for so many years, and where post-war austerity was still biting hard – it must have all seemed like another world. From the hardships of everyday life in England, to the luxury on board the *Queen Mary* and meeting his jazz idols. It must have felt like the realisation of all his dreams. It only lasted a few months and at £10 a week, it was hardly a career, but he never forgot it.[5]

(II)

Through all the connections Dad was making, things started to move fast. Once the adventure on the *Queen Mary* was over, he dedicated himself to getting as many paid gigs as he could. After he returned to London, he was offered a regular club gig down in Bournemouth and it was during this period that he met and fell in love with my mum. She had two daughters but wasn't happy in her marriage and was about to get a divorce.

Dad eventually had to break the news to his parents that he was going to marry a Gentile girl with two small children. He figured there would be a terrible fuss, as in his family no one had ever married outside of the faith. For a son to marry out was particularly upsetting for Jewish parents, as under Jewish law, children take the mother's religion, not the father's. His family were not particularly orthodox, but they did uphold all the traditions. As a child, he had of course followed suit, but after the age of about sixteen, with music dominating his thoughts, he just hadn't been as bothered. His brothers and sisters were good Jews; they observed all the feast days, the Sabbath, and on the whole the dietary laws. Dad wasn't really doing any of that, plus he didn't see anything wrong in mixed marriages, but then

---

[5] My first trip to New York with my own band Cocteau Twins was, by contrast, quite a let-down. I got mugged down near 42nd Street on the night we landed and I spent the rest of our week there in the hotel room, too anxious to go out.

he'd never been that big on religion. It wasn't as important to him as it was to the rest of his family. He'd always imagined he would get married when he found the right person, when he fell in love, and her race and religion was of no consequence to him. In their heart of hearts, his family all knew what he was like. They were already prepared for the news when he sprang it on them.

Dad and Nita got married as soon as they were able. Ivor did his best to provide for Mum and her two daughters, Gail and Linda.

By 1955, all his recent networking and friendships with other arrangers like Wally Stott and Reg Guest seemed to be getting him somewhere. They would all look out for each other and if a job came up that one couldn't do, they would pass the information on to the others. In this way, Ivor was commissioned to write the signature tune for a new TV series *Great Scott – It's Maynard!* . . . starring Terry Scott and Bill Maynard.[6]

This led to a friend of Dad's from the television series putting him forward to play the piano on a TV advert for Black Magic chocolates. He also suggested it could help him get an Equity

---

[6] That makes me smile now because in the early '80s there was a sitcom called *Terry and June* with the aforementioned Terry Scott and June Whitfield. They play a middle-class married couple living in suburbia. When my brother Nick and I would visit Mum and Dad together at weekends in their own middle-class bungalow near Woking, on the way home we always referred to them as 'Terry and June'. Dad didn't really look that much like Terry apart from his little belly, but Mum was the absolute spitting image of June Whitfield.

card as he'd heard word that they might well ask him to appear in the ad itself.[7]

Ivor's exploits in his early thirties became of great interest to me when *I* was in mine.

In the early 1990s, I was a *huge* fan of old black-and-white American TV shows like *The Honeymooners, Car 54, Where Are You?, The Phil Silvers Show* with Sergeant Bilko and our British shows like *Hancock's Half Hour, The Prisoner* and *Callan*. I'd tape them off the TV and take them to our studio for Robin, Elizabeth and I to watch if we had some time to kill.

The Hancock show began on radio in 1954 and ran until 1959 before it switched to TV. It starred the comedian Tony Hancock playing a version of himself. I joined the fan club (the Tony Hancock Appreciation Society), and even had a special leather binder with 'The Lad Himself' on the front, with all the newsletters inside. Proper anorak. Still got it actually.

---

[7] After much digging, to my absolute delight I found this ad recently on YouTube and there he is, around thirty years old in a tux, sitting at this white grand piano playing the theme, looking like a proper Charlie. Fantastic.

Search YouTube: 'Rowntree's the Old Black Magic I Knew I Had to See You Again 1960'.

The Ivor Raymonde Orchestra also released 'It's the Real Thing' on Coca-Cola Records in 1971, which is an orchestral instrumental version of the New Seekers' track that was being used in the TV ad campaign. I had no idea about it until 2001 when DJ Shadow and Cut Chemist used the breakbeat from that Ivor Raymonde Orchestra single on their *Product Placement* album. In rather an odd coincidence, Cocteau Twins wrote two jingles for Coca-Cola in the '90s for a new drink they were launching called Fruitopia. Us and Kate Bush composed the music for a series of thirty-second commercials.

The Hancock show was pioneering for the BBC. Written by Ray Galton and Alan Simpson, who also created *Steptoe and Son*, it centred each week on the surreal life of one Anthony Aloysius St John Hancock of 23 Railway Cuttings, East Cheam. Tony is an out-of-work actor who is convinced that he's far more famous than he really is. His character is crabby and pompous. He is out of touch with the world he sees around him. I lapped up every episode I could find. The fact that in real life Tony Hancock had some major demons, and was crippled by nerves and stage fright, made me appreciate the show even more, knowing that the shows back then were all recorded live.[8]

I bought a book on *Hancock's Half Hour* that I found in Foyles bookshop on Charing Cross Road that listed every episode, all the cast and a summary of each show.

One night in 1993, I found myself lying in the bath digesting as much of the Hancock arcana as I could, in particular *any* facts about the episodes I hadn't yet been able to find. In the fanzines I subscribed to, there were always people trying to sell you VHS copies of rare and out-of-print episodes. While scrolling through all the info for one of these hard-to-find shows – '*The Tycoon 6/11/59 recording at Studio 1 Riverside Studios, broadcast 13/11/59, audience 11.2 Million*' – I did a double take:

'*Tony's Barber: Ivor Raymonde.*'

---

[8] Elizabeth suffered badly with stage fright. I did too to a lesser degree, but while I tried to be a tough guy and not show it, most nights I would heave and gag in the bathroom minutes before we'd go on. I never really enjoyed being onstage as much as I would have liked to because the nerves were always too much of an obstacle to overcome.

What the literal fuck?

I looked again, and then at the previous episode, '*The Big Night* broadcast date 6/11/59'.

'*Man in Cinema: Ivor Raymonde.*'

By the time I had gone through the rest of the episodes listed in the book, the bathwater had gone cold. He had been in *loads* of these shows, and I hadn't known a bloody thing about it.

I desperately wanted to call him up to ask him about it. I wanted to know *everything*. But this was impossible. I called Mum instead.

Typically non-plussed and blasé about it all, she sighed and wearily responded:

'Of course you knew about it. Oh come on! You *all* knew about that, Simon!'

Mum wasn't someone you could contradict or argue with, and I knew better than to say what I was really thinking: ('*I think I would know if my own father was in* Hancock's Half Hour, *Mum! Jesus!*')

I didn't get much from her as you can tell, other than admonishment that I clearly hadn't been listening, but I set about seeking out every single episode that I could find that he had been in. Some of these very early episodes had been lost by the BBC and yet some collectors had VHS copies, usually in pretty ropy condition, but still I treasured every one, often watching them through tears, not always just from the emotion of seeing my old man up on the screen but in hysterics at the scenes. He would have been thirty-two, exactly the same age I was then. He was only an extra, sometimes with a very small speaking part, *always* in a deep, booming Cockney accent, and he was

definitely never going to win any awards for acting, but I loved
that I could find something else to connect me to my dad. I
treasure all those episodes to this day.

During the first three years of their married life, he was often
working round the clock: appearing in television shows, making demos for music publishers, singing and arranging for vocal
groups, playing piano for various gigs. Whatever he was asked
to do, if it was humanly possible to fit it in, he did it. In his early
years of breaking into music, he believed that when you were
offered work you should take it as it might not come around
again. But then when I was a child, he also told me to never do
a job that I didn't want to do! So I don't think he had it quite
as worked out as he thought. He was certainly making plenty
of money, but didn't see much further than the end of his nose.
Now with a young baby son Nicholas to add to the two girls, it
was Mum who finally suggested he might be spreading what talents he possessed too thinly. She told him he was driving himself
into the ground, and asked where it was all leading. What did he
really want to do?

*'That stopped me in my tracks. What I really loved most, I realised,
was arranging. The whole concept appealed to me; taking a song, cap-
turing its melodic structure, getting my ideas down on paper, hearing
the sounds in my head and later the ultimate experience of hearing an
orchestra of top-flight musicians bring all that to life. That was a
bigger thrill than anything else I'd ever done.'*

His first big hit had been 'Halfway to Paradise' by Billy Fury
in 1961, where he was musical director/arranger. This meant

that he would decide on the orchestration, the backing vocals, choose which instruments to use and ultimately determine what was eventually heard on the radio and on the vinyl record. The song remained in the UK charts for twenty-three weeks so it definitely put his name on the map. Once he established himself as a songwriter, musician, singer and an arranger, more work followed as a producer, and an A&R man too. But I think he did manage to take Mum's words to heart and during the next decade he became one of the UK's top arrangers.

(III)

By 1958, he found himself working with Johnny Franz at the Philips label. They enjoyed several number-one singles in the UK, working together with Frankie Vaughan and Marty Wilde with Dad producing and arranging. At this time, Philips was one of the biggest and most successful labels in the country and it was there that Dad's career as an arranger exploded.

Wally Stott, whose elegant arrangements Dad really admired, was under contract at Philips and when he was overloaded, he began asking Ivor to ghost arrangements for him, with the approval of Franz, passing 'B sides' on to him. This was great news for Dad as he would get a credit on the label irrespective of the songs' priority ranking on the disc. Arrangers generally don't receive royalties, but as your reputation and prestige mounts, so does the fee. When Dad first met him, Wally already had a string of hits to his name, including those with singer Frankie Vaughan – 'The Green Door', 'Happy Days and Lonely Nights', 'Garden of Eden' and 'Kisses Sweeter Than Wine' – but Wally was never particularly interested in the pop side of the business.

He preferred the more complex projects, and composition on a much grander scale. And much later, of course, he would work with Scott Walker.

Stott aimed to go freelance when his contract ran out, leaving the field at Philips wide open.

Being so in demand, Wally now had the freedom to pick and choose his jobs. But he was always generous with his time and took an interest in Ivor's progress.

Dad's first Philips artiste was Marty Wilde, Britain's newest teenage sex symbol. Johnny Franz had wasted no time in signing him up. Marty was also spotted by Josephine Douglas, the BBC television producer, who put him on their new pop show *Six-Five Special*. He became an overnight sensation. Wilde was a tall boy with a cheeky face, a snub nose and a deeply dimpled chin very much in the Kirk Douglas mould. With his backing group the Wildcats, he was precision-tooled for the teeny-boppers.

Alongside his work with Marty Wilde, the Springfields were a country folk band that Dad and Johnny were developing together. The growing interest in the group was due in large part to the voice and presence of lead singer Dusty. It became clear to everyone that Dusty was the next breakout star. After returning from Nashville where the group had recorded a number of lacklustre country and western ballads, and with her appetite for country folk dwindling, the Springfields as an ongoing concern never stood a chance. Simultaneously, while in the US, Dusty had been able to indulge her passion for R&B and soul, and as soon as she announced she was going solo, Dad and Johnny were bombarded with songs for her first single. But the song search would momentarily have to be put on pause as Dad took a break from work to be with his new son.

And like that, I am born.

Mum and Dad had rented a holiday home at West Wittering in Sussex. It had a garden that led directly on to the beach. It was intended to be our first real family break. Mum, Dad, me as a newborn, Nick my brother, now six, and our half-sisters Linda and Gail. But as he carried all the bags in from the car, he saw that the old house had an equally ancient piano in its living room, and he just couldn't help himself.

'*This piano, a collector's item rather than a musical instrument, made such a horrendous row that everyone within earshot headed for the beach as soon as I began to play. The keys were yellowed with age, it was completely out of tune, and the hammers so worn out that I had to bash the livin' daylights out of it to get any sound at all. But I just had to get this song out of my system, and by the time I'd played it several hundred times, I thought I'd got a winner.*

'*Considering the dreadful racket I'd been making, it was hardly surprising that none of the family agreed with me. They were not impressed or at all convinced. Regarding theirs as strictly untutored opinion, I simply played it some more, only louder. Stubbornness is a family trait and in this case, I refused to let myself be put off. Dusty and her debut single was always in the back of my mind as it was coming together and I think this must have sparked me off in the first place, because to be honest I'd done very little song composing throughout my somewhat varied career to date and here I was, suddenly filled with inspiration.*

'As soon as I got back to London at the end of the holiday, I rang Johnny Franz and made an appointment to see him and Dusty. I didn't have a lyric, but that was a problem easily solved. Or so I thought.

'A few months prior to all this, I had begun sharing some office space in Denmark Street with Mike Hawker, Jean Hawker of the Breakaways' husband. The Breakaways were a British all-girl vocal group who were the go-to backing and session singers of the time. They performed the background vocals on both "Hey Joe" by the Jimi Hendrix Experience and "Downtown" by Petula Clark. Living about twenty-five miles out of London, I needed a base in town where I could land between sessions, do some writing, and where people in the business could drop in to see me. Mike was a newly successful lyricist, having recently co-written "Walking Back to Happiness" with John Schroeder for Helen Shapiro. Even though we shared this space, we didn't really see much of one another. Mike was either writing or on the telephone. I was usually rushing to finish an arrangement or hurtling off to a studio. But it was a convenient set-up and it suited us both.

'When I was writing the song in Wittering, I had a little hook that I kept returning to. Songs about dances were very much the thing at that particular time, and the hook I had was: "I Only Want To Dance With You". That was all I had in the way of a lyric.

'So the following week in Johnny Franz's office, with Dusty standing next to me at the piano, I played the song through a few times, la-la-ing it all, except the few words I had for the chorus. Soon Dusty was moving about, getting in the mood, humming along with me. She loved to dance and was always hopping around when we routined numbers. She seemed pretty happy and so was Johnny. But what about *the lyric they wanted to know? Rashly, I promised to get Mike Hawker to write it. This was just what they wanted to hear, being well aware of his recent chart successes and we set up a further meeting for a week later when I assured them I would present the finished article.*

"'The dancing theme. I like that. Keep that going."

'Back in the office, I found Mike as usual, crouched over a pile of score paper. When I asked him to come over to the shared piano, Mike groaned. He was far too busy, he said.

'Mike was hot right then, with his Helen Shapiro record. Everyone wanted a Mike Hawker lyric. He listened to what I had written, said it was good, but didn't see how he could possibly come up with a lyric for it in under a week as he was snowed under.

'This was a bit disheartening. But I remained optimistic. I didn't ever consider approaching anyone else. As the days passed and nothing was forthcoming, I began to get a bit twitchy. Every time I broached the subject, Mike said he still hadn't done anything about it. It was no use pressuring him. I just hoped he would come through. At 7.30 a.m. on the morning of my deadline, Mike rang. He sounded exhausted.

"'I've got your lyric," he said.

'It's funny remembering it now. He dictated the words to me over the phone, and being a somewhat complicated lyric, it took a long time. As he painstakingly enunciated every word, I realised something very important was missing. The dancing theme had gone right out of the window. "I Only Want To Dance With You" had become "I Only Want To Be With You".

"'It's great, Mike," I said.

"'Really, it's a fantastic lyric. The only thing is, what happened to the dance theme?"

'Mike sounded weary and disinclined to discuss the matter. He'd been up all night, writing it.

'"It just didn't work out," he said.

'And that was that.

'The more I pored over Mike's lyric, however, the more I liked it. I didn't know what Dusty's reaction would be. As it happened, when I played it to her later that day, she never even mentioned the change. She didn't quibble at all, and neither did Johnny. The song suited her perfectly. "I Only Want to Be With You" would be her first single release.'

Ivor Raymonde, recorded in 1983

So, they recorded the single the following week. Dad brought twenty-six musicians into the Philips studio at Stanhope Gate, plus a three-girl backing group, and within a couple of weeks, this recording of 'I Only Want To Be With You' reached number four when it was released on 8 November 1963. A few weeks later in 1964, Dusty became the first artist to feature on the new BBC TV show *Top of the Pops*, opening the first-ever show with 'I Only Want To Be With You'.

Of all the great songs that she was to record during her career, Dad could never have imagined that it would eventually become *the one*. This annoyed her at times, certainly according to some of the press interviews I have read.

The song has attracted many singers over the years, and not just female. It's been recorded hundreds of times and been in the charts on six separate occasions, with six different artists: Dusty with her number four in 1963; the Bay City Rollers, also number four in 1976 (who slightly changed the title to 'I Only

Wanna Be With You'); the Tourists, number four again in 1979 (Dad's favourite version); Nicolette Larson – engaged to Andrew Gold – who came up with a typical Gold arrangement and got a US top twenty hit in 1982; and Samantha Fox, with a number sixteen hit here in 1989 produced by Stock, Aitken and Waterman. In France, a good friend of Dad's called Richard Anthony went to number one with his own version 'A Présent Tu Peux T'en Aller'.

Mike and Dad went on to write three more songs for Dusty: 'Stay Awhile', 'Your Hurtin' Kinda Love' and 'I Wish I'd Never Loved You'.

As her career took flight, Dusty was inevitably always linked romantically with someone, and at one point it was American songwriter Burt Bacharach. Dusty was to record many Bacharach/David songs. Her voice was *perfect* for their material.

'I was summoned to Johnny Franz's office to go through some songs with Dusty for a forthcoming album, and I was sitting at the piano with her when out of the blue, Johnny announced that Burt Bacharach would be dropping by shortly. He was in England, it seemed, placing some of his songs with various artistes, and wanted her to hear a song he'd written especially for her. It was a complete surprise. I'd always admired this genius, and now I was about to meet him. I was quite star-struck.

'There was a tap on the office door, and Johnny's secretary Moira – later to become the second Mrs Franz – announced the arrival of Mr Bacharach. He was indeed quite a striking man, charismatic, with unusual eyes, very American white teeth, and a burly build. As the introductions were made, I couldn't help also noticing he seemed

pretty loose; relaxed to an unusual degree, considering it was only around eleven o'clock in the morning.

'Burt was charming to me, complimenting me on the songs I'd written for Dusty, and of course I told him how much I admired his own numerous compositions. Being already at the piano, he suggested that I play his song. Naturally, I insisted he play it. Eventually, he agreed and sat down at the piano. The song was 'I Just Don't Know What To Do With Myself'.

'With a flamboyant and highly impressive introduction, he made a grandiose sweep of arpeggios from the bottom of the keyboard to the top, and to our absolute horror, fell straight off the piano stool on to the floor. Victor Borge couldn't have done it better and Les Dawson would have given his eye teeth to see it, but this was no comedy routine; this was for real.

'We rushed to pick him up, dust him down and make sure he hadn't broken anything. With profuse apologies he re-seated himself and played it over again beautifully, a song which was and still is, as we all now know, fantastic. Dusty recorded it later that year and it went to number three in the British charts. It was perfect for her. A truly great song by a brilliant writer. But I can't listen to it without remembering Burt's inimitable rendition that morning.'

(IV)

In my late teens when I first began frequenting record shops, I heard about Joe Meek and how ahead of his time he was, but there wasn't a huge amount of his work available other than singles in the second-hand shops.

In the '80s, I remember reading in the *NME* about Joe's bizarre death in 1967 when he was just thirty-seven. He had shot his landlady dead before turning the gun on himself. No one seems to know to this day exactly what happened, but the tabloids had a field day. Every aspect of Joe's private life was dug up for hand-wringing public scrutiny. Like his neighbour, the playwright Joe Orton, who also died in 1967 in similarly strange circumstances, Meek was persecuted for his homosexuality. When the Sexual Offences Act received royal assent in the same year, a moment that signalled the first liberalisation of the law to legalise sex between men, it was sadly too late for the two Joes.

Casually, over one Sunday on a family visit in the early '80s, 'Telstar' came on the radio in the kitchen as Mum was serving up lunch.

'Lovely man, Joe Meek,' he muttered.

'You knew him?' I asked.

'Yeah, I worked with Joe on a ton of songs in the '60s,' he offered matter-of-factly.

Who are you?

Dad said that some of those close to Joe had uncanny premonitions that he would die an unnatural death and certainly the circumstances surrounding that night were weird and inexplicable, in certain aspects not dissimilar to that of the late Marilyn Monroe. Because of this, Joe has become something of a cult figure. For good reason. As a producer he was a true pioneer, an innovator and way ahead of his time. He was one of the first British sound engineers to go out on a limb and set himself up as an independent operator outside of the big West End studios and he did this all in a tiny flat in Islington.

Robin once found himself in a studio with the dub maestro Lee Perry, and after the session described him as a 'mad genius'. Meek was too.

Although Joe was not exactly a household name at the beginning of the '60s, his 1962 recording of 'Telstar' with the Tornados changed all that. The record became a worldwide hit, and for a while at least was the most successful instrumental pop record ever made.

Joe had set up a studio in a couple of bedrooms in a flat over a leather goods shop in Holloway Road and was actually producing records from these most unlikely of premises, putting them out under his own label imprint (RGM), and flogging them to major record companies like Decca.

Eventually, all the majors were fighting to get their hands on a Meek production, which was surprising as he wasn't well liked in the business. He was a rebel and a successful one. But he was also a genius. It was all jealousy and envy.

After Telstar, Joe approached Dad about MD-ing one of his sessions. He already had the rhythm track laid down by his regular musicians – the boys who would subsequently become the Tornados, and the group who backed Billy Fury: Clem Cattini on drums, a friend of Dad's called Alan Caddy on guitar, George Bellamy on rhythm guitar and Heinz on bass guitar. Joe would ask Dad to augment his track with strings, brass and sometimes voices.

'The first time I visited "The Bedroom" as I called it, it was a revelation. I had to laugh. The set-up comprised two rooms: the front bedroom which served as a studio, and the back bedroom which was his control room, with a door in between the two. The approach was up a flight of narrow stairs, and these needed to be negotiated with considerable caution, particularly on the way down. Loose carpet and

missing stair rods could cause an unexpectedly rapid headlong descent, resulting in concussion or broken limbs. The whole place was a tangle of wires, electric cables, reels of partially wound tape, strewn records, out-of-date equipment, and bits and pieces that seemed to have been assembled by a mad scientist. The soundproofing consisted of egg-box packing and strips of carpet tacked over windows to cut out light and noise. There was an antiquarian piano propped against a wall, which he eventually replaced with a Lowrey keyboard, and the echo system, so I understood, was concealed in the bathroom. In spite of the complete lack of modern recording equipment, he had made a rather touching attempt to give the place an air of authenticity. It was inspirational and fascinating to think that from this tiny, scruffy top-floor flat with its apparently cobbled-together sound system, Joe was producing records that had the whole industry buzzing.

'He would play me a tape of his backing track, tell me what he had in mind for it, and ask my opinion. Did I feel three violins and a cello would be good, for instance, or some other combination? If he wanted some brass, he'd suggest a tenor saxophone or a horn maybe, and again ask me if I thought that would be good. He usually liked strings to follow the melody line. If he wanted backing singers, it might be just one girl or more usually three or four girls, or two girls and two boys. In the early half of the '60s, there was a certain format when deciding the line-up for pop records; rhythm section, strong string sound, horns, trombone or saxes. Joe Meek used the same formula, but it was what he did with it after we'd all gone home that made the difference. Having got the general picture from him, I would take his tape, go away, write an arrangement, book the musicians and singers, and on the appointed day, up we'd all troop to The Bedroom.

'The strangest thing about my collaboration with Joe, I guess, was that never did I know who the artiste was or even the title of the song. The voice would be put on at a later date. When the record was finished and about to be released, he would send me a copy, and only then would I found out what I'd been involved in. He played his cards very close to his chest.

'He was good about paying everyone and was very complimentary about our input. He always asked how I wanted my name to appear on the label, and that's how it would be done. I wish I could say the same for everyone I worked for. It was amazing how often one's name "accidentally" failed to appear on a record label in those days. Not much use making a fuss after a record has been released, unless you enjoy lawsuits.

'As I was never there when he did the mixing, exactly what he got up to I've no idea, so it's only guesswork. But I often saw him edit tape, which he did by cutting it in mid-air with a pair of kitchen scissors in seemingly the most haphazard fashion and then join the bits together again where he wanted. No editing blocks, no modern aids at all. It looked most alarming, but he knew exactly what he was doing. It was just a natural instinct he had.

'There were always rumours about his terrible temper but I never saw it. Once I'd written an arrangement, he let me get on with my job without further interference. Maybe he was on his best behaviour, but I think he liked the kudos of professional session people working in his much-maligned makeshift studio.

'The only time I saw him show any kind of temper was with his own backing group. He got a bit cross when they tossed their cigarette butts and ash all over the place. I suggested it might help if he bought a few ashtrays. The next time I went up there, several large ones were in *evidence, and notices on the walls: "ALL MUSICIANS WILL USE THE ASHTRAYS PROVIDED".*

'One thing I did ask of Joe was that he would get his group to tune their instruments to the Lowrey organ before laying down the backing track. They weren't too fussy about tuning in the beginning, and it had caused me some problems. From then on, another notice went up: "ALL MUSICIANS WILL TUNE THEIR INSTRUMENTS TO THE LOWREY BEFORE RECORDING".*

'Sometimes during a session, he'd come flying out of the control room and shout at his group, "DON'T DO WHAT YOU THINK! DO WHAT IVOR TELLS YOU!"*

'In the winter months, it was absolutely freezing up there. The musicians had to keep their overcoats on. If they'd been able to play wearing gloves, they would have done that too. I said to Joe one day that he really ought to put in some form of heating, and the next time we went, there were portable heaters all over the place. He always kept us well supplied with tea or coffee and biscuits, and we'd have these sitting downstairs in his front parlour, which was furnished with a few easy chairs and some coffee tables. He ran round after us in fact, making sure we were quite happy, pretty chuffed with his "studio facilities".*

'I've no doubt in my own mind that the reason Joe was so delighted with the work I did for him was that after struggling for hours on end to get a result with his own largely inexperienced musicians, we would go in for just one three-hour session and he'd have three or four titles completed. This was a luxury he couldn't afford in his early days, but once he'd had a little success, he was very keen to improve the quality of his records. And I think he craved the respect of the "legit" element of the business. The expression "genius" is perhaps too loosely applied these* *days, but I would certainly have no hesitation in using it to describe Joe's extraordinary talent.'*

Ivor Raymonde, recorded in 1985

(V)

As the twenty-first century progressed, I started to collect as many of the records Ivor was involved with from anywhere in the world. A real passion project. As an insomniac, late nights sitting at my computer, discovering a new gem that I'd never heard of, was my way of trying to get to know him better through this musical connection we had. It was *our* secret language. Song by song, night by night, he was sharing his skills, telling me stories, helping me piece together the puzzle of who my father was, one that had eluded me for so long. His death had left me with a blurry, out-of-focus monochrome image, and now finally there was definition and some colour.

The volume of work I would keep discovering was astonishing. I would type 'Ivor Raymonde' into YouTube and then just keep on scrolling. Pages and pages of versions of 'I Only Want To Be With You' (the metal version by Volbeat, currently at 14 million views, is one of my favourites), reams of Dusty and Walker Brothers stuff until maybe on page 156, some mad obscure B-side would come up that had 129 views. Yes, THIS was the magic right here. Then I would head straight to Discogs and try to track a copy down on vinyl of this rare find in mint condition.

After a while it struck me – obvious really but I can be a bit slow on the uptake – that I should, because I *could,* release a proper collection of his work on vinyl on Bella Union.

Paradise: The Sound of Ivor Raymonde Vol I,[9] which came out in 2018, was all put together lovingly with the help of a good friend, the writer Kieron Tyler. Kieron, also a music historian and specialist in reissues, helped me acquire all the rights and wrote most of the words in the booklet. We worked with Bella Union's art designer Luke Jarvis on the design, and I think we produced a really beautiful package.

It made me so happy to be able to show a new audience what a brilliant career he had. To give life back to a lot of songs that hadn't been seen or heard in a long while. And, perhaps most importantly, to show how inspirational he was for me.

A year later, aware that we hadn't even scratched the surface of his catalogue of work, I decided to make *another* double album. *Odyssey: The Sound of Ivor Raymonde Vol II* was released in 2019.

---

[9] The track listing is here:

'Halfway to Paradise' – Billy Fury; 'I Only Want to be With You' – Dusty Springfield; 'He Doesn't Love Me' – The Breakaways; 'He Knows How to Love Me' – Helen Shapiro; 'Giving up on Love' – Sonny Childe; 'Black is Black' – Los Bravos; 'Love You Till Tuesday' – David Bowie; 'Make it Easy on Yourself' – The Walker Brothers; 'Mylene' – Ivor Raymonde; 'Chahawki' – Burr Bailey; 'Little Lonely One' – Tom Jones; 'He's Sure the Boy I Love' – Cindy Cole; 'Jealous Heart' – Ottilie Patterson with the Ivor Raymonde Group; 'Your Hurtin' Kinda Love', Dusty Springfield; 'I Got the Feeling', Dave Berry; 'Now It's My Turn', Jon Gunn; 'I Love Her', Paul and Barry Ryan; 'Grotty', Ivor Raymonde and His Orchestra; 'Beautiful Friendship', Barbara Ruskin; 'Sueperman's Big Sister', Ian Dury and the Blockheads; '(I'm Not Your) Stepping Stone', The Flies; 'It's the Real Thing', The Ivor Raymonde Orchestra; 'Wait By the Fire', The Majority; 'She Sold Blackpool Rock', The Honeybus; 'I Found Out Too Late', Alan David; 'My Ship is Coming In', The Walker Brothers.

I thought that this equally fabulous package should have a beautiful photo of my mum on the front. Mum had passed away in March 2018, a few months after *Paradise* came out, and it was my way of showing not just how important she was to his career, but to mine too. He died in 1990 and in those twenty-eight years before her own death, she never went out with another man. I asked her about that a few times.

'Why don't you ever go out on a date, Mum?'

She would always say the same thing: that no man could come up to his standard so why bother. She had gone on a couple of those solo Saga cruises with the idea that *maybe* she could find a little romance, but she said all the men she met were just after one thing. She did conclude by saying that should I ever find myself on a cruise – unlikely as I hate ships and boats and being at sea – that if there is an upside-down pineapple or a pink flamingo pinned to or hanging on the door, it means that the inhabitants of the cabin are up for a bit of swinging. Quite why she thought that might be information I had a need for, I have no idea.

I found it sad that she felt no one could compare to him, but at the same time, I totally understood the essence of the sentiment. After Cocteau Twins broke up, I didn't want to be in another band. It took me twenty years to get over this idea that 'no one is going to be as good as Elizabeth, so why bother?'

Researching this second volume of Ivor's work, I made a critical discovery on that last page of Google before you don't get any more suggestions. My eye was drawn to this particular result because it was a .pdf file, not something you see in that many searches.

It turned out to be a ten-page document with hundreds of columns, numbers and text. It was a log from Decca Studios spanning 1960 to 1967. Column A listed catalogue numbers, Column B the song titles, C the date of the recording, and D the names of *all* the protagonists who were in the studio at the time of the recording.

Dad had worked at Decca exclusively from 1965 for a couple of years as A&R/producer.[10] Dick James had offered him this role as a way of allowing Dad to bring his own projects into the studio and to give him some structure now he was a dad to four kids. Ivor wasn't sure about it initially. He had worked so much with Johnny Franz at Philips on Dusty, the Walker Brothers, Marty Wilde, Frankie Vaughan and Susan Maughan – as well as with other producers at other labels – that restricting his work to *one* label seemed risky. But the offer of stability was of course more attractive and he went with it.

This document I had found was really something. Not only did I discover which sessions Dad was on, but also how many

---

[10] Dad was always a classy whistler, and in 1967, during his time at Decca, he adopted the pseudonym of Whistling Jack Smith for a record he and his colleague Noel Walker dreamed up called 'I Was Kaiser Bill's Batman'. Written by Roger Cook and Roger Greenaway and adapted from the original version called 'Too Much Birdseed', it became an earworm hit, getting to number five in the charts and staying there for twelve weeks. Dad said it was 'irritating'. Although some sources claimed John O'Neill was Whistling Jack Smith, Dad was the whistler on the record, but he did not go on television once it became a hit. The actor Coby Wells mimed on *Top of the Pops* and subsequently appeared as WJS on tour.

tracks were recorded and which ones were given full Decca catalogue numbers but then never actually made publicly available to buy. When I was growing up, all my demos were on cassette, but in Dad's day, demos from studios like Decca would always end up on acetate, a thick lacquered vinyl, only really suitable for a few plays and never available for sale. Today you might hear them also described as dubplates.

This discovery was like seeing his actual work diary for his whole time at Decca. It was like unearthing a holy ancient parchment.[11]

The last track on this second compilation was 'Where's the Girl' by the Walker Brothers. A month or so after Ivor died in 1990, I drove down to see Mum one day, and 'saw' Dad on at least three occasions. There's nothing stranger than seeing someone you just cremated a month earlier walking down the street. But it got weirder still. I was alone in the car and had Radio 4 on at low volume in the background, a repeat of an episode of *Desert Island Discs* with boxer Joe Bugner as the 'castaway'

---

[11] 'Little By Little', Dusty Springfield; 'Simon Smith and his Amazing Dancing Bear', Alan Price Set; 'Brand-new Baby', Los Bravos; 'Don't Ask Me to Mend Your Broken Heart', The Eyes of Blue; 'Wearing A Smile', The Chants; 'That Other Place', Susan Maughan; 'The Way of Love', Kathy Kirby; 'Blackness of the Night' Cat Stevens; 'Odyssey', Paul Slade; 'Tower of Strength', Frankie Vaughan; 'Time to Say Goodnight', The Martells; 'Please Stay', The Cryin' Shames; 'Pretty Paper', Roy Orbison; 'Swingin' Low', The Outlaws; 'Chain Gang', Ronnie Carroll; 'From Me to You', Del Shannon; 'Loo-Be-Loo', The Chucks; 'Tequila 68', Olé Jose and the Golden Leaves ; 'Memories of Missy', The Rogues; 'Endless Sleep', Marty Wilde and His Wildcats; 'Thursday Morning', Giles, Giles and Fripp; 'Michael Hannah', Twinkle; 'Girl in the Mirror', Christopher Colt; 'I Feel Lucky Tonight', The Stylistics; 'Where's the Girl', The Walker Brothers.

guest. At the exact moment I passed by the doppelgänger for Dad, host Roy Plomley asked Bugner which of his choices would be the one song he'd be allowed to take on to the desert island. Joe picked 'Where's the Girl' by the Walker Brothers, and as it played, even though I had never heard it before, I just *knew* that those beautiful strings and harp were arranged by Dad. I slowed down and pulled over just as it began to pour. One solitary tear scribbled my cheek as raindrops ran clear across the windscreen. I wasn't sad.

An obsession with Scott Walker was born that day. It seems that so many moments of great significance in this life of mine are signposted and soundtracked by Scott's music.

It took me a long time to make peace with losing my father. I never told him how much I loved him until he was on his deathbed and unable to hear me, and it took me thirty years to realise that I didn't need to always be trying so hard to make him proud of me. It's not the worst thing to use him as a yard-stick, but I have spent a lot of this life asking myself, 'What would Ivor do here?'

Now I don't ask that question so much.

CHAPTER TWENTY

Bella Union: Early Years

Following the collapse of the studio and all our possessions being taken by the receivers, Robin – who had made a fist of being involved in the label for a while – and his French wife Florence moved to Rennes, and I picked up the baton.

I dropped it quite a lot in the next few years as I struggled to cope with running a label with no experience, but thanks to some amazing friends who helped me fathom it all out, Bella Union somehow survived. Pete Townshend, our landlord, kindly let us stay in the building for free for a while until we worked out what we were going to do.

Like it or not, the label had to be the focus now, and while I was still working it all out slowly, we continued as best we could to keep putting out the music that we loved. The reception to the debut album by the Czars had been pretty mixed. A few journalists adored it. Most didn't acknowledge it. I didn't pause to worry about it and moved on as best we could. I believed in John Grant and felt that we just needed to stick with him.

The second Czars album *The Ugly People vs The Beautiful People* was recorded and mixed in the beautiful city of Denver, Colorado in 2001. When we arrived, it was midwinter and thick snow covered the ground. With the Rocky Mountains to the west and the High Plains to the east, the views from the city are breathtaking. Giles and I once more reunited for co-production duties and were excited to be here, especially given that our studio back home was no more.

The album was another step forward. John's position as a really unique songwriter was developing fast and the harmonies he was unsure about a couple of years ago were now seemingly effortless.

Those first two Czars albums were deemed by many as altcountry, Americana, sitting in some dusty corner of our global record shop along with Lambchop, Smog, Whiskeytown, Ryan Adams, 16 Horsepower, Handsome Family and many others. I feel there are limitations in this type of description, but regardless of what I think, the sad truth is that neither album broke through in the way they should have, and that was massively disappointing to me, and no doubt to John.

I was not going to give up on him though. I knew people would wake up to his gifts sooner or later, and in 2004 we released the third album *Goodbye*, John's thinly veiled rejoinder at not just the end of his band, but the heartbreak at the death of a personal relationship that he had invested so much in. Listen to 'I Am the Man' and 'Trash' for two of the album's best spite songs. Irresistible country-esque tones inhabit 'Paint the Moon', which was a minor radio hit here in the UK.

Goodbye had some wonderful press, and I hoped its reception might provide some comfort to John. I could see that things were very difficult for him at the time and yet I was struggling with my own stuff and wasn't there for him as I should have been.

Artistically, the label was getting better and better but was still losing more than £100,000 a year. My marriage was over. I had just been diagnosed with the brain tumour. And I was totally deaf in one ear. And whilst I tried to put on a brave face, I was a mess inside. I found myself often sliding out of focus. I tried seeing a therapist, but I couldn't get on with that at all. I took every session as a competition and resented the invasion. I tried dating, thinking that might help, but I was too full of negativity to be much use to anyone.

As the Czars' final chapter was approaching its conclusion, a new storyline was slowly developing, one that would later have a significant impact on the John Grant story.

Every March, I would head to Austin, Texas for a festival called South by Southwest. It was quite unique in that it was mostly for unsigned and unknown bands from all over the world to play a showcase for an international audience. The attendees were a mix of the general paying public and the music industry, but when I first came in 1998, only a few people from the UK were aware of it. I have barely missed a year since.

I first saw Denton locals Lift to Experience in Austin, whereafter I quickly signed them. A few years later I was back again for SXSW and Lift to Experience drummer Andrew Young told me I should go and check out *another* Denton band called Midlake.

I fell deeply for this band. Hook, line and sinker. I connected with them immediately and I believe it was reciprocal. I loved the demos and duly signed them in 2003. When they delivered their debut album, I was thrilled with the music. Everyone was. Strange and compelling. Not really like anything else, but with *flavours* of other artists we all loved like Mercury Rev and Flaming Lips. And in singer/lyricist Tim Smith, they had someone very special. One of *those* voices. When the band eventually sent the artwork and the title over, however, we were all a bit bemused. Perhaps a little disappointed. The album title was *Bamnan and Slivercork*. It didn't roll off the tongue. The artwork was equally odd. There were some noises in the office that we should see if they would be open to a new title and new art.

I did partially broach the subjects delicately but just didn't feel that this was the right way to start the relationship − by squashing their creativity and putting restrictions on what we thought was acceptable and what wasn't. I told everyone that we should let this go. I remembered our own Cocteau Twins artwork discussions and debates with 4AD, and I felt this was the time to be supportive. In hindsight, I can't regret it. And while I still don't love the title or the sleeve − I think that they *were* possibly a minor obstacle − the album *was* liked; most notably in France and Norway where Jean-Daniel Beauvallet at *Les Inrockuptibles* and Claes Olsen at the Øya Festival in Oslo were both significant advocates in those early days when, to be honest, any support at all is a welcome boost.[1]

---

[1] The actor Jason Lee had contacted me to profess his love of Cocteau Twins and we met up in Austin when he happened to be filming there while I was at SXSW. Through our connection and his fondness for discovering new music, like me he grew very fond of Midlake and offered to direct a video for the Dentonites. His film for

Pre-Drowning Craze, 1979. Paul Cummins on guitar and Adam Peters on keyboards. (Adam arranged strings and played cello for Echo and the Bunnymen during the *Ocean Rain* sessions in 1984.)

After Drowning Craze, Paul and I had a short-lived band called Wild About Harry. We didn't record anything, but we played one show. This is a rare shot from that gig.

Tiffany's Newcastle in April 1984 with support from the incredible Felt.

Right: I had just turned twenty-two and this was my first show in Liverpool at Mountford Hall, within the University of Liverpool.

Below: Dad and I in his garden in 1985, West Byfleet, Surrey.

In a hotel room with Ray Conroy our erstwhile tour manager in Japan, 1985.

Soundcheck in Japan, 1985.

Dressing room, Japan, 1985.

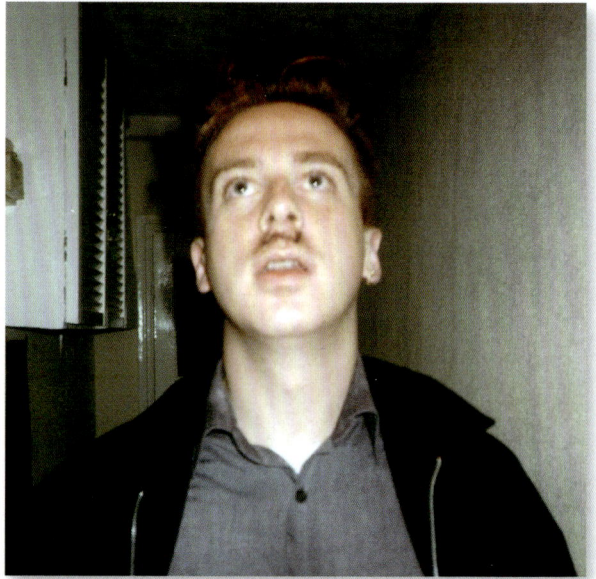

A few days after getting glassed in a pub in Shepherd's Bush, London.

Japan '86 with Vaughan Oliver (above) and Ray Conroy and Lincoln Fong.

Above: Heaven or Las Vegas tour, Detroit 1990.

Left: Recording Robin at September Sound.

Below: I have no memory of this at all...

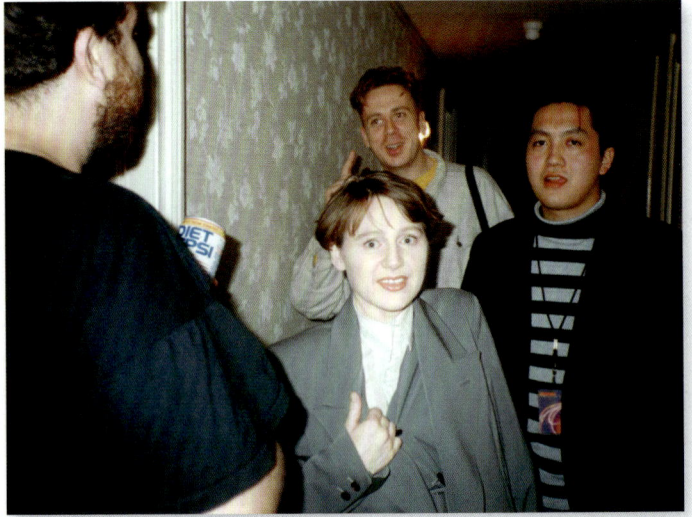

In an unknown hotel in the US, 1991.

Brazil, April 1991.

September Sound, St Margarets, near Richmond.

Stan (*Milk and Kisses* T-shirt) and Will in Menorca in 1996.

Mum and me in 1997.

Left: The adorable John Grant in our original vinyl shop in Ship St Gardens, Brighton, 2017.

Below: The magnificent beast that is Bodhi.

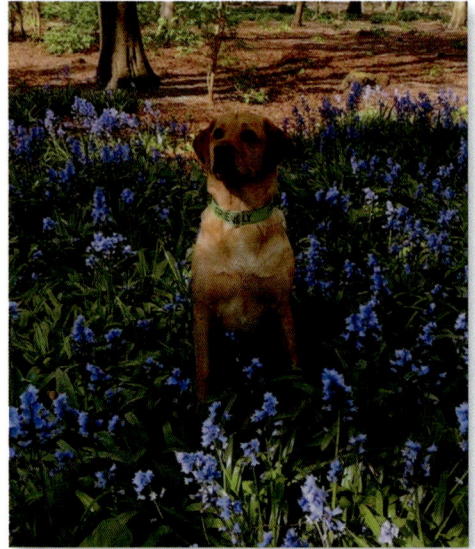

With my Ivor Novello 'Visionary Award' taken outside 4AD by Fiona Glyn-Jones in 2022.

As for any reticence I had over art and title, I figured that 'the music will shine through'. And with an equally strange album title and sleeve for the *next* release, the band's quirks would simply become part of their make-up and their character.

The band were making this beguiling music themselves in their own space in Denton, on a limited budget and on equipment that was not state of the art. When I received the first rough mix from the second album, I was sitting at my desk in our new label offices in Church Street in Twickenham.

I used to sit by the window with my pack of Marlboro Lights and would puff away while staring out on to the cobbled street below with my headphones on, blaring into my one useful ear. The office was on the first floor, and we had about six desks in there; Fiona, Duncan, our in-house head of press, Mark Byrne, who initially came on as Duncan's assistant, Pete Hill, Johnny Brocklehurst, Paul Trueman, the brilliant Anne Müller and me. To round it off, we had a revolving chair of assistants and interns who all in their own unique way contributed greatly to these difficult early days.

So, it was one sunny late afternoon in spring when I lit a fresh cigarette and pressed play on the MP3 that had just arrived in my inbox from the boys in Midlake.

'Balloon Maker' was strange and wonderful, just like the band. I was to play a significant part in Jason's life a few years later when he came over to London to celebrate our tenth anniversary at the Royal Festival Hall in London. A friend from Australia was also over in the UK for a modelling assignment. I invited her to our event. Jason texted me after the show, asking for her phone number. I sent him her number and it makes me very happy that they have four children together and have been together ever since that day seventeen years ago.

The cigarette burned all the way down to my fingers without me taking a single draw on it. As the song finished, I turned around to look at everyone in the office. Some beavering away on their PCs consumed in their work with headphones on, some wandering about the room on the phone, others making tea at the sink. All oblivious to the glorious music I had just been privileged to hear. I pressed play again. I needed to listen again. I needed that feeling again.

Anyone who works in the arts where the job is, in its purest essence, to develop and nurture young talent, will know that the hope is always to see *some* progress from project to project. In music, I know well that some artists develop incredibly quickly over a year and others take a few years to get where you want them to be. Some of course *never* get there; that's the gamble and that's life. When I heard the rough mix of 'Roscoe' by Midlake, I *knew*, there and then, in my head with no one else's opinion needed.

I waited a few minutes until everyone was back at their desks, took my headphones off and played the song again on my speakers. After a minute, Duncan, our head of press, whose desk was opposite mine, looked up from his computer and said quizzically and enthusiastically, 'Is that a new Midlake song?'

More songs started to arrive over the next few weeks. We could all tell that this was in a different league to *anything* we had released up until now. It may not have been recorded in a fancy studio with a 'name' producer, but to this ear, it sounded like it cost a million dollars.

The Trials of Van Occupanther eventually proved to be our most successful to date in this our first decade – 40,000 copies in that first twelve months – and without doubt it also directly influenced the band Fleet Foxes who would release their debut for us a couple of years later in 2008.

Back at SXSW earlier that year, I was with Laurence Bell, a very nice gentleman who owns the label Domino Records. We were having a heart-to-heart about how impossible the business sometimes seems and how close you always seem to be to a near-disaster. I had co-produced James Yorkston's debut album, some tracks with Archie Bronson Outfit and an album by Clearlake, all for Laurence at Domino, and even though the fees I received were tiny, almost shockingly so, I was happy to do the work and still saw Laurence as a shining light in the independent label scene in the UK. I asked him how he remained positive when the chips appeared to be down.

'It's all about the eleventh year,' he said cryptically.

'What do you mean?' I asked.

He smiled, kindly.

'You'll see. Once *you've* been in business eleven years, something will happen. In *our* eleventh year, I was here at SXSW when I got a phone call telling me that Franz Ferdinand's debut had just sold its millionth copy – 2004. So that's it. Just *hang on* until your eleventh year.'

Our eleventh year?? Well, that's like . . . next year . . .

With Beach House the year before, Midlake *and* Mercury-nominated Fionn Regan all releasing brilliant albums but *still* only scratching the surface of what Domino's Franz Ferdinand achieved, I went into a slow spiral of depression. This was then accelerated by not one but two huge financial disasters that

I am still not quite sure how we recovered from. Whether it was genetic stubbornness, those beatings at school, the collapse of our studio, bankruptcy, my beloved band breaking up, 9/11, divorce or people just telling me 'you can't be friends with your bands!', I had developed a very thick skin and a determination to prove everyone wrong.

When the chips are down, I subconsciously adopt a kind of 'will not be beaten' mentality.

First up, our distributor Pinnacle suddenly went bust, owing us more than £100,000, and within a year our licensing partners in Europe – V2 Records – *also* suddenly went into administration owing us a similar amount.

We are totally fucked, I thought.

Just before these seemingly fatal body blows were dealt, I was invited to Øya Festival in Norway by the owner Claes Olsen who had championed Midlake that first year they signed to Bella Union. On the first night, we were sitting at the boathouse on the banks of the Oslo fjord, surrounded by happy smiling faces. I was trying my best to have a nice time but was just overwhelmed by a feeling that I had utterly failed with the label. Being physically, as well as mentally, away from the office maybe gave me a little space to have some much-needed perspective. The stress of keeping the label afloat, ensuring all the staff were paid each month, all the bands' royalties settled and our office rent covered was causing me increasing ill health and too many sleepless nights. I was in and out of hospital with stomach problems and then a burst ulcer, so I viewed this trip as much recuperative as reflective.

However, as I looked out across the still water, a stark contrast to the churning of my feeble insides, I thought that maybe the best thing for everyone would be for me to knock the label on the head and try something else. I'd given it my best shot and we had some incredible bands, but without enough money left over after making the records to market them as effectively as I wanted to, we would only ever get *so* far. We could get to 40,000 sales with a band like Midlake but never had the resources to turn that into 100,000+. I went up to my bedroom thinking maybe I wasn't as good at this as I had kidded myself I was.

Before I fell asleep, I went on to MySpace on my laptop and checked my messages. I had something from the US booking agent Trey Many, whom I worked with on Beach House. He sent me the link to a band he had just seen in the US; it was only their third show, but he said he thought I might like them.

I was about to close the laptop and just be done with it, but out of habit I clicked the link that took me to the band's page. There was just one demo, a song with only a handful of plays.

It was called 'White Winter Hymnal' by Fleet Foxes.

It was the slap around the face I needed. By the end of the first play, I knew that *this* was what I was meant to do. I decided there and then, that if I *didn't* sign this band, I would stop doing the label. I listened to it at least fifty times more into the early hours of the morning, whilst writing a love letter to the band.

On once-beloved MySpace, there was a facility for sending a message to the band you were listening to. A little blank box appeared, and I introduced myself. A little bit about me and the label and the bands we worked with, and then mostly gushing about the music. It was quite a long gush. I didn't pause to edit or reread it once I had finished, I just pressed SEND.

I slept soundly for the first time in a long time.

When I woke up around 7 a.m., I already had 'White Winter Hymnal' echoing around my sleepy head. I jumped out of bed, opened up the laptop and saw that I had a new message.

It was equally long. I figured that was a good sign. Once my eyes had begun to fully open and focus, I read the response.

The only feeling I can relate this to – which I guess explains the 'love letter to the band' – is when I find music that affects me emotionally, physically *and* spiritually – *my* holy trinity – the feelings *are* comparable to those early dopamine moments you get in the first throes of a romance.

Singer Robin Pecknold replied to say that he knew and loved the label *and* my old band, and that he was 'also in Norway right now visiting the birthplace of his ancestors with brother Sean and sister Aja, and would love to meet up'.

I mean, fate isn't something I subscribe to, but this crazy coincidence did knock me sideways for a minute.

So, Robin and I did indeed arrange a meeting, and we got on famously. And so the courtship began. We talked often and shared many similar feelings about the business and loved many of the same artists. When he sent me the finished album, it was better than anything I could have imagined. Yes, 'White Winter Hymnal' was still beautiful of course, but the quality of songwriting, Robin's voice and the musicianship across the whole album *and* first EP 'Sun Giant' were exceptional. Initially there was only one other suitor, Hardly Art, a subsidiary label of Seattle's legendary Sub Pop Records. I made Robin Pecknold an offer to release his next two Fleet Foxes albums in Europe. I think I offered to manage him as well; I was that smitten. Within a couple of months, I heard rumours that Sub Pop themselves had come on board also wishing to sign the band, as well as a few other labels now expressing an interest. Once the frenzy to sign a band escalates, I usually lose interest, but this time waited eagerly for a response to my offer. I had invested such a lot of emotional energy into this. The depth of feeling I had about the band was intense.

I woke up one morning to an email I had been dreading. The gist of it was 'I *would* love to work with you, but Sub Pop have made us an offer for "The World", and don't seem willing to budge on that. They're not *just* a great label, but they're local to where we all live and it will keep everything simple and under one roof I guess.'

I felt a hollow forming in the pit of my stomach. I immediately replied, writing without pausing.

'Hi Robin, I totally understand why you would feel that, and it makes a lot of sense of course. Nice and easy, one contract, one signature, one set of people to deal with, an office you can pop into anytime you like. I get it, I really do. If I was in your shoes, I am sure I would feel and do the same. But I do want to say this before you finally sign off on it and I am really only saying this as a "friend" or even as an "artist to a fellow artist", rather than "some dude at a record label" who is trying to twist your arm to do something:

Sub Pop is one of the best US labels, no doubt about it.

But they don't have a European set-up like I do. I've been there as a musician when you arrive in a city in Europe where you know no

one and don't speak the language. Just having a team on the ground to
collect you from the airport, take you to the radio station, take you out
for some food etc., makes such a difference to the experience of being on
tour. Sub Pop don't have such a set-up, but I do. Teams in every major
city in Europe, and Japan and Australia too. I believe that Fleet Foxes
will be adored here, and I just want you to enjoy that experience and not
feel in a couple of years that you missed out. That's it really. It would
be such a shame if the album didn't get the exposure it deserved. But
listen, you know what I think of you, Robin, and I couldn't be more of
a fan of your music. I know that whatever you ultimately decide, I will
still be your number-one fan here in Europe, and support you in any
way I can, from near or afar. Your friend, Simon.'

I went for a very long walk with Molly, my yellow Labrador, my
'therapy' dog. But I was still thinking that if they signed with Sub
Pop for 'The World', I may not have the strength to continue.

The following morning, I received an email from the band's
lawyer, with a signed contract attached and a cover note to say
the band would be delighted to sign with Bella Union for the
UK and European territories. I didn't know whether to, but I
laughed *and* cried at the same time.

We released the self-titled debut by Fleet Foxes in June 2008,
and from the very first moment, the love for this band was at
a different level to anything I'd seen before. Their first-ever
London show quickly sold out at the 250-capacity Hoxton Bar
and Grill following the buzz that they created at SXSW a few
months earlier. It was a great vibe, but less than a month later
they were playing at ULU, University of London Union, capacity
800, again sold out in no time at all. As the room began to fill up,

this palpable sense of anticipation grew in the crowd, an almost religious fervour. But I gradually realised a most remarkable thing. At most Bella Union gigs I attended, I would recognise a lot of the same faces, and the audience would be generally white, beardy, thirty-to-fifty age group, but tonight, the whole world was represented within the tiny sphere around me. A young gay couple holding hands, an old man and his wife, women of all colours and ages, teenagers, hipsters and, of course, lots of beards and beanies. And as the band walked onstage to the most rapturous welcome, I thought to myself, *OK, this is new. Something is going on here that I haven't seen before.*

The album got off to an incredible start at press, and while radio took a little time to warm up, the sales were increasing day by day. And as we approached the winter, with significant showings in the end of year 'Best Of' lists, a whole *new* wave of sales happened. We began to spend heavily on the marketing of the record at retail and within the print press.

There were a couple of crucial moments that changed the course of the prevailing winds.

In early December, I was having a meeting with our team when our label manager Stuart Giles from Pinnacle, our distributor at the time, got a call on his mobile. I looked over as he was talking and noticed that he was slowly turning a whiter shade of pale. He returned briefly to explain that this very morning, while 50,000 copies of the Fleet Foxes debut album were in a van on their way from the manufacturers to the distributors' warehouse – the first stop on their journey into the shops, homes, hearts and charts – Pinnacle had gone into administration. He turned, mumbled something and then was gone. My heart was just with Stuart and all the fine people at Pinnacle that we had become so friendly with over the past year.

With inspired quick thinking, one of our team, Vincent Clery-Melin, the boss of our label services company Cooperative Music, realised that if that van continued on its journey and delivered its cargo, the receivers would 100 per cent impound them and we would lose all that stock and in the process hundreds of thousands of pounds, and the band would certainly not have charted that week. Vincent made an urgent call to someone he knew in logistics and somehow found the driver of this van and diverted it to a different warehouse. Miraculously this action ensured we were still able to chart the record the following week.

Tiny margins.

The collapse of Pinnacle did still result in us losing more than £100,000 that they owed us, but thankfully Vincent and I were able to pull together a deal in a matter of days, and the full transition to Cooperative Music was relatively smooth and no sales were lost.

In addition to the self-titled album, the band had a stand-alone EP that we had released called 'Sun Giant' which was also selling in vast quantities. There was a song on the EP called 'Mykonos', which over the summer of 2008 was fast becoming such a big tune at their live shows that it was clear to me that if we were to keep the momentum building through to the end of the year and into 2009, *this* was the track that we needed to get 'playlisted' at radio. There was one big problem, however. 'Mykonos' was *not* on the album. Radio would *not* support a track from an EP while in the middle of an album campaign.

Our head of marketing Jason Rackham had an idea. If we could package the album *and* the EP together in one convenient double

CD case and have a sticker on the front that said '*Includes* the singles "Mykonos"', etc., we might be able to get away with it. Radio might 'buy' it. But first I had to get the band to agree to it. I figured the only way to explain it properly was in person, so I flew out to Zürich that day where they were due to play a show. I knew it was possible, even understandable, that Robin would fight it, as in one sense it could be seen as a bit of a crude marketing ploy to get around the rigidity of how UK radio works. I explained to him that the design of the 'new' CD package would be exactly the same as the album, so to all intents and purposes it would *look* identical, but just have a sticker on the front saying, 'Deluxe Double CD edition, includes the singles "Mykonos", "Your Protector" and "White Winter Hymnal", plus the "Sun Giant" EP'. To my surprise and delight, Robin agreed immediately.

This meant that we could now go to radio with the message that here is the 'new single "Mykonos" from the new Fleet Foxes album'. Which was technically true, just maybe a little bent.

Radio bought it. We went on to the A-list at BBC Radio 1 (unheard of), A-list at Radio 2 (impossible), as well as the A-list at BBC 6Music. I couldn't believe this was happening.

Over the next few months, we went from silver to gold to platinum, then double platinum here in the UK and more than a million records sold across Europe. It easily became our biggest selling album. The knock-on effect of the success of the debut album by Fleet Foxes no doubt led to us being able to sign artists of the calibre of Spiritualized, Flaming Lips, Mercury Rev and Patti Smith.

Yep. A million records in our eleventh year.

Laurence Bell is clearly some kind of fucking crazy wizard sage.

The follow-up album *Helplessness Blues* was released in the spring of 2011 and since their debut three years earlier, I had met and married a beautiful American woman, Abbey.

But I'll come to *that* soon.

We both felt pretty close with Robin, his sister Aja who managed the band, and brother and visionary film-maker Sean. All the momentary anxiety about what I was doing with Bella Union before I heard that one Fleet Foxes song 'White Winter Hymnal' in Oslo back in 2007 was long gone, and the relationship between everyone at the label and Robin had grown into something special, like it had with all our artists. I had even met the Pecknolds' lovely parents several times over the years. After the album campaign for *Helplessness Blues* finished, Robin, Sean and Aja all came to our wedding in Carmel, Monterey in March 2013. The next day, Abbey and I drove to Big Sur for a couple of days' honeymoon, and unexpectedly met up with them all again as we decided to drop into the Henry Miller Memorial Library. This wonderful non-profit arts centre had been almost totally destroyed the night before during a wild storm when a huge redwood tree had fallen just inches away from the building. It had still wrecked so much of the surrounding grounds. As we got out of our car, burly lumberjacks with plaid shirts and safety helmets were cutting the sequoia wood into huge slabs and selling them at the top of the drive in a bid to raise money for the museum. The foreman invited Robin and I to cut one of the slabs ourselves with their massive double saw. After thirty minutes of hard graft, we had cut a beautiful slab, the size of a whopping great conference table. I think each slice was selling for about $7,000. They scribed our initials on it in chalk, 'SR/ RP' and perched it up against the wall on the roadside with a 'FOR SALE' sign. So if anyone *has* that piece and is eating dinner off it right now, *that* was cut by Papa Fleet Fox. I can't say that would make it worth any *more* than $7,000 as that seems like a shit ton of wedge for a bit of ragged wood, but California has some mega-rich folks so who knows where it ended up. It was a lovely spontaneous unplanned moment and as Abbey and I drove off to enjoy the rest of our honeymoon, all felt very right in the world.

So, I can't deny it hurt like hell – and still does – when Fleet Foxes returned a few years later after an extended break and Robin chose to leave Bella Union for the major label Warner Brothers. The reasons he cited publicly were not the same as those he gave me privately.

Listen, Cocteau Twins left 4AD for Universal. Bands leave labels all the time. I have no problem if any band wants to leave for a plausible reason, if they're unhappy with us, or if they have an offer of significantly more money elsewhere. In fact, I encourage it; no sleep needs to be lost if things aren't working. I understand why things can fracture between artist and label better than most. But it was for none of these reasons. They *loved* being on the label and it was a hugely successful relationship. We would have given them any amount of money that they wanted. So, when it happened, in the way that it did, via an email, it felt like a massive kick in the teeth. I really fooled myself into thinking they were our friends. I fought it and tried to get Robin to reconsider his stance, but it had no impact. The anger and disbelief I felt initially has dissipated over time and been replaced by a small bubble of sadness that floats forlornly in the pit of my stomach somewhere.

Had there been any contact from Robin in the intervening years just to say, 'Hey, sorry for what went down, but thanks for your part in our story,' etc. I would have welcomed it. Been comforted by it. Knowing and understanding that even though artists are often sensitive and complex people, sometimes decisions are made from the heart not the head. Or vice versa. But not one word has been forthcoming. Does that sour the experience of working with them during those two albums? Thankfully not. I learned way too much invaluable stuff. About myself, trust, friendship and about working as a label at that higher level. And the success Robin's music brought the label is something of course I am eternally grateful for. But I just can't listen to their subsequent releases with the same open heart as I would have done before. Robin is one of *the* great songwriters of his generation and our part in elevating and nurturing that status is something I value highly.

I thought it might affect how I operated the label in the future, in terms of getting too close to the artist, but it hasn't changed that much. I can't really do this kind of work without having a genuine connection with the artist, and while I don't expect it always to be perfect, it is one of the foundations of the label. I know it is a 'business' but it is also my *family*, so the feelings are always going to be strong when things go well, *and* when they don't.

CHAPTER TWENTY-ONE

John and Josh

Around the time Fleet Foxes were exploding, circa 2008, I was talking to the lovely Midlake boys – the two Erics, McKenzie and singer Tim Smith – about their next album plans and they mentioned they had heard that our mutual friend from the Czars, John Grant, wasn't doing so well. A discussion followed between John and the band, the gist of which was:

'Hey, friend, we love you. We have always enjoyed playing shows with you and you're amazing. Why don't you get out of New York [where John was working, translating Russian medical dictionaries into German], come to Denton, Texas for a few months, you can couch surf with all of us and we can help you make a new record in our studio?'

This beautiful gesture from one of our bands to another sums up Midlake as people, perfectly. Generous and kind, and full of love. There was already a musical mutual respect, so John flew down to Denton, and over the next few months lived on and off with various members of the band. During the day, while Midlake were in the studio making their third LP for us, John would be writing lyrics at the house, then in the evenings they would work with John in the studio on *his* songs. Occasional nights off would take place at one of the local Denton bars where he would play the old school arcade games and drink his beloved Diet Coke. The Midlake boys clearly adored John and the recording sessions were pure joy for them. They were finding their own album stressful to make. The songs were sombre and full of melancholy, and relationships a little strained, so I can see why the sessions with John seemed so free of pressure and blissful to be part of. Eric Pulido told me a lovely story of how they would do their vocal warm-ups with him by all singing ABBA's 'SOS', John at the piano.

Eventually Midlake finished their own album, the expectation high after *The Trials of Van Occupanther*. I loved it. If *Van Occupanther* was colours, it would have been green and russet. *The Courage of Others* was monochrome. It was like going from a summer drive along the Pacific Coast Highway with the rooftop down listening to your favourite songs on the radio, to then suddenly finding yourself in the cloudy icy terrain of eastern Oregon in winter.

The Bella Union office had now moved from Hammersmith to Hackney, on Oval Road where, after receiving the new Midlake LP, I arranged to play it to *Mojo* editor Phil Alexander, a fine young man who had been very supportive of the label over the last few years. He seemed to genuinely like what we were trying to build.

'Do you remember that Denver band, the Czars?'

I explained to Phil the broad strokes of what Midlake had been doing at their studio with John Grant and started playing him a track called 'TC and Honeybear'. He listened intently.

The song ended and Phil shook his head.

'That is one of the best things I have heard in a *long* time.'

'It's no big deal but how about I do a little ten-minute Q&A with John on the phone soon, and we could put it in the next issue. Just like a little square inch on one page. Nothing major but a nice little bit of pre-release blurb? Get things moving?'

We set John and Phil up to chat on the phone a couple of weeks later.

'It was just like a big old therapy session for John,' he told me.

'He's just an amazing guy. Brutally honest and full of emotion, but also terrifically funny.'

Yeah. He is *all* of those things.

In February of 2010, *Mojo* overtook *Q* magazine as the biggest-selling music magazine in the UK, selling around 100,000 copies a month. Phil's enthusiasm for John Grant could not have been better timed.

In the April 2010 issue of *Mojo*, John Grant's *Queen of Denmark* album was their 'Album of the Month'. Out of nowhere, an artist who was in such a dark place barely six months earlier, who was not on *anyone's* radar anywhere, was now receiving the press attention his huge talent deserved. For his debut solo record. By the end of the year, it had beaten Arcade Fire to the number-one spot as *Mojo*'s Album of the Year.

If I had to pick just one story from our twenty-five years in business, this one gives me the warmest, fuzziest feelings inside, a beautiful story in both its inception and reception. Midlake's contribution would of course have attracted a certain interest in the album to begin with, but it was that *Mojo* interview and subsequent album review that lit the blue touchpaper for everything that has happened to John since then. He is dearly loved by so many people. His honesty as an artist, delivered with his notable wit and intellect, is unyielding. As a solo artist, finding your *sound* can be elusive. And it should never be definitive. John has a curious mind and is an adventurer. He is always experimenting and never resorts to settling for the thing that comes easiest. There are parallels with Scott Walker in that they both have that 'voice' – the velvety croon – but more so that neither are afraid to fuck with the convention.

As I say, John's story is perhaps the most significant of all in the long Bella Union history. Not just because we still continue to work with John to this day on all his brilliant music, but more for the love and friendship that bonds us all.[1]

* * *

Around 2007, shortly after Midlake's *The Trials of Van Occupanther* had begun to weave its magic spell on so many of us in Europe, I signed the artist J Tillman after receiving a tip-off from Brian at

---

[1] Fiona, initially Cocteau Twins' manager's assistant and Bella Union's first-ever label manager, is also now John Grant's *and* Elizabeth Fraser's manager. It makes the fuzzy even warmer.

Western Vinyl, at the time one of my favourite small independent labels in the US.

I sure am a sucker for a beautiful voice. A lonesome tune with sparse backing. More melancholy than you can shake a mood stick at. And J Tillman records (and this was I think his seventh) hit all my buttons. I had high hopes that Josh could become a big part of our second decade.

After Seattle's Fleet Foxes debut was released, they set off on their first headline tour in the US, which saw original drummer Nicholas Peterson abruptly leave the band. Josh Tillman, also living in Seattle at the time, was meanwhile dating singer Robin Pecknold's sister/manager Aja and, as fortune would have it, he was not *just* a brilliant singer/songwriter but also a fantastic drummer. The rest, as they say, is history.

Having sat behind the drums night after night, watching this phenomenal band in front of him grow into one of the world's most-loved and cherished groups, Josh no doubt decided that for his own sanity and fiercely creative mind, he needed to ditch this temporary stand-in drummer job and resume his own music-making which, after all, he had selflessly put on hold since he agreed to help Fleet Foxes out back in 2008. It had been a great ride. Josh's dark humour and playful mind was a great onstage foil for Robin's oft doleful demeanour. No doubt to my mind, the range and power of Josh's voice was also crucial in their development as a mighty live band. Anyone who saw them between 2008 and 2011 will attest to this.

Within every story there is always a ton of other subplots, many of which have no bearing on anything much. But every now and then, as with the John Grant/Midlake hook-up, a collaboration just clicks and immediately bears fruit.

In 2011 as Josh was leaving Fleet Foxes, I signed an artist called Jonathan Wilson to release his album *Gentle Spirit*. It was adored by the music press. Jonathan and Josh met that year and decided to work together on the new music that was now pouring out of Josh like a dam had burst. With Jonathan as co-producer with his own studio in Los Angeles, Josh had found his perfect partner. Josh had felt like he needed a whole reset and what was coming out of these sessions with Jonathan had really very little in common with the sound and style of his previous 'J Tillman' records.

It took the world a little while to catch up and get their head around his new sound and this flamboyant onstage personality. Social media – exploding around this time – was a gigantic playground that a man of his intellect and playfulness couldn't resist to visit. The reverential attitude of artists and labels to the might of media entities like Pitchfork – due I guess to the perceived power they had in breaking or destroying bands – was of little interest to Josh. Instead of engaging with them, he sneered at the folly of the whole construct of music journalism. Interviews were funny, obtuse, bizarre but never anything less than entertaining. If his music had been mediocre, I am sure this would have been viewed simply as attention-seeking by somebody who couldn't back up the talk with talent. But the albums were staggeringly good. The sincere folkster J Tillman was now writing songs as Father John Misty where *he* was the target.

The whole 'Who Is Father John Misty?', 'Will the real Father John Misty please stand up?' trope was rife initially. Josh simply responded, 'It's all of me and none of me, and if you can't see that, you won't get it.'

I Love You, Honeybear (2015), his second, was a huge break-through album. His performance of the first single 'Bored in the USA' on *The Late Show* with David Letterman sparked that huge viral buzz that blew the whole thing up. Abbey and I had flown over to New York for the taping of the show at the famous Ed Sullivan Theatre in midtown Manhattan. It was an astonishing performance, one that managed to trifle with the convention of showmanship *and* the artifice of performance, whilst simultane-ously delivering such a beautiful heartfelt rendition. It showed the world that this was a unique talent, blossoming live on the most-watched late-night TV show in US. It really was a moment.

Until this point, for many he was just 'the drummer guy from Fleet Foxes'. But to all of us at Bella Union, here was Josh Tillman, the artist we fully believed in.

A lovely man with an incredible gift and an insatiable appetite for songwriting. That is a dream combination right there.

CHAPTER TWENTY-TWO

Montreal

My girlfriend Stephanie Dosen and I had decided to end our relationship earlier in 2011. We'd been together for about five years and worked on a lot of music together and enjoyed every second of it. But I think that we both realised just after we had finished our Snowbird album *Moon* that love wasn't quite there in the way we both needed it to be. She returned home to Wisconsin and we parted as great friends.

After we broke up, I figured that I should just stop trying to find someone to share my life with. I was fast approaching fifty years old, overweight and bald. Since I broke up with my wife Karen almost ten years ago, I had gone out with a number of beautiful and special people. After Stephanie, I figured that if I couldn't make it work with her, then I should just give up entirely. I am happy enough on my own, I thought. As long as I have a dog.

About six months later, I was invited to the M for Montreal festival to speak on a panel. I flew to Quebec excited and keen to see some new bands.

I hadn't been to Montreal since 1994 when Cocteau Twins played the Metropolis on the *Four-Calendar Café* tour. Four years earlier, when we played the beautiful Église St Jean Baptiste, the church was lit that night by a thousand candles. It was something to behold as the flames flickered gently between the balustrades and reflected softly on the stained glass.

So to be coming back to Quebec after such a long break felt good. When I arrived in the hotel lobby, some people I knew were getting ready to head off to the welcome dinner across the road.

The restaurant had long tables and chairs laid out and folks were getting settled in. Feeling brave, I decided to go and meet some new people that I didn't already know and walked over to a table with a couple of spare seats and sat down.

I got chatting to the woman next to me. Her name was Abbey. And before I realised it, the place had emptied out and there we were still gassing away with the staff already wiping down the tables and clearly hoping we would hurry up and leave. We wandered over to one of the venues to watch some music.

That night as I lay in bed I couldn't help thinking about Abbey. I had a word with myself. *C'mon, don't be daft. You're here to work. You're not looking for a 'holiday' romance. Behave and go to sleep.*

As I opened my eyes in the morning, she was the first thing I thought of.

The next few days we spent almost every spare minute together. Record shopping, eating meals, going to gigs and panels together. When the festival was over, I was heartbroken to be leaving. Abbey lived and worked in Manhattan, and while she had indicated that we would see each other again soon, I wondered really if it was ever going to work. She was a brilliant live concert photographer and also had her own two-hour daily radio show for Virgin Mobile, while my work was centred in London where I was needed to look after the label and all our bands. I also had two young boys back home so I accepted that the more likely scenario was that it would peter out naturally, too stressful and expensive to maintain.

But I couldn't stop thinking about her.

I flew to New York to see her a couple of weeks later and as I was preparing to go home, I asked her if she would like to come to Australia with me. Fleet Foxes were playing three nights at Sydney Opera House. I had never been there before, so what better opportunity to spend some more time together?

We had a magical time. On New Year's Eve 2011, five weeks after we first met in Montreal, we were staying at this lovely romantic cabin on the beach and I had decided a few days before I was going to propose.

When you know, you know, right?

I asked Abbey half-heartedly if maybe we should go for a little stroll on the beach before bed, trying very hard to give nothing away, but she just wanted to stay in, so I played it cool and put the ring I'd bought back in my pocket. I'll have another go in the morning I thought.

Knowing she would be invigorated after a lovely sleep, I tried again in the morning to suggest a little wander before we had to leave.

'I'd *love* to but I've got to pack if we are going to leave on time!'
Maybe I needed to be less subtle.

But try as I might, there was not one moment in the next few
days that was perfect for a proposal. So remarkably I returned
home to England with the ring still in my pocket and not on her
finger.

In February, she came over to stay, and thankfully the next
moment I got to propose on Valentine's Day, she accepted.
I told her about the aborted attempts in Australia and she was
mortified. I remind her of this as often as I can when she needs
time to pack a bag.

Over the next twelve months, we spent as much time together
as we possibly could. I'd go and stay with her in New York for
a few weeks at a time and a couple of months later, she would
come to London for a few weeks. It felt easy and real. I didn't
like being apart from her at all. We would *definitely* make it work.
My kids loved her instantly, her natural warmth and genuine
interest in them and, to be honest, I knew they would. Since
breaking up with their mum, I know they just wanted their dad
to be happy and they could see that I was.

The travelling back and forth was never tiresome because we
knew we would be together again soon.

In that year leading up to our wedding in March 2013 and
following a glorious couple of years of transatlantic to and fro, a
chain of events started that saw things get very dark, very quickly.

Driving back home to Twickenham one day, around the
back streets of Chiswick, sitting in slow-moving pre-rush hour
traffic, I saw a motorcyclist approaching fast behind me in my

driver's door wing mirror. He momentarily disappeared from view until I saw him sliding along the road past me with the bike some yards behind.

I turned off the road, pulled up and ran over to him to see if he was OK. I could see through his helmet that he was very young, but he wasn't moving. I stayed with him, in the middle of the road, talking to him constantly, while I called 999. Two people started running towards us. Strangely they turned out to be connected to him. One was his sister and the other a friend of the family. They had been driving behind my car and saw the whole thing unfold. I stayed with them, trying to remain positive until the ambulance finally arrived. He was put on a stretcher and driven away. The medics were lovely. They reassured me he would be fine and as they'd spoken to the sister who had veri-fied that no one was at fault I could probably go. But if I *wanted* to wait, the police were on their way and I could give them any details they might want.

I waited. Felt like the right thing to do.

Two police came and we had a brief chat about the accident. They had spoken to the ambulance. Broken leg. Not great but nothing more serious.

They said they would need to run a check on my vehicle just as a matter of procedure.

One went back to their police car and returned a few minutes later.

'Have you got insurance on this car, sir?'

'Yes. I am with Liverpool Victoria.'

'Our checks suggest that the vehicle is not insured.'

They ask if it's possible that I had cancelled my insurance and if I could call Liverpool Victoria.

I ring them. They explain that as I hadn't responded to their letter about renewing, the policy had expired.

As you can then imagine, lots of confusion and irritation about not having received the letter, followed by profuse apologies for my genuine error, and an offer to immediately renew there and then, so that I was fully insured moving forward.

The police then explained that as I *was* driving without insurance at the time of the incident, it would have to be reported. At worst, a driving ban but probably just some points on my licence.

I got the ban.

Six months.

I did appeal it, but the appeal was rejected.

Fuck my old boots.

The car would now have to remain parked off the road near the place I was renting in Twickenham at the time.

In 2003, Karen and I had split up after twenty-three years together. With our children just ten and eight years old, I made the decision to move out and rent a flat nearby. Karen had left her job doing graphic design and was training to be a teacher, so now would be in a precarious financial position. We were still pretty friendly as we wanted the boys to see that this needn't be a contentious, dramatic battle with them being pulled this way and that. It was agreed that they would live with her during the week except every Wednesday and come to me every other weekend. We sold the house, paid off the mortgage and then I offered for Karen to keep my share of the house sale to help set them up in a new place. It wasn't a difficult decision. She was a brilliant mum, and I needed to step up and make this work for the boys. I initially rented a small room at the top of a flat in Teddington, and then year by year moved around that area – a flat in Twickenham, one in Hampton – but determined to stay close to the children until they left school or home. I remained in this neighbourhood until ten years later when Will had left for university and I was dating Abbey.

Abbey and I spent as much time together as we could but she had a fabulous job, presenting a new music show on radio in New York. She would come and visit me for a few weeks and then I would go and stay with her for a few, and that's how it was. She was also a successful live music photographer, a passion with a *very* transferable skill wherever we might be in the world.

So although the wedding was fast impending, we had not been able to see each other for a couple of months. I was at home in Twickenham and Abbey was working as usual in New York. Originally the plan was to wed in Big Sur – her family were from California – but, blimey, what a racket that is. Stupid amounts of money that neither of us had just to erect some wobbly pagoda on a hill. We decided upon getting married at a small chapel in Carmel and with a reception in a hotel nearby after. It seemed perfect.

I had for a long time suffered with migraines, but recently they had multiplied in frequency and strength. I had my next bi-annual MRI scan for the brain tumour coming up so I was curious to see if this was related. Previously, a couple of pink pills would generally do the trick, but recently these migraines were of a different level. One morning I was barely able to get out of bed; my head thumping like it was being kicked by an angry elephant. Even just walking slowly to the bathroom was an ordeal. I was horrified to find that I had no medicine left in the house and somehow had to get to the chemist in town. It was only 500 yards from the house, but there was no way I could walk there. I was all over the place, felt sick and was desperate for something to ease this pain. *Fuck it*, I thought, *I'll just drive; I'll be there and back in two minutes.*

Before I even got to the end of my road, a police car (with 'This Car Is Fitted With ANPR' plastered on the side) pulled me over and even with this thick black fog enveloping me, I knew this was gonna be bad.

I was handcuffed and put in the back of the police car and driven off to the station while my car was impounded and taken off somewhere else.

Being arrested, and having fingerprints and mugshots taken, yards from your own home in broad daylight, where all my sons' friends' mums and dads lived, and in a community where everyone knows everyone else's business, where I had lived on and off for twenty years, wasn't how I saw this day playing out when I had woken up half an hour earlier.

I felt numb. All I could think about was the wedding and how it would all have to be cancelled. How disappointed Abbey would be in me. How disappointed I was in me.

What a total fucking idiot I had been to even consider getting in the car.

The shock of the arrest had taken my mind off the migraine a bit, but it still felt like a crew of carefree campanologists were merrily swinging their tuneless bells against the delicate insides of my head.

The police at the station were surprisingly kind, even sympathetic, and I think they swiftly realised that I was not a criminal mastermind. Not *any* kind of mastermind clearly, and once I had been fully charged with driving without insurance *whilst banned from driving without insurance*, I was eventually released on bail later that day.

Waiting for the court date was like a sentence in itself. I resisted telling Abbey immediately. I was just so ashamed of my stupidity and knew that the wedding and honeymoon was in jeopardy if the court hearing was delayed for some reason.

I found a legal firm who took my case on, and at the lawyer's suggestion procured some personal endorsements from friends and colleagues who submitted letters of support and testaments to my apparent good character. The lawyer was honest and frank with me and said the case was 50–50. If the magistrates wanted to make an example of me, I could get a prison sentence, but he was hopeful that the overwhelming support and clean(ish) record I had would swing it in my favour. The court date was finally sent through. If I got off, I'd make the wedding. If I went down, well, we'd definitely have to rearrange.

I heard Charles Bronson (not the actor) got married in prison. Twice! But I kept that to myself.

I felt sick for a full week leading up to the hearing. My brother Nick met me at the magistrates' court in Wandsworth in the morning for moral support. He was the only person, outside of the friends who had written letters, who knew about this incident.

I didn't go to jail.

I got 250 hours of community service to be served and a hefty fine. Abbey was, of course, kind, loving and understanding. Because she is.[1]

Over the next six months, my community service was served working in the mission's homeless shelter in Whitechapel. I'd cycle the two miles from my new flat in Hackney to Whitechapel Road for a 5.30 a.m. start. It was humbling and rewarding and I was grateful.

Every morning of the year, they would serve a free hot breakfast from 8 a.m., with showers and free clothes available to anyone who needed them. I was on a team of about five people who would make breakfast and serve, wash up and, sort out all clothes down in the basement. I would hose down the bathrooms and showers before leaving the mission around 11.30 a.m. I may have been feeling a bit sorry for myself when I first arrived, but hearing the tragic stories of so many of the folks who stopped into the mission every day made me realise how truly lucky I actually was.

'Don't accept your dog's admiration as conclusive evidence that you are wonderful.'

Ann Landers

---

[1] A year or two later at a family Christmas lunch, I came clean to the boys about it.

'Dad, we already knew! It was in the local paper!'

CHAPTER TWENTY-THREE

Brighton

From the moment I met Abbey in 2011, my life drastically changed for the better. Before Abbey, I felt that the label was in danger of sucking me dry. I wasn't making any music on my own, I wasn't producing much, and everything I was doing was for other people, although helping other people is something I'm quite good at. I've made enough mistakes, seen enough friends in bands *way* more talented than me disappear from music and seen the tragedies, so trying to stop anyone else make those same mistakes feels like the best way of paying it forward. And running an independent label, managing bands I love, putting out their records, connecting them with *other* great people that I have become close with over the years – be they publishers, booking agents, radio presenters, festival bookers or other labels – it's what I do best.

But I think it was beginning to take its toll.

311

I didn't have a balance. I was starting to wonder, '*Who am I?*'

Falling in love with someone whom I respected and admired, who was way smarter than me, who loved me for all the right reasons, and gave me the confidence to look after myself, my own happiness, my wellbeing, allowed me to gain the equilibrium I desperately needed. Abbey was the catalyst for everything starting to fall into place.

Moving out of London was our first accidental brainwave.

I can honestly say that I never considered leaving London. I just assumed I'd always be there. Spurs every other weekend, a new label office in London Fields, seeing my sons, friends, going to gigs, galleries . . . having spent all of my adult life there, it never crossed my mind to leave.

In fact, we'd recently moved the label office into this massive building in London Fields that Ed from Radiohead had purchased. He was looking to turn it into a kind of hive mind for creatives with studios, labels, publishers, filmmakers, artists, designers, PR all under the one roof. Ed is a lovely chap who had also played guitar on my Snowbird album in 2011 and he was keen for Bella Union to be one of the first businesses to set up there. The space was cool. Freezing in fact. Everyone put up with it for a while but working in thick coats, hats and gloves in the office when you're trying to type emails really isn't ideal. I bought a couple of those Dyson heaters but even when they were blowing warm air directly into your face, it made barely any difference.

By this time, I had also moved out of Twickenham into a beautiful little flat in Hackney on Morning Lane, a ten-minute bike ride to the new office. Abbey was still in New York, Will was at university in Bath and Stan was travelling in India so it made sense for me to be nearer to work. And then one morning I opened a letter addressed to 'The Occupier'.

The gist of it was as follows:

Dear Sir,

We are writing to you from the local council to confirm that the demolition order for the property at 89 Morning Lane is set for March 27th. We will be in touch in due course.

Yours sincerely,
Charlie Farnsbarn
Hackney Council

I reread it numerous times to make sure I was not indeed going mad.

Seething, I called the landlord who only a few months earlier had been happy to take a hefty deposit off me as I signed my one-year lease.

'What the fuck is *this*?'

'Yes, sorry, I was meaning to tell you about this, but figured it probably wouldn't be happening for a year or so. It will be in a couple of months and I do have a six-month contract break in your contract so yes, I will have to be enforcing that I'm afraid.'

From that day, forth my time in Hackney seemed to be jinxed.

The staff at the office were about to mutiny if I didn't get them out of the Arctic conditions.

My old Labrador Molly hated Hackney. I would take her out for a pee before bed to this patch of grass down the path by my flat, but unfortunately the other folks who were also on this path at midnight were not as friendly as me. I had a knife pulled on me once by a drunk lurking behind a bush. Molly was then bitten on her neck by some untrained and seriously aggressive dog and it seemed like every night I was just doing my best to avoid getting into a fight with someone or someone's dog. I quickly began to hate and despise Hackney and didn't look forward to coming home to my lovely little flat at all. After twenty years in leafy Richmond and its surrounding suburbs with parks full of deer, squirrels and strollers, I had clearly gone soft and was just not equipped any more for the intensity, unpredictability and competitiveness of daily urban life.

Fed up, I toyed with the idea of moving out to somewhere quiet like Suffolk where I had some good friends who all encouraged me, saying that the commute was easy and very doable, so I spent one afternoon looking at flats to rent and at the train times from London to Suffolk, but as I climbed into bed that night, I just wasn't feeling it.

So, with the clock ticking, and on a complete whim, I decided to get the train down to Brighton the next morning. As I walked out of the station, I saw the sea, and a thick black cloud moving mysteriously across the promenade. It was a murmuration of starlings, as customary a sight in Brighton as pigeons are in Trafalgar Square.

After seeing some nice affordable pet-friendly flats to rent, I opened the door to a café on nearby Western Road, and seeing several dogs inside, shut the door behind me. Molly was greeted with a friendly 'hello' and a warm smile from the barista behind the counter. *That's nice*, I thought. I sat up at the counter and looked around. The place was called Salvage and the vibe was that *everything* in the café was for sale, so even the stool I was perched on could at any moment be sold to a customer. It was full to bursting with antiques and interesting furniture. Old mirrors hung on the wall, an upright piano sat in the corner, a turntable next to a pile of second-hand LPs and a box of old sheet music and manuscripts. No two chairs were the same, there was a lovely old green leather Chesterfield sofa in the centre of the room, board games and books filled the shelves. It was curated by someone with excellent taste. The owner and barista was a chap called Tazz whom I immediately got on with. I moved into a flat a few days later and put the last few months behind me. Salvage became my regular spot and I went in there every morning with Molly for my coffee. It was full of great people. That first year I moved down, I guess it became my office.

And then, my studio.

Back in New York, Virgin Mobile shut down their US operations. Abbey would be joining me in Brighton. No more transatlantic commuting; we would finally be living together under one roof.

CHAPTER TWENTY-FOUR

The Flaming Lips

A mini-obsession with Denton, Texas took hold of me in the first decade of the twenty-first century when I signed Lift to Experience, Midlake, Mandarin, Jetscreamer and Robert Gomez. At that time, the total population of Denton was only 80,000. The University of North Texas is situated there and is the city's largest employer with around 7,000 staff. Its music courses are legendary, and a huge number of successful jazz musicians are alumni of UNT, like Bill Evans and Lyle Mays. Midlake all met there and were once a jazz outfit called the Cornbread All-Stars. I loved the community spirit in Denton and visited there whenever I could. If we took a few bands over to Austin's South by Southwest festival each March, we would try to detour to Denton, a couple of hours' drive, and play a Bella Union showcase event there with some of the Midlake boys involved.

It's not the same now, but in the early 2000s, it seemed to me like the city had a particularly unique make-up. It was an odd mix of old people and young people and with not much else in the middle. The young loved and respected the old, and the old loved to pass on their wisdom to the young. I found that charming and inspiring, a generational love fest that I couldn't see happening in the UK.

My fascination with Texas didn't end there, and in 2002 one of the *best* signings I ever made was the Austin band Explosions in the Sky, whom we still work with today. Abbey and I got married in Monterey and 'Your Hand in Mine' from their *The Earth is Not a Cold Dead Place* album was the song that Abbey walked down the aisle to. By the time she reached my best man Dave and I, we were all in floods of tears. That music is emotional enough even on a normal day, but on your *wedding* day, it probably wasn't the smartest choice. But I wouldn't have changed it for the world.

The story of Baltimore's Beach House is also an important one, not just for me, but for *all* young musicians. I first saw Beach House in Austin, Texas at a tiny Tap Room in 2006, the year we released their self-titled debut. They were a delight, hypnotic and enchanting. The album only sold a couple of thousand copies. The following year they came to London to play at one of our two tenth anniversary shows at the Royal Festival Hall, and then in 2008 we released the follow-up. Back home in the US where the band were based, the reception to and the sales of their second LP *Devotion* – released on Carpark Records there – were both significantly better than ours here in Europe. We had worked hard on the release but compared to the US, things just felt like they were stuck in second gear. The following year, they were due to play with Explosions in the Sky down on the big stage at the river shores in Austin, again at SXSW. With their minds beginning to think about album number three, they had asked me and Mark (their project manager at Bella Union) to come to meet them, to talk about things and maybe understand why things hadn't gone as well in Europe. Our two-album deal was now finished, and we heard 4AD were circling. Mark and I reassured the band that we absolutely adored them, our international team adored them and that they were really on the cusp of something in Europe. We dearly hoped that they would feel all that love and stay with us for the next album, to allow us to continue building what we had started. Being with them right then in that moment was important – to the band and to me. This wasn't just some email or text exchange. It was the least we could do.

All the credit must go to the band for believing in us. Now as we are in our seventeenth consecutive year of working together – and with Beach House our biggest selling artist – you can see that those early years were so crucial for developing and strengthening those bonds. Figures don't tell us everything, but Mark and I strongly felt that on their third LP, something would snap into place for them in Europe. And sure enough it did. *Teen Dream* became their breakthrough album and set them on a path whence they have never looked back. Every new release from Beach House is a gift that I will never tire of.[1]

Music as therapy.

* * *

---

[1] 'Space Song' from the 2015 release *Depression Cherry*, just hit its 1 BILLIONTH stream. For some perspective, 'White Winter Hymnal' from our million-selling debut release by Fleet Foxes has streamed 215 million.

Like me, Scott Booker used to work in a record shop in the 1980s, although his was Rainbow Records in Oklahoma. Back then he was also promoting small shows in Norman and Bricktown as well as Oklahoma City itself, bringing bands like Superchunk, Firehose and Nirvana to the state. When local band the Flaming Lips dropped a cassette into his record shop and asked if he would manage them, he initially said no because he didn't know the first thing about it, but the band persevered. In 1990 he relented. He remains in that post today.

Scott and I first started working together when he contacted me regarding a new venture he began in 2003 called World's Fair, a company that helped labels self-release. Bella Union wasn't yet established in the US but Scott was a fan of Midlake, as were the Flaming Lips, so we did a few things together before World's Fair collapsed as the fast-accelerating streaming culture trampled over every small start-up in its rush to global music dominance. Instead he set up a brilliant music college in Oklahoma City and became the dean. The dean *and* the don.

Scott and I kept in touch, and on one call he asked if I was a fan of the Flaming Lips. Even though signing and developing new bands had been my sole focus in the first ten years, this was mainly because I didn't have the cash or the CV to sign an established act even if I wanted to. In interviews over the years, I would often be asked, '*Who would be your dream signing?*' Once, without pause I said, 'Patti Smith.' Another time I offered, 'Kate Bush.' And after seeing the Flaming Lips for my fourth time at the London Forum in 2006, *they* would have been the answer.

Scott explained that Warner Brothers, who had signed the band back in 1990 after seeing them almost burn down the

American Legion Hall in Norman, Oklahoma, were doing a great job for them in the US but less so in Europe, and he wondered if ever a day came in the future where they *might* leave WB, who might be a good label for them in Europe?

I replied that of course it would be an honour to release their music on Bella Union.

Scott said he would think about it and obviously he still needed to talk to Wayne Coyne. But he had just wanted to hear what I thought about it in case it should ever come to pass.

And it did. Scott called after Christmas to say that they had discussed it and that Wayne would like to meet me. On the call he stressed one thing:

'Obviously I'd love it to happen as I think Bella Union is the perfect home for them, but you should know that if Wayne doesn't like you or get a good vibe, it just won't happen. Sorry to be so blunt but I wanted to be straight with you.'

In 2011, Scott, by way of mashing two potatoes with one fork, invited me to Oklahoma to do a masterclass at ACM@UCO. It was fun. Scott interviewed me onstage in front of a class of students. He asked me about running an indie label, being in a cult indie band in the '80s, stuff like that.

The other potato was for me to meet Wayne Coyne.

I don't usually get nervous meeting people no matter who they are, with the notable exception of footballer Chris Waddle, the former Newcastle, Spurs, Marseille and England winger. My old pal Pat Nevin knew my adoration of the skills of the Geordie and espied him at one of the PFA dinners that he'd invited me to. 'Oh, look, Chris Waddle. Let me go get him!!' I pleaded with him not to, but he sprinted up the grand staircase of the Dorchester ballroom when he saw Chris heading off into the night, and physically dragged him back down the stairs to where I was standing.

He introduced us and as Chris and Pat awaited for me to say something, my mouth just wouldn't work. My top lip had somehow curled up and got stuck on my gums and I just stood there silently unable to do anything, just baring my teeth like a sniffing horse.

A more uncomfortable silence I could not have imagined.

Chris shook my hand sympathetically. And then as quickly as he arrived, he was gone. *Great job, Si.*

If I could just get through my meeting with Wayne without baring my teeth at him, then I was sure it would be OK.

We met at a café in town. Wayne made quite the entrance. He walked in carrying a curious black box, holding it carefully like it was a new kitten and laid it on the table. He shook my hand strongly and welcomed me to his hometown, full of his own mix of nervous energy, enthusiasm and zest for life.

For the next half an hour, I listened intently to a most fascinating tale of the mystery box and its contents.

He had found a place in town that specialised in real and replica skulls and skeletons. He was after a real human skull, and while the shops' customers were generally from the education and research sectors, Wayne was able to use his formidable charms to have the shopkeeper go and fetch one from behind the curtain. The Lips' anthem 'Do You Realise?' was after all voted the Oklahoma State Song beating 'Heartbreak Hotel' in 2002, so I figured Wayne was pretty much like royalty around these parts.

The skull he purchased was laid out in this special carrying case, and I asked what the plan was. Was he collecting all the other body parts as well? He said he was working on something. We talked about brains, bodies, Native American burial rituals, everything in fact except music.

I left Oklahoma feeling energised. Wayne loves life as much as I love music. I thought we could do something great for them in Europe, but having been with Warner Brothers for more than twenty years, I didn't imagine for a second it was going to be an easy decision for him to leave.

In 2011, the band released a limited edition 'Gummy Song Skull' EP, a USB of music embedded in a cherry-flavoured gum brain inside a pineapple-flavoured gummy skull.

Ah.

In 2012, we released our first Flaming Lips release *Heady Fwends*, a collaboration collection featuring guests like Bon Iver, Tame Impala, Nick Cave, Erykah Badu and Jim James of My Morning Jacket. This was swiftly followed by 2013's *The Terror*, which was as bold a statement as they could have made: bleak, dark, experimental and electronic, unafraid to break the euphoric Lips model of the past, with its themes of anxiety and depression.

Abbey and I went to Austin to see the band perform the whole *The Terror* album live, a month before its release, on the Lake Auditorium river stage at SXSW. If the album was bold, the live show was even more audacious for a Friday night festival crowd. The audience was unprepared for the unrelenting mechanical beats and stark presentation, but watching from the side of the stage was an education in witnessing first-hand the awe in which this band are held. Wayne Coyne was centre stage, not in his usual big transparent zorb ball rolling out across the audience's heads, but now attached to a custom-built synth that was moulded into a prosthetic baby with illuminated umbilical cords shooting out of its body like tentacles. Working with an established band unafraid to take huge risks was exactly what I relished.

In 2020, we released their eighth album for us, *American Head*, which was rightly acclaimed as one of their finest albums of all time and was their best-selling album in the UK since 2006. Band and management were a sheer joy to work with, and no hesitation the Flaming Lips are one of my favourite signings to the label.

After working with an artist for a long time, hindsight allows me to look at the relationship in its entirety. By that point I'm not just measuring it primarily by how well the band 'does'.

Most album deals these days are one- or two-album agreements; in other words, once the band have delivered on their contractual commitment, they are free agents and can go elsewhere.

As a label, deciding to offer a band a renewed contract is not straightforward. If I and/or the staff find the band or a manager too difficult or obnoxious, we won't prolong the agony no matter how successful they are. It's never easy. If the artist is adorable but they have a manager who is rude, overbearing, impossible to please, then that's also a real dilemma. You want to carry on working with this artist, but you can see the damage this negative handler is having on all of the surrounding relationships. However close you might be with the artist, you cannot steam in and tell them what you think of their manager. I have wanted to do that more than once. Indirectly, there is *a lot* of damage they are doing to their artists' reputation, unbeknownst to them. Discretion forbids me to dish the dirt at this point, but it can go nuclear.

But they know who they are.

There are still a lot of thug managers in my area of the industry. Always male, always white, always misogynistic, always over fifty. They have either consumed way too much cocaine – or still do – and think that the best way to get results is to bark at people, and to belittle young women in meetings. Now those demographics do apply to me as well, including the cocaine part, so I realise the thin ice I am skating on, but we won't sign a band now if we don't get a good vibe from the manager, even if they're the talk of the town. Those tactics may work elsewhere, or have worked elsewhere, but it just doesn't work for us. I know how stressful it is for the staff who have to put up with that kind of intimidation and insidious bullying.

We love demanding managers who push us to be better, as long as it is done constructively and from a place of mutual respect. It just needs to be fair.

I don't look at streaming numbers, Facebook/Instagram/Twitter/YouTube/TikTok likes, or any of that data before I sign a band because it doesn't interest me. I cannot change how I am now. I sign bands because they make me *feel* something inside. It is a guttural, instinctive approach that doesn't even consider algorithms or data. That doesn't make me stupid or clever or insightful. It is just the way that works for me and the team of beautiful people who work tirelessly behind the scenes at Bella Union. *Nothing* happens without them.[2]

---

[2] These are the quiet angels who are ethical, culturally aware, politically and socially considerate, love the music I sign, and take the time to get to know the artists and each person at Bella Union contributes hugely to our effort to make the world a slightly less painful place to exist. Most of all, though, they are all lovely human beings and while

After twenty-seven years, you'd think I would have worked out by now why some bands make it and some don't, but I am still entirely unable to make much sense of it. Of course artists and managers want to know what is happening, but fundamentally, while it doesn't sound very exciting to them I am sure, basically the *same* things happen for every release. The *same* journalists and radio people receive a PR document with a CD or link to listen, the *same* shops receive advance copies of every album to gauge their interest, and while the weight of support can differ from release to release, why Steve Lamacq, say, chooses one band over another to support is really down to him, not me. It is frustrating of course, intensely at times when you cannot fathom why a track or album appears to have fallen between the cracks, and you can build up all sorts of conspiracy theories in your mind about certain media people and how they view you or the label, but probably most of it is nonsense and well, even if it *is* true, there's really fuck all I can do about it. If Mary Anne Hobbs doesn't want to play a new track on her BBC 6 Music show, then whingeing about it won't make her change her mind. As an avid listener to these shows over twenty or so years, maybe I kid myself that I know their taste, and when I do sign a band that might actually have a song or two that I can hear being

---

this core team of Duncan, Mark, Anika, Luke and Danielle has been the same now for years and years, we have a secondary team who recently joined us down in Brighton, who are hopefully the future of our next twenty-five years, helping us with management and the social media side for those bands who need help. We all appreciate how lucky we are to work with artists we love and when things go well, we have a shared pride in our work and when they don't, a determination to keep trying next time.

played on a particular show, it is momentarily annoying when I discover that they don't feel the same as me. But never annoying enough to sway me from my own belief in the artist.[3]

I have grown to accept that you just have to keep believing, even in the face of seeming total apathy from the industry and the general public.

I always hope that every time I sign a band / an artist that they would have enormous success and certainly believe that they all absolutely *could*. But the reality is that most don't, and no matter how many times they don't, it's always a crushing blow to the confidence and of course the stark harsh reality of your own failure at championing something that no one else appears to like lives within you, until . . . you hear something else that blows your mind and all the belief comes surging back.

* * *

When I was eighteen, my friend Stan and I saw the Birthday Party for the first time and it changed everything. It was at the Rock Garden in Covent Garden, one of our least favourite venues to go to, but nevertheless it was the start of a love affair that for me has lasted more than forty years. Over the course of the

---

[3] Lowly are actually a brilliant case in point. I know with every atom of my being that they are one of the greatest bands in the world ever, but as yet, the world hasn't caught on. Everyone who saw them at Ypsigrock Festival in a medieval castle in Castelbuono, Sicily in the summer of '22 will agree with me now, and I know more and more people that feel similarly to me than did a few years ago, and will in even greater numbers in the future.

next month, they played several times at the Moonlight Club in West Hampstead, again at the Rock Garden, and at the Clarendon in Hammersmith, and Stan and I would be at every show. A year later when 'Release the Bats' became a minor hit, the shows got bigger and the band, already artful *and* heavy, were now *thrilling*. They fully replaced that anger and energy that made punk so vital and had been missing from my life ever since the original scene had gradually evolved into something more cerebral. Nick Cave was as compelling a front person as I'd ever seen live.

I snapped up everything they released, on 4AD and then Mute. I found every release, whatever the guise, as magical as the last. The quality never diminished. Every major artist has a duff moment or two and while I kept expecting that to happen with Nick, it never did. And never has.

Working with Nick Cave's musical partner Warren Ellis on all Dirty Three releases since 1998, and having lived in the same town as them both for many years, I am lucky to have had the opportunity to catch up with Warren when time allows. What he and Nick have created together over all these years on film and on record is monumental. But here is what is truly beautiful about these people, regardless of their unquestionable talents.

An eleven-year-old girl from Calgary called Nell went to a Flaming Lips show with her dad a few years back. She was dressed as a parrot. If you know the Lips, you will understand this is not as strange as it may sound. Their shows often have characters onstage in Superman outfits and you may see audience members dressed as dinosaurs, rabbits, superheroes, sharks or astronauts. Singer Wayne Coyne often climbs into a see-through inflated zorb ball mid-set and walks out across the audience, who then hold him up and move him back and forth over their heads all the way to the back of the venue. It is a magical sight and just one part of the Lips' live experience. If you knew the world was ending next month, I would want the Flaming Lips to be the last band I ever saw. The euphoria and connectivity between fans and band is truly unique. It's not a circus – their songs are often sad and reflect the complexity of the human condition – but the message comes out loud and clear that we are all in this *together*. And that is both unifying and perhaps even more important now than it has ever been.

So, young Nell was on her dad's shoulders, in her parrot outfit, and she found herself eye to eye with Wayne inside his inflated zorb ball singing the words of a Bowie cover in perfect sync. Wayne saw her again a year later at another show and remembered this. He invited Nell and her dad backstage to say hi. Nell's exuberant nature left a mark on Wayne and he gave them his phone number and they promised to keep in touch. 'We thought it would be one of his agent's numbers or something but it was his actual phone number,' Nell later said.

A few months later, Wayne called from their studios and suggested they do a cover together. Wayne decided on the Nick Cave song 'Into My Arms' as the band were fans. He asked if she would like to try it. Nell at this point didn't know the song. Nor indeed *any* of Nick's songs. Covid intervened so plans to record together in Oklahoma were initially scuppered, but Nell learned the song, recorded it and emailed it to Wayne.

They went back and forth on ideas for a follow-up track but before they knew it they had made a whole album. Of Nick Cave songs. Nell Smith, now thirteen years old, with the Flaming Lips.

Scott asked if we'd like to release it. I was *completely* knocked out by it. So we did. *Where the Viaduct Looms* by Nell and the Flaming Lips. We sent an early copy to Nick's team.

A few days later, Nick Cave posted the following on his blog the Red Hand Files in reference to Nell's version of 'Girl in Amber':

'This version is just lovely. I was going to say Nell Smith inhabits the song but that's wrong, rather she vacates the song in a way that I could never do. I always found it difficult to step away from this particular song and sing it with its necessary remove, just got so twisted up in the words I guess. Nell shows a remarkable understanding of the song, a sense of dispassion that is both beautiful and chilling. I just love it. I'm a fan.'

Then, unprompted, his designer wife Susie (the Vampire's Wife) sent us a message to say she would love to send some clothes for Nell and the band. The *next* day, Warren Ellis messaged me to say how much he and Nick love the album. Soon after this, Wayne asked Nell to come and play some shows with the Lips, coming on in the middle of their set to do a version of 'Red Right Hand'. Nick and Susie Cave subsequently invited Nell and her family to come over for Nick's show at All Points East in 2022, and they all met up afterwards. The circle was complete.

No one pushed for any of this. Music happened and it was authentic and done for reasons of love and passion.

It is why we get up in the morning.

Nick Cave is inarguably one of the greatest artists of the twentieth *and* twenty-first centuries. But I don't think I have heard of many artists of Nick's stature that would actively seek out someone who covered one of their songs that they genuinely loved and go to the lengths that they did. To be so effusive and generous in public like that was beautiful of him. When something happens so organically without any label or marketing teams involved, you just have to marvel at it, and be thankful that this *can* still happen. It's a business I have often felt very cynical about. It's easy to sneer at things and the questionable motives behind them, but when things come from a place of love like this, it does make the dark days a little brighter.

Music as therapy.

CHAPTER TWENTY-FIVE

Mum

'Cry Cry Cry til you know why, I lost myself, identify.'

Cocteau Twins

Music allows me to feel things and express the emotions I seem unable to show in real life. I'd been swimming for years in a pool of unwept tears. I was on the verge of going under about ten years ago when I walked into Shepherd's Bush Empire to see one of our bands, Beach House. It may have taken a while for the tears to start to fall, but when they did, I didn't see them coming.

I was sitting on the balcony on the first floor directly above the stage, in perfect close proximity to both the band and the audience. This was the first time I remember literally sobbing at a show. Weeping uncontrollably. My body shaking so hard that I wondered if I had actually been possessed. Initially I didn't understand what was happening to me. I had seen Beach House many times before, but as the music poured over me, I had a revelation, a moment of enlightenment. It had been building during the show, songs predominantly culled from the recent release *Depression Cherry*. They had just played a beautiful version of the song 'Silver Soul' from *Teen Dream*, their breakthrough album here in Europe, and then they launched into 'Space Song'. That's when it hit me. It was the perfect storm: my emotional state and their affecting music. It was that adoration the audience had for Victoria and Alex in the room that night. I recognised that exact 'look'. I'd seen it every night on tour for the best part of thirteen years, on the stage as I looked up from my bass and into the crowd for a second or two at the end of each song. I'm not sure I really knew what it was back then. But a lifetime of experience later and I could now recognise and comprehend that expression. It was one of pure love. My tears tonight were in part from a place of empathy that I had for all the fans who adored Elizabeth so similarly, so deeply. They were for the loss of the band that meant *everything* to me that I hadn't allowed myself to mourn. And for all the music that I was no longer creating myself.

People had said to me before that Beach House are the closest thing these days to Cocteau Twins. I never really gave it a minute's notice as I just loved them for who they were. But now I get it. It wasn't anything to do with the music per se. It was the *feeling* that it gave me, that overwhelming emotion that just hits you without warning like a punch to the chest.

I was a little concerned that this new maudlin reaction to music might not be discerning. What if every time I sat on a sofa for my daily ten-minute trawl through dog videos on Instagram, I'd start weeping uncontrollably if a clip popped up of Britney singing 'Email My Heart'?

The dog videos though . . .

As I have mentioned, my love and respect for Nick Cave and his music is boundless. I put him up there close to Scott Walker. Because of his friendship with Warren, I've met Nick a few times of course over the years. He's always been perfectly affable but I have never been my best self.

A few years ago, Abbey and I were in Los Angeles for some business meetings. There was a small rooftop pool at the hotel and we'd popped up there one afternoon for a wee dip. Naturally we were delighted to see there was only one other person up there, a man asleep on his lounger. We ordered some drinks and some chips and as I was munching away in the sun, idly taking it all in, I looked down at the man sleeping. *Fuck me, that's Nick Cave.* It was surreal, seeing the prince of darkness in swimming trunks on a lounger. I don't know why I found it so odd. Later we saw him with his sons Arthur and Earl in the lobby. He was dressed in tracksuit bottoms, a black tank top undershirt and flip-flops. Again, I found it hard to compute. *Come on, man, he's a fuckin' Aussie. In Los Angeles. It's about 90 degrees here. What did you expect him to be wearing?*

It was lovely seeing him out of context. Being a dad.

As a father of two beautiful sons, when Arthur died so tragically in 2015 so close to where we all lived, I felt terrible. I walk our dog past that spot most days so the physical proximity only accentuated the sadness I felt for Nick, Susie and Earl.

I have worked with Warren Ellis for more than twenty-five years now and whenever he is in Brighton we try to arrange a get-together. A few months after Arthur's accident, I met up with Warren at Salvage Café in Hove where my studio was at the time. We talked for a couple of hours. With his *own* two boys who were close to Arthur and Earl, this was hitting them all so hard. He talked and I listened and then we had a lovely hug.

Listening to the music Nick has written himself since Arthur died has not been easy, because of the pain that he is clearly feeling. But to see the musical relationship and friendship with Warren blossom even deeper than before, you can't but feel that it is one of the greatest love stories in modern music, creating more magic than even Johnny Cash and June Carter.

Just after they had finished *Carnage* in 2020, Warren was over in Hove and texted me to go for a coffee at Salvage. He was so full of excitement about what they had just done. He said he wrote and recorded large sections of music on this tiny little thirty-six-note Yamaha keyboard, a keyboard so small it would fit in your backpack. And when Warren texted me a few years later to see if Abbey and I wanted to come and see Nick and him play *Carnage* at Brighton Dome, I was thrilled.

As the show began, and without warning, I felt the water drowning my eyes, and wept quietly, behind my glasses, more during this show than I had at any other. I wasn't prepared for that. It was moving of course because of the nature of the material, but it felt more like a spiritual communion than a show. An introspective one but nonetheless immensely powerful. With music having been the sole focus of my life for over forty years, and my deep connection with the sad, emotive and melancholy corners of it, it does seem odd for someone who has been so adept at keeping emotions bottled up and just 'getting on with it', that it would only be in more recent years that these feelings would be so strong, so frequent and unexpected.

The brutality of boarding school and distant parents who would rather not talk at all than talk about 'feelings' meant that any hope of discarding my carefully constructed cloak of invincibility was delayed by several years. The lack of tears at Dad's funeral in 1990, the inability to show emotion with even a loved one, let alone to myself, took a long, long time to remedy, but I am glad to report that now in my sixties I will cry at literally *anything*. Seeing my beautiful wife Abbey walk down the aisle towards me as 'Your Hand In Mine' by Explosions in the Sky played in that lovely chapel in Carmel on our wedding day in 2013 was the first time I actually remember tears falling, but it was still a one-off at that point. Now, more than a decade later, it takes very little to set me off. When that little boy is surprised by his parents with a puppy, a stirring string section, a heart-warming story on the radio, when Spurs walk out to the Champions League music, at *any* Bella Union gig and feeling proud, when I'm thinking about our dog not being with us any more, even a fucking HSBC ad, I can be a veritable showerhead of emotion. I don't fully understand it. I am always conscious of being manipulated by film and TV images, but I think it's because I am happier than I've ever been, knowing that I am loved. Or I just don't care what people think. Mum told me that *does* happen when you get to a certain age. And she *truly* didn't give a fuck.

I believe it was the death of my mum in 2018 that was the fissure that allowed the water to start to flow. Slowly at first, but surely. People talk about the hole in your heart that appears when you lose a parent. I was able to eventually heal some of the pain of Ivor's death in 1990 by honouring his life twenty-seven years later by releasing those two compilations of his work. Dad went quickly but Mum's decline was slow. The years and years of illness she endured were painful to watch. In her mid-eighties, she was diagnosed with pulmonary fibrosis, to go along with her leukaemia and glaucoma. We were always being told to expect the worst. The rest of her life she would be permanently hooked up to a tube, an oxygen machine would be installed at home and if she wanted to go out, she would need to take a portable version with her. Her cherished independence was curtailed.

To be frank, though, Mum had always had a pretty shit time of it on the health front. In the 1970s, she was prescribed Mogadon (Mogadon tablets contain nitrazepam, which is a type of benzodiazepine, a hypnotic drug that acts like you're being shot by a tranquiliser dart) and she remained on these for about thirty years. Not a good idea as we now all know. They provided some relief from her anxiety and insomnia, but she became wholly dependent on them. Any suggestion over the years from family, husband or doctor that she wean off them a bit was never heeded. No one ever wanted or cared to get to the root of her problems. And to be honest I don't think she did either.

Things were difficult for her at home growing up. In the mid-nineteenth century, her own mother would have been committed to a lunatic asylum like Bedlam, but after the Mental

Treatment Act was brought in in the 1930s, such stigmatising language thankfully became obsolete when *lunatics* officially became *mental patients* and *asylums* became *mental hospitals*. Pre-1930, her mother, Marjorie Nona Charlesworth Page, may have been classed 'insane', but after the new act, she would simply have been 'of unsound mind'.

As the youngest child of four, I was always the last to know anything, but when I *was* old enough to understand (in Mum's mind, that was when I was in my forties), I heard the stories and saw the utterly mad letters Marjorie wrote to Mum, denouncing her as an evil child. An 'unsound mind' actually seems quite a *kind* definition.

I never met my grandmother, but with her as a role model, it didn't take me long to work out why Mum's skills as a mother were more hands-off than hands-on. There was no hugging or kissing, not even in later life. Mum always favoured the turned cheek and the mwah noise to *suggest* affection rather than to actually *demonstrate* it.

I had initially wondered if they shipped me off to boarding school just because I was such a massive pain in the arse. And while that *was* probably true, I am sure there was more to it than that. Mum had fended for herself after her own abandonment as a child and maybe she felt that history would repeat itself if I remained at home during my teenage years. Possibly this was her way of protecting me.

She wasn't really one for discipline, but she did always threaten to wash my mouth out with soap and water if I told lies. Sounded totally ridiculous. On one rare occasion where I *was* actually telling the truth, she followed through and *did* wash my mouth out with soap. I couldn't believe she was doing it, and I hated her for a long time after that. My brother had beaten me up on the stairs and run off and when Mum asked me why I was crying, she didn't believe my answer.

She was a brilliant cook though. At the start of each term, Mum would make this amazing tiffin cake that she'd wrap in silver foil and slip into my bag. *This* was how she showed her affection for me, I figured. And it *was* quite out of character. Growing up, I noticed that she wasn't really a 'do things for other people' kinda gal. After the first batch of this biscuity, fruity manna from mamma, word was now out, and the minute I arrived back in the dorm the following term, my cubicle would be packed with sugar-junkie teens, only too willing to forget about their troubling acne for one more night.

My dad's work had dried up in his last years. It was sad for me to see this great musician and arranger playing piano in the bar at his local golf club, and while he would never say so, I am sure it was agony for him. In the 1980s, not many people were using real strings as synths and machines were the fashion, so while his name was still known, the phone never really rang any more. It did ring once though. Ben Watt from Everything But the Girl asked if he could come down to the house and meet him in regard to an album he was about to make. Ben arrived and stayed for most of the day, but sadly it turned out that he was just picking Dad's brain rather than wishing to do any actual work together. None of this was helping their dwindling finances, so Mum found work in her fifties and sixties making lunches for company directors in posh offices. It was a practical way for her to help. I think it actually made Dad feel *worse* though. Having been the sole breadwinner since the 1960s, he felt emasculated by their new circumstance.

My relationship with Mum was, for many years, quite distant. This was probably my choice. She was often very blunt and argumentative, while I was over-sensitive, sulky and stubborn, so weekend trips down to their bungalow would often be tense. But after Dad died, everything gradually changed. And then when Karen and I divorced, I spent more time with her and the visits became relatively free of drama. She was generous and thoughtful, and her wit, wisdom and intelligence always astonished me. In her eighties, she joined the DVD mail order club LoveFilm and rented about five movies a week. After she finished each one, she would get on her computer to review it. She loved writing. Her body was falling apart but her mind was as sharp as ever. I remember on her eighty-third birthday I went down to visit and we started talking about films. She was waxing lyrical about the director Kaneto Shindô and how much she loved his films, especially *Onibaba*. I had tried to watch that film many years before, but I didn't get through it. It's a complex piece and every single scene seemed to be a comment on *something*. To hear her talking about it in such depth took me entirely by surprise. I don't think I had ever had a conversation with her in my forty-seven years about sex – certainly not sensuality or eroticism; in fact I am sure we never even had 'the birds and the bees' discussion – and yet here she was telling me all about this erotic horror film in quite graphic detail. She couldn't believe the director was a man. I couldn't believe this was my mum. Fascinating woman.

As her health deteriorated, my brother Nick and I spent more and more time with her. I certainly grew closer to her. We never quite got to the hugging stage, but who knows, maybe a few more years and we would have.

She was a medical enigma, and even the hordes of specialists and doctors she had for her various ailments were often astounded by her. She loved her trips to the shops in her little yellow Honda Accord, though we were all quite worried that she was still driving at all given how terrible her eyesight was becoming. On a Sunday afternoon visit in 2009 with my sons Stan and Will, Mum announced she was going to take us all out to lunch so we all piled into the car. Now, I am not into rollercoasters or any kind of thrill rides, but I would happily take New Jersey's Kingda Ka ten times in a row over a trip with Mum, or Mrs Magoo as she became known after this short excursion. We all exited the car for lunch, paler and a lot older than when we got in.

I went to visit her in hospital when the pulmonary fibrosis was first confirmed. She was hooked up to an oxygen machine for several weeks and we made arrangements to install one at her flat so she could come back home. Mum also bought a portable oxygen system so she could at least be pushed around the supermarket in a wheelchair while still hooked up to her machine. Her greatest fear was never ever leaving the confines of her flat; heavy and inconvenient though the portable machine was, this at least gave her some hope that her life wasn't now entirely pointless. Of course, as a naturally beautiful woman, who even in her eighties and nineties looked twenty years younger than she actually was, the idea of permanently having tubes up her nose was depressing. Mum got dressed and put make-up on every day, whether she would see anyone or not. She took pride in her appearance and wouldn't have dreamed of even answering the door to the postman in her dressing gown. We all visited as much as we could to try and keep her spirits up. Taking the boys down to see her made her happier than anything, but the last year of her life was very tough. We found her a nearby nursing home where she could see out the rest of her days. I helped her move in sometime in early December and on Christmas Day we had a lovely time. It was all laughs and smiles and a great relief for all of us. But within a few weeks of the new year, it all began to spiral out of control. Who knows what really happened, but she kept calling us in tears. She believed they were mistreating her, said they were not checking in on her for days, and all had it in for her. Their story was that she wouldn't answer the phone, when they came to the door she wouldn't respond, had asked for no visits, was sleeping all day long, wouldn't ever come downstairs to socialise and then when they *did* come in to bring her food, or to wake her and clean the room, they found all the pills she was meant to have taken in various places hidden around the room. She would call in the middle of the night and leave messages that were upsetting to hear. We took turns to go down and find out what was going on and try to settle her down. But nothing worked, and one night she called Nick in distress to say she couldn't stay any longer and was going to try and get a taxi and go back to her flat.

I am sure this whole depressing experience contributed to the rapid deterioration in her health and, a month or so later in March 2018, she was admitted to hospital again. We were in Texas at SXSW when Nick called and suggested we should get back to the UK as soon as we could. We caught a red eye flight back. When we got to the hospital, I found her on her bed, looking bewildered and scared, the hospital gown loose and barely covering her modesty, the pallid skin now thin, almost translucent, and her face contorted like a terrified child who had seen some unimaginable horror. She tried to speak but no words were coming out, I assumed because of the morphine. I held her hand and talked quietly to her, and for a few brief seconds I felt she was maybe comforted that I was there. But there was a look of fear in her eyes and despair creased across her beautiful soft face that I'd never seen before and hope I never see again. The doctors came around and asked that I give them a moment. I said I would go and get a cup of tea.

I am still trying to work it all out. Death that is.

Mum's and Dad's ashes are buried side by side in a small churchyard.

I visit on birthdays and on their wedding anniversary and whatever the season, whatever the reason it will always be raining. I went there last week and as I stood by the blue-grey slabs that cover their ashes, a lone horse in the sloped field behind the cemetery suddenly started galloping gleefully around the field, nodding its head and swishing its tail. As it slowed to a canter, I heard the uplifting rush of small birds departing the hedgerow into the darkening sky above. For a minute it felt good to forget and to smile than to remember and feel sad.

Whether it was her death alone that explained my sudden emotional fragility (or should that read 'maturity'?) I cannot say, but letting it out does feel a lot better than keeping it in. Outward expressions of emotion have been discouraged for such a large part of my life that I am still getting used to this new version of 'me'. So if you're out at a show and see me, don't be afraid to come over and put an arm around my shoulder.

A year later in 2019, I was shocked to hear of the passing of Vaughan Oliver, the widely influential graphic designer who started the company 23 Envelope with photographer and film-maker Nigel Grierson. The maverick artist was as synonymous with the indie giant 4AD as most of the bands themselves.

The arrival of Apple Macintosh and PCs in the analogue recording studios of the 1990s was initially greeted with suspicion and distrust. But like all things new and unknown, early adopters quickly showed the potential, and before long, most studios began shifting towards a more digital-savvy approach. In the graphic design universe, it seemed that soon after the candy-coloured iMacs were launched in 1998, every designer had one.

All but Vaughan Oliver.

His designs for the label throughout the '80s and '90s were as iconic as Peter Saville's were for Factory. During those final two decades of the twentieth century, perhaps only Germany's ECM Records had such a distinctive in-house style. His designs for Lush, the Wolfgang Press, Colourbox, This Mortal Coil, Ultra Vivid Scene, Pixies, Throwing Muses and my own band elevated these record releases to works of art that people wanted to own. For my generation, 23 Envelope sleeves were regarded with a similar reverence to that of Hipgnosis in the '70s, who were behind the sleeves of bands like Yes, Pink Floyd, Led Zeppelin and Genesis.

One great difference, to my mind, was that Vaughan's work was always the perfect visual companion to the aural delights within the sleeve. Until much later, Vaughan also preferred the traditional draughtsman's board, using it almost like a bedroom wall to pin his ideas on to, where he could shuffle them around, overlaying and overlapping bits of paper and photographs until his mind's eye was in focus.

Working with us on Cocteau Twins' artwork wasn't always easy, but then everyone said that. Label, writers, promoters, all found us a bit of a challenge, but Vaughan was always trying to find the perfect solution and he did so with great humour and no end of patience. And he truly *listened* to the music – intently – until the appropriate vision came to him.

Designing for a whole label, he was often able to use his dark humour and wicked eye for controversy, even when the hope may have been to have a commercial hit. With the swell of popularity accompanying new signings Pixies, they now had a band that could also deliver proper top twenty singles. But Vaughan was not one for seeking compromises.

Thankfully, Pixies singer Charles was very open to his ideas, and whether it was a crying baby, a monkey, a man with a back as hairy as a Vivienne Westwood mohair jumper or a flamenco dancer naked from the waist up, his sleeves for Boston's finest are certainly among his best work. I would vote for the Breeders' *Pod* as a personal favourite. It's like a Francis Bacon painting, but I do believe that the image was actually a blurred photo of Vaughan himself with a belt of dead eels tied to his waist. However, his penchant for the subversive wasn't only reserved for them. At first glance, his artwork for Ultra Vivid Scene's debut single 'She Screamed' seemed innocuous enough. But the eagle-eyed amongst you might spot a row of tiny clitorises that he used from a set of centrefolds from porn mag *Hustler*.

The best album sleeves get picked up by curious record browsers initially, regardless of the artist, and I'm sure that many 4AD artists from the '80s and '90s were discovered as a consequence of their incredible packaging.

That his artwork defined an era was arguably as important to 4AD as the music they signed, and that it had a longer-lasting influence on both vinyl *and* book cover design is indisputable. Vaughan Oliver was a one-off who is still sorely missed by his wife Lee, and children Beckett and Callum. We may never see his kind again, but it is a comfort for me to think of all the millions of unopened vinyl albums still sitting patiently on shelves all around the world, waiting to be picked out by unsuspecting folks who will now have the same joy I have had, of hours poring over his intricate and sumptuous designs.

CHAPTER TWENTY-SIX

Shaken to the Core

Thanks to my dad, Spurs play a significant part in my life and that of my youngest son Will. I'll happily admit to spending far too long reading all the same daft Spurs gossip on social media most days, and by Wednesday I am already counting down the hours to the game on Saturday.

Seeing Will every other week is a joy I hope to experience for many more years. We have been through some shocking times watching Spurs. But we experience this *together*. It is our bond. Once we even got to the Champions League Final and Will and I travelled to Madrid, where of course we were beaten by Liverpool. We had a terrible trip. The policing was unnecessarily brutal and we couldn't wait to get back home. For most football fans, we are told it's a game of highs and lows, but mostly it is just lots and lots of lows. When you share the lows with a family member, it feels slightly easier to stomach, and for the last twenty-five years, Will has sat next to me at every Spurs home game. We walk for half an hour to the station and then, after a few stops, go our separate ways. It will be like this until I am too old or unable to make the trip, but I am hopeful that will not be for a good few years yet. So when I got an early-morning call from Stan my eldest in late 2023 to say that Will was unconscious in the ICU at Charing Cross hospital after having a seizure at 2 a.m. that morning, my life started to come away from its moorings.

Becky his girlfriend was thankfully with him when he collapsed. She called the ambulance and twenty minutes later he was in hospital. Sitting next to his bed that day – his mum/my ex Karen, Becky and Stan – we had no idea if he would come out of his coma. And even if he did, what kind of state his brain would be in? So many questions all remaining unanswered for a few days as the doctors struggled to get to grips with what had caused his seizure. As I drove back home to Brighton, I felt guilty that it was him there and not me. I've lived a good life. He is just starting his. Now in my sixties with mortality a pressing issue, I had perhaps briefly imagined a future of Will going to games without me, but not me going without *him*. That was absurd. He remained unconscious for three days, but on the third day he did momentarily come to. He didn't recognise anyone and had no idea where he was. The doctors finally started to work out what was wrong, how to combat it and how to improve his vital statistics, and within a few days he was fit enough to transfer to one of the main hospital wards. Will has a rare form of diabetes, something he's had since he was five, and the result of him missing a hormone in his pituitary gland. He has always managed it successfully with the medicine the specialists prescribed him as a child. In the hospital he told us that it hadn't been working as well recently and neither his GP nor the doctors at A & E that he spoke to a week earlier had any idea what the issue was and sent him away. Naturally, with no help from the professionals, he just took a greater dosage of the medicine. I would have done the same thing. And it was actually *this* that caused his system to eventually crash and totally shut down. Becky's quick thinking definitely saved his life. If she had been asleep and unaware of his collapse, he would certainly have died.

When Will finally came out of hospital, while there was enormous relief, I felt a need just to run away somewhere to switch off my already overactive brain. Accepting that the mental stress of Will almost losing his life had affected me more than I realised, Abbey and I decided that getting out of England to a new destination neither of us had visited before would do us the world of good. We arrived in Morocco in the early evening. It was still warm and humid. The short drive from Marrakesh airport past Menara Gardens with its long lines of olive trees just hinted at the immeasurable beauty of this ancient walled medieval city. We talked excitedly about all the places we would go. We checked into our room, ordered some room service and Abbey fell asleep around 11 p.m. I stayed up putting all my clothes away and tidying away my suitcase – an unnecessary fussy little habit that I have developed late in life that I don't care for at all.

I closed the cupboard door, but suddenly stumbled and lost my balance as the whole room started to shake uncontrollably. My first thought was an explosion, but as the building was still shaking from side to side, it could only be an earthquake. We had to get the fuck out of there. Abbey was already halfway out of bed as I got to her. I grabbed our passports and in our underwear we joined the hundreds of guests running down the stairs. Many were screaming but we held hands tightly and made our way down to the ground floor. The shaking stopped, but already a huge crack in the wall of the hotel staircase had appeared as we descended.

We ran out into the street. It was just panic and confusion. No one from the hotel was taking the lead, and as we stood opposite the entrance, Abbey and I knew a second tremor was likely. Late-night revellers, some coming back from a party at the nearby Buddha Bar in their best Friday night clubbing attire, mingled with half-naked hotel guests in bathrobes and slippers. Phone reception remained strong as calls were made to loved ones back home, and guests searched for news and pictures of the earthquake that had begun to flood the internet. It had been 7.0 on the Richter scale, and the first earthquake of any significance in Morocco in decades. We were about 30 kilometres from the epicentre, one of the reasons we survived. First reports were of 'hundreds dead' which days later tragically rose to more than 3,000.

We watched some staff inside breaking down in tears – no doubt receiving some awful news from family in nearby homes – and we saw some guests rush to their rooms to hurriedly pack their bags and head to the airport. But there would be no flights for the next seven hours at least. By about 3 a.m. the street was beginning to clear a little and more and more guests were sheepishly re-entering the lobby.

Some people were settling down on the sofas and chairs in the reception and restaurant areas, seemingly reluctant to go back up to their rooms. We were too tired to think straight and went back to our room and lay in bed just staring at the huge crack in our ceiling until the light began to seep through the curtain.

In the morning, the hotel was attempting a 'normal' service for breakfast. We asked Yusseff the general manager for his advice on what we should do. He suggested for the next couple of days we should stay in the vicinity of the hotel while the city mourned its dead and began the massive clean-up.

By day three, we tentatively ventured out and booked a taxi to the Bahia Palace. Due to road closures, we were dropped off in front of a small market square bustling with activity. As we slowly wandered through the square, families were huddled on blankets laid out in front of the rubble where their homes once stood. It made me think back to being in New York for 9/11. The dust, the dazed looks, the shock and loss stay with you, but equally so does the resilience and stoicism that humans exhibit when faced with awful adversity. The city just seemed to be dusting itself off and getting on with it. As New York did.

I had come away to try to get over what happened to Will but hadn't imagined that I would be having to overcome another trauma so soon.

CHAPTER TWENTY-SEVEN

Scott

BBC PROMS SCOTT WALKER – July 2017

Even writing that down makes the hair on my arms stand up.

I'll go back to the beginning briefly. To remind you, in the mid-'60s, Ivor did the orchestral arrangements on the Walker Brothers hits 'The Sun Ain't Gonna Shine Anymore' and 'Make it Easy on Yourself' as well as several others. My intense love affair with Scott Walker remains unsullied to this day. The significance of Dad's work with Scott and Dusty Springfield cannot be underestimated. It must have been an incredible period for him to be arranging orchestras for two of the most significant voices of the time.

However, when Scott Walker comes to your house and you are barely five years old, it means nothing.

If I have one regret, more than fifty years later, it's that I didn't call out to him as I looked out of my upstairs bedroom window to where he sat in the garden, angelic in his white shirt billowing in the light spring wind. *'Hey, Scott, I might only be five but know this, we are going to be on the same record label, not once but TWICE! How do you like THEM bananas?!'*

The strangest parts of that apparent fantasy are not that Scott was at our house or that he was wearing a white shirt, as both of those are true, but that my *own* band Cocteau Twins signed to Fontana (Scott's label) after years on 4AD, and that Scott then signed to 4AD years after being on Fontana. Indeed, no fantasy at all.

Thanks to Julian Cope's *Fire Escape in the Sky: The Godlike Genius of Scott Walker* CD release in 1981, many more of my contemporaries became aware of him. Culled predominantly from the four albums *Scott 1, 2, 3 and 4*, the twelve songs Julian picked were perfect as an introduction to the introspective Walker.

My love was rekindled all over again.

Once I had relaxed a little into what I was trying to do with Bella Union, I looked into licensing all four Scott Walker albums for a box-set release and, with my friend Kieron Tyler who helped me with the Ivor Raymonde releases, we put in a request to Universal. I spoke with Charles Negus-Fancey, Scott's manager, and he said Scott loved the idea too. Amazing. I liked Charles a lot. We had been in touch previously around the release of *30 Century Man*, the excellent Scott documentary that my beautiful friend Stephen Kijak made.

A few months rolled by and then we heard that Universal had decided to do their own box-set. I was gutted. I think Charles was disappointed too and worried that Universal might botch the box-set but he needn't have been. They actually did a really beautiful job.

An excellent Dutch writer called Dick Hovenga, who had been in touch with me several times over the years, had begun a new blog 'Written in Music'. He was a huge supporter of Bella Union and we always tried to meet up whenever he came to London. We shared a lot of the same music tastes and also a lot of the same frustrations from working in the industry. One of our joint passions turned out to be Scott Walker, and we often spoke about trying to arrange an orchestral tour of his songs with some of Bella Union's finest singers, like John Grant and Father John Misty. Now, speaking about it and actually *doing* it are totally different things. Whenever I would speak to agents, it would usually get knocked back due to scheduling clashes or some such stuff. Dick was friends with Jules Buckley, an accomplished arranger/conductor/orchestrator who had co-founded his own sinfonietta, the Heritage Orchestra. He had mentioned to him our fanciful idea of this 'Songs of Scott Walker' tour.

On 4 January 2017, while on a call to the BBC Proms people about another project they were working on together, Jules mentioned *our* concept and had very positive feedback. I called Scott's manager and by the end of the day, Scott had given his blessing. Within a few days, Dick and I were brought on as creative directors for the BBC Proms 2017 – 'The Songs of Scott Walker'. It seemed unreal that our preposterous idea had come together so beautifully and organically.

The next six months flew past. The cast list of singers was the first thing we needed to secure.

Scott himself had requested Jarvis Cocker be one of the sing-ers, and that felt entirely appropriate given their existing friend-ship. Fellow Sheffield legend Richard Hawley was also favoured. John Grant was always going to be my number-one choice and not just because he was on Bella Union, but because of his voice, presence and his ability to convey the deepest emotions. The choice of the fourth singer was not so easy, but I insisted it had to be a woman. Four middle-aged blokes just seemed unbalanced and disparaging. It was all liable to be rather . . . grey.

The BBC offered up some suggestions – Jehnny Beth and Siouxsie were two that I remember, both incredible artists – but I was adamant that the fourth singer needed to be a wonderful *singer* with range and not just a charismatic individual. To that end, I suggested Susanne Sundfør and the initial reaction, which I of course expected, was '*Who?!*'

Privately I had sounded out Susanne. She was already a mas-sive fan of Scott's and having seen her live, I knew with all my heart that she was the right person and persuaded them to at least listen to her music; ironically, her debut LP for Bella Union was due out the following week. Any accusations of nepotism please send to youdontknowme@sofuckyou.com.

That night I wrote to Scott and his manager with a link to Susanne's new LP with a note outlining exactly why I wanted her to be the final singer. By morning, Scott had come back to say he had listened to her album, loved it, totally agreed that her voice would be perfect and approved her inclusion. Knowing this, the BBC felt comfortable with the decision and our cast list was complete.

The next task was to pick the songs that would both best serve the Prom and the voices. For an artist with a career spanning five decades, there were always going to be dissenters, people who wanted a broader choice from both his early *and* later work. That was to be expected, but we all agreed with Scott that a show focusing on *Scott 1–4* and *'Til the Band Comes In* would work best with the Heritage Orchestra. Jules, Dick and I exchanged some ideas and spoke to the artists. After some to and fro, we settled on the following tracks and running order.

Jarvis Cocker
'Boy Child'
'Plastic Palace People'

Susanne Sundfør
'On Your Own Again'
'Angels of Ashes'

John Grant
'Rosemary'
'The World's Strongest Man'

Richard Hawley
'It's Raining Today'
'Two Ragged Soldiers'

Jarvis Cocker
'The War is Over'

John Grant
'Copenhagen'

Susanne Sundfør
'The Amorous Humphrey Plugg'

Richard Hawley
'Montague Terrace'

Jarvis Cocker
'Little Things (That Keep Us Together)'

John Grant
'The Seventh Seal'

Susanne Sundfør
'Hero of the War'

Richard Hawley
'The Old Man's Back Again'

Everyone
'Get Behind Me'

In conversations with Scott, one thing he kept emphasising to me was that the new arrangements had to have 'power'. He had seen the Bowie prom the year before and felt it lacked horribly in that department. Jules noted this and made the brilliant move of inviting the London Contemporary Voices to add some depth and volume if needed.

The original arrangements on *Scott 1–4* were done by a combination of Peter Knight, Reg Guest and Wally Stott (who later in 1972 transitioned to Angela Morley), while production duties were handled by one of my dad's great mates, Johnny Franz.

Now the task for Jules Buckley in 2017 to meticulously recreate arrangements from exactly fifty years earlier was a mammoth one. None of those original orchestral arrangements exist, and nor have *any* of these songs ever been performed live in this way before, even at the time. The only performance was on the day of the original recording sessions.

I'm no expert, but nor am I a total dummy, and even I, after thirty-five years of doing this music lark for a living, found it hard to imagine how one could dissect these songs in such granular detail and know with any certainty what instrument is playing what. Remember, there are no studio tapes in existence, where Jules could, say, pop into a studio in 2017 and have a listen to the orchestra parts in isolation. I'll be honest, I kept my fears to myself. But I did wonder how it could be done. But he clearly did it, and my admiration for this craft, *his* craft and that of my dad, and the likes of the formidable Fiona Brice, Andrew Skeet, Hannah Peel, David Arnold and all the other brightest arrangers in the world, could not be greater.

We only had a couple of days' rehearsal with the orchestra and singers before the event, so it was all done fairly by the seat of our collective pants.

While rehearsals were going on, I called Charles to see how many tickets he would need and to enquire whether *maybe* Scott would likely make an appearance. He asked for some tickets for himself and for Scott and his family 'just in case he decides to come. He may but he may not.'

On the day of the Prom itself, I was a fidgety nervous wreck, in a constant blur of caffeine and dog walking. Never once sitting still, all I could think of was that it was going to go spectacularly wrong – whilst going out *live* on the BBC.

Abbey and I got the train up to London and headed to the Royal Albert Hall early. We went for a little dinner first, but I didn't eat a thing. My stomach couldn't take it.

We went to our seats, stupidly early. I was looking around for Charles and any clues that Scott might be in the house when I espied Stuart Maconie in the BBC box. He beckoned for me to join him, and I popped in to have a chat with him live on air. He was excited about the event and as the room was now almost full, I began to calm down a bit.

I have to be honest, at the time the concert was happening, I have *no* idea what I thought of it. I could tell how nervous all the singers were, as these were very big Walker shoes to try and fill, but all my usual high-functioning critical faculties had completely deserted me. I make my living by having an opinion about the music I hear and deciding very instinctively, very swiftly whether I like it or not, and if it is connecting with me. For the first twenty minutes or so, I had no idea if this was good, bad or indifferent. My thoughts were scrambled. I just kept thinking of my dad, of how proud he would be that I'd pulled this off (not just me of course but you know what I mean). I thought back to Scott Walker coming to the house when I was a boy and then to Scott now and if he was here and if he was hating or enjoying it. Did he watch two songs and then slip out the back in disgust, or was he like me shedding a tear at the enormity of it all? Was it powerful enough for him? I was a ball of confusion.

By the time John Grant, and then Susanne, came on, my heart rate began to settle to its usual pace, between eighty and ninety – funnily enough around the same beats per minute as most Cocteau Twins songs – the numbness in my legs began to disappear and I felt more confident that it was going well. Really well.

The realisation of what was happening was starting to dawn on me – that for the first time anywhere, those arrangements of the finest orchestrators of their era were being heard live just as they were written, just as they were intended with a worldwide audience in one of the UK's elite concert halls. It wasn't Scott singing but it was the next best thing, with four artists who all loved the material and were doing everything they could to make their interpretations honourable and authentic to the writers and authors.

The reaction from the audience inside the Albert Hall was stunning.

Abbey and I stayed in our seats and watched as people gathered their coats and began shuffling towards the exits. As the room began to empty out, we walked down towards the left of the stage to go back to see everyone.

It was already busy backstage. There were a lot of people in this unique production all with friends and family coming back to say hello.

We walked into John Grant's dressing room first. And the first face I see is Scott Walker's. He came up to me before I had a chance to say anything and gave me a massive hug. 'How was it?' I said quietly as he held me. 'Everyone did an *amazing* job. Thank you so much! We all loved it. Beverly, Lee, this is Simon.'

I was introduced to his partner Beverly and his daughter Lee.

'Was it powerful enough?' I checked.

'It was. It really was. Better than I could have hoped for.'

Scott Walker loved his own Prom.

So now I can retire and go to my grave happy, satisfied that one of the most important musical figures in my entire life loved a show I played a small part in organising, an event I was sure he probably wouldn't even attend, a concert of songs I believed he no longer had feelings for.

In case you're wondering, I never spoke to Scott Walker about my own version of 'It's Raining Today' when we saw each other at the BBC Proms event. Nor did I find the right moment to bring up my dad doing the Walker Brothers arrangements for 'The Sun Ain't Gonna Shine Anymore' and 'Make it Easy on Yourself'. I am not sure why. Charles and I discussed it many times on the phone, so it doesn't really make sense. I've thought about it a lot, but I just think when in the moment of speaking with him and hugging him, *that* was plenty enough for me. But truly, what did that all matter now? I didn't want to spoil this precious moment with him.

After half an hour backstage, we let everyone in the cast and crew know that we had arranged a free bar around the corner from the Albert Hall and we'd love to see them all there. I told

Scott and Beverly about it, not imagining for a second that this shy man that we had all been led to believe was some sort of Howard Hughes recluse would actually come and hang out with everyone.

But they did. And they stayed until 1 a.m., chatting and laughing with everyone and having a thoroughly fabulous time. I had to do a double take a couple of times, sitting in the corner with my glass of water, looking over to a room filled with maybe forty people, one of which was Scott flippin' Walker.

His death twenty months later deeply shocked us all. When it hits, cancer can sear through the body like a laser. Ivor went the same way, fast. Here one minute seemingly in good cheer, and then gone.

I was honoured to be invited with just a few close friends and colleagues to attend his funeral in a secret wooded location. It was a beautifully sombre and elegantly curated Walkerian event. Moving and profound, thought-provoking and unique. Like everything he put his earthly hand to. Gone but never forgotten.

And I should have known better than to assume that would be my last entry on Scott Walker.

On Valentine's Day 2023, I was sitting in the bath when the phone rang. It was arranger Jules Buckley. He explained he had the Barbican on hold in May for an event with the BBC Symphony Orchestra and thought maybe we should do something together again with the songs of Scott Walker. I remained sitting in that cold bathwater like a defrosting turkey for the next two hours, and by the time I finally exited the tub, this bird was ready for basting. I only had two conversations. One with Jules and one with Josh aka Father John Misty.

In just three short months, Jules would create eight brand-new arrangements for Josh. They had together come up with a brilliant setlist, not just from *Scott 1–4* as we had done previously, but with Scott compositions from each of the next three decades, from 1970 to 1995: 'Thanks for Chicago Mr James' from the 1970 album *'Til the Band Comes In*, 'The Electrician' from *Nite Flights* in 1978, 'Sleepwalkers Woman' from *Climate of Hunter* in 1984 and 'Farmer in the City' from the 1995 album *Tilt* released on 4AD.

The evening of the concert came along so quickly, Abbey and I arriving early to soak up the atmosphere. I didn't have the nerves like before, perhaps having had Scott's personal blessing from the Albert Hall Prom that we were doing things the right way had helped, and I was able to enjoy every second just as a diehard fan would. I knew within the first few seconds that we had made the right choice asking Josh – an artist with great presence who would not resort to pale impersonation and would rather inhabit the songs in his own way, his own inimitable style. The new orchestral arrangements blew me away.

There was a beautiful symmetry with the original BBC Prom night, meeting up with Josh in the pub across the road from the Barbican after the show, just like we had with Scott six years prior.

I woke up the following morning to a voice message from the hospital. I'd been for my annual MRI scan the previous month over at the Brighton and Hove Albion football stadium in Falmer, and the doctor was calling me back – in, I should add, an infectiously cheery voice – to say that there was no significant growth in the tumour since the previous one in 2023. He was happy not to see me again until 2025. What a lovely start to the day.

And as Abbey and I drove over to see my own son Stan and his fiancée Georgie, my thoughts drifted back to the previous night's show, to Scott and then to Dad.

As I look down upon this life so far, as I must do to write this memoir, these once imperceptible thin threads with the past via an artist that my *own* father first worked with fifty-seven years ago, now feel like bridges I can actually follow, tracing the paths of both our lives and finding them converge. I always wanted to do my own thing, intimidated by his prodigious talent and success as a writer and arranger, that I never stopped to consider that perhaps we had a lot more in common than just a love of Spurs and Tony Hancock.

I always keep coming back to the time he sat me down for 'a father–son chat', admittedly a good few years before my brain was large enough to understand it.

'All I can say is never start a career that you don't absolutely love. If you have a burning desire to be a bin man, then whatever it is as long that makes you happy then that is all you can ask for.'

I haven't worked it all out yet, but despite all early attempts to distance myself from Dad's career and deny myself the wisdom of his years of experience, the echoes of his past seem now to be reverberating loudly in my present. And I am embracing that.

Maybe the parallels I dismissed before are closer than I realise.

And it seems that my *own* past is no longer just a shoegazey blur of distant lights receding in the rear-view mirror; it is clearly visible in my present too. Cocteau Twins have *never* been as popular as we are now, almost three decades after we stopped making music.

As the great pianist Vladimir Horowitz once said, 'My future is in my past and my past is my present. I must now make the present my future.'

In this, our twenty-seventh year of Bella Union, the world is still on fire and there is still uncertainty about the future of our industry, but what I am sure of is that discovering new music is what helps me forget the dread for a moment, what *still* gives me that shot of adrenaline that I've spent all my life auto-injecting.

I keep waking up wondering if that desire to listen to the next demo in my inbox will have deserted me overnight.

So far it hasn't.

So as long as my one good ear still works, I'll keep listening.

Goodnight.

Acknowledgements

Thanks to Pete Selby for wisdom, honesty and an editing knife sharper than a Harley Street surgeon. Warren Ellis for initial encouragement to go for it, Abbey Raymonde my wonderful wife and David Allison my best pal for almost fifty years, for their support whenever I questioned myself. Matthew Hamilton my literary agent for his calm intelligence. Big hug to the staff at Laughing Dog café in Brighton for tolerating me sitting at the same table, every morning from 9 a.m. until 2 p.m. every day for about six months as I wrote the lion's share of this book. Thanks to my beautiful sons Stan and Will for their love and friendship, Spurs for being a place for me to dream and let off steam, and to Bodhi the fox-red Labrador and best dog friend I have ever had.

Thanks to Chris Bigg for the cover design, Jurgen Teller for the cover photo, Rory Lethbridge for organising prints of all the inside photos. A hug to everyone below who has at one time or other left a lasting impression on me, even if they would have no idea why, plus additional thanks for photos and help in jogging my memory must go to many named here, not solely but including Miki Berenyi, David Evans, Deborah Edgley, Linda Bateman, Matthew Kelly, Ray Conroy, Lincoln Fong, Russell Fong, Duncan Jordan, Mick Cartledge, Sheila Rock, Jim Seigel, Luciana Camargo, Nina Jackson, Tetsuro, Tom Sheehan, Paul Cox, Nick Hider, Paul West, Simon Harper, Nigel Grierson, Natasha Youngs, Sean Forbes, Jimmy and Charlie Allen, Kevin Westenberg, Hazel Savage, Zach Tenorio and Jocie Adams, Josh and Emma Tillman, Nanaco Sato, Chris and Sadie Anderson, Steven Drozd, Tim Keegan, Ed Riman, Beth Cannon, Helen Ganya, Bic Hayes and Jo Spratley, Simon Taffe, Jonathan Caouette, Esteban Ray, Chris Hrasky, Michael James, Mark Smith, Munaf Rayani, Tam Coyle, Rich Thane and Grace Goddard, Peter Van Der Velde, Anna Bronsted, Dan Monsell, Vic Galloway, Gideon Coe, Alex Southam, Gary and Chris Deveney, Sarah Louise Green, Tessa Harris, Veronica Gretton, Wren Hinds, Helen Weatherhead, Craig Charles, Jake Read, Melting Vinyl, Melissa Woods Maskan, Marisa Baldi, Innerstrings, Ruth Kilpatrick, Claire Courtney, Claire Southwick, Scott Heim, Chris Roberts, John Robb, Ondine Benetier, Nuno Da Cruz, Nayfe Slusjan, Joshua Knight, James Yorkston, Amber Millington, Lana McDonagh and Wayne Murray, Joss Yebury, Personal Trainer, Wayne and Katy Coyne, Derek Brown, Patti Smith, Plug Edwards RIP, Seymour Stein RIP, Tony Wilson RIP, Lawrence Bell, Chris Blackwell, Stuart Braithwaite and Elisabeth Elektra, Ed Harris, Melanie Dawn, Tom Verlaine RIP, Cinder Flame, Liela Moss, Toby Butler, Luke Ford, Ollie Betts, Pat, Simon and Annabel

ACKNOWLEDGEMENTS

Nevin, Katja Rackin and Sam Stacpoole, Ivo Watts-Russell, Steve Homer, Tim Anstaett, Christy McNaughton, Colin Wallace, Fiona Glyn-Jones, Hamish Mackintosh, Michael Borum, Fiona Brice, Dec Hickey, Misha Anderson, Pete Townsend, Scott Rodger, Mick Conroy, Claudia Stanten, the family of Leesa Beales, Vinnie Lammi, Dave Palfreeman, Courtney Chavanell, the whole Denton-Midlake clan (Eric and Kristen Pulido, Mckenzie and Felicia Smith, Eric and Rachel Nichelson, Joey McClellan, Paul Alexander) Tim Smith and Kathi Zung, Vashti Bunyan, James Minor, Keanu Reeves, Colin Daniels, Thomas Golubić, John Kennedy, Wendy Rose, Sofia Hagberg, Perry Farrell, Wendy and Lisa, Lauren Down, Tony Harlow, Michelle Cable, Christophe Basterra, Jonathan Wilson, Rosie Blair, Will Stratton, Jonathan Donohue, Jose Cadahia, Paloma Cordon, Darren Revell, Sean 'Grasshopper' Mackowiak, Jesse Chandler, Geoff Travis, Jeff Barrett, Maria Porcaro, Mark Bowen and Roxanne Oldham, Gianfranco Raimundo, Christopher Storbeck, C Duncan, Jim White, Mick Turner, Luisa Gerstein, Roy Harper, Van Dyke Parks, Rachel Goswell and Steve Clark, Susanne Sundfør, Stephanie Dosen, Clams Baker, Maria Linden, Cillian Murphy, Hannah Cohen, Paul Trueman, Kirk Hammett, Romy, Molly Rankin, Trevor Horn, Liv Willars, Robert Linney, Ed Simons and Tom Rowlands, Adrian Sherwood, Mark Stewart RIP, the Kissaway Trail, Sean Hughes, Marisa and Oli Isaacs, Sharon Van Etten, Joanna Pickering, Alex Scully and Victoria Legrand, Mark Byrne, Anika Mottershaw, Luke Jarvis and Danielle Carr, Mathieu Pinaud, Ben Blakeman, Bill Heggie, Pete and Katie

Hill, Claes Olsen, Siggi, Glenn Larsen, Richard Thomas, Stan and Georgie, Will and Becky, Karen Raymonde, Stephen Mallinder, John Grant, Stephen Kijak, Simon Toombs, Scott Booker, Cathy Negus-Fancey, Beverley Foster, Lee and Emmy Engel, Mitsuo Tate, Lauren Fisher, Debbie Tucker Green, Dick Hovenga, Mark Cleveland and Viva Seifert, Anne Mueller, Miwa Okumura, Vinita Joshi, Estella Adeyeri, Stephanie Phillips, Tristi Brownett, Simon Crisford, Alex Drysdale, Adam Peters, Paul Cummins, Lowly, Lynda Fotheringham, Pom Poko, Sandy Leigh, Paul Gregory and Hazel Wilde, Philip Selway, Danny and Daniel Chavis, James Yorkston, Bryan Mills, Richie Thomas, Huw Stephens, Steve Lamacq, Helen Weatherhead, Cameron Neal, Karl Blau, Alison Wenham, Pete Paphides, Tim Keegan, Patch Hannan, Nick Hannan, Dave and Harriet, Dave and Alan Curtis, Gary Bromley, Toby L, Kieron Tyler, Keiran Evans, Marc Geiger, Jean-Daniel Beauvallet, Gary Bales, Cam Pia, Vincent Clery-Melin, Justin and Alexandra Meldal-Johnsen, Elia Einhorn, Hale Milgram, Matt Aberle, Phil Costello, Steve Sutherland, Laura Veirs, Grímur Atlason, Jack and Lily Wolter, Ben and Dottie, Tom Coyne, Chloe Spence and Louis Bradshaw, Penny and Mike Wolter, Frankie Nardiello, Robert Fantinatto, Tom Robinson, Hebe Silva, Russell Yates, Mig Morland, Martin Raviraj, Jon Turner, Keith Mitchell, Johnny Brocklehurst, John Madden, Jon Fryer, Billy Mackenzie RIP, Paul Buchanan, Sean Keaveny, Kim Deal, Brian Eno, Daniel Lanois, Danny Kelly, Danny Baker, Mark Radcliffe, Bob Harris, Simon Hotchkiss, Jason Pierce (J Spaceman), Wolfgang Press, the Walkmen, Elton John, Vinta Joshi, James

ACKNOWLEDGEMENTS

Oldham, Jeanette Lee, Bambara, Chris and Sadie Anderson, Chris Madden, Adrian Cooke, Will Stratton, Takiaya Reed, Marcus McDonald, Vanessa Govinden, Tim Hampson, Our Girl, Peter and Katie Hill, Sumie Nagano, Brian Christinzio, Sofia Hagberg, Roland Brown, Shirley Manson, Annie Clark, Jane Weaver, Phil Howells, the Bella Brighton crew, Jeremy Lascelles, Pierre Hall, Ben Rimmer, Alice McLean, Steve and Peter Kent, Samantha Connaughton, Panos Polymatidis, David Kittlety, Noreen and Phil, Alex Kennedy, Amine Ramer, Ed Marquis, Catherine Grieves, Pablo Clements, James Griffith, Mark McQuillan, Dominic Jones, Andrew Singh, Alex Gatt, Martin Aston, David Fricke, Darrin and Julie Robson, John O'Connell, Phil Alexander, Martin Aston, Charles Negus-Fancey, Cinder Flame, James Petralli, Russell Jones, Michelle Choudhry, Michael Turbot, Justin and Mew Welch, Pom Poko, Tony Benn, Don Letts, Kevin 'Moose' McKillop, Nigel and Sally House, Jae and Alyssa, congratulations, Melissa Thornley and Kenn Goodman, Francine Gorman, Faith Vern, Sophie Galpin, Anna Donigan, Nic Harcourt, Cameron Cook, Bill Pearis, Sat Bisla, Stuart Roberts, Jane Roberts RIP, Kevin Cole, Ariana Morgenstern, Chris Douridas, Celesté and Chad Peterson, Claire and Tony Morpeth, Ineke Daans, Gemma Dunleavy, Damon Reece, Euvin Weeber, Terry Edwards, Emma Tricca, Sophie Jamieson, Laura Groves, Finn Eisles, Dave Wrench, Lee Widdows, Nick Raymonde, Laurie Ganes, Iggy B, Clark Staub, Ray Coffer, Robin Hurley, Steve Webbon, Andy Gershon, Ural Thomas and Scotty Magee, Ezra Furman, Spencer Davies, Matt Biffa, Emily Baughman, Marissa Nadler, Beryl Braden, Kat and

Larry Braden, Lucy Holliday, Paul Anderson (Tram), Marc Riley, Amy Krawczyk, Martin Mills, Judy Leighton, Adrian Thrills, Dirk Van Dooren and Graham Wood, Kim Hyunggun Ssako, Rich Walker, Jason and Ceren Lee, Phi Murphy, Stan Frankland, Lambert, Jah Wobble, Don and Karen Peris and finally my hero Niall Harbison for always restoring my faith in humanity.